ROUTLEDGE LIBRARY EDITIONS: SOUTH AFRICA

Volume 10

CLASS, RACE AND GOLD

CLASS, RACE AND GOLD

A Study of Class Relations and Racial Discrimination in South Africa

FREDERICK A. JOHNSTONE

LONDON AND NEW YORK

First published in 1976 by Routledge & Kegan Paul Ltd.

This edition first published in 2023
by Routledge
4 Park Square, Milton Park, Abingdon, Oxon OX14 4RN

and by Routledge
605 Third Avenue, New York, NY 10158

Routledge is an imprint of the Taylor & Francis Group, an informa business

© 1976 Frederick A. Johnstone

All rights reserved. No part of this book may be reprinted or reproduced or utilised in any form or by any electronic, mechanical, or other means, now known or hereafter invented, including photocopying and recording, or in any information storage or retrieval system, without permission in writing from the publishers.

Trademark notice: Product or corporate names may be trademarks or registered trademarks, and are used only for identification and explanation without intent to infringe.

British Library Cataloguing in Publication Data
A catalogue record for this book is available from the British Library

ISBN: 978-1-032-30347-5 (Set)
ISBN: 978-1-032-30834-0 (Volume 10) (hbk)
ISBN: 978-1-032-30836-4 (Volume 10) (pbk)
ISBN: 978-1-003-30691-7 (Volume 10) (ebk)

DOI: 10.4324/9781003306917

Publisher's Note
The publisher has gone to great lengths to ensure the quality of this reprint but points out that some imperfections in the original copies may be apparent.

Disclaimer
The publisher has made every effort to trace copyright holders and would welcome correspondence from those they have been unable to trace.

This is a reissue of a previously published book. The language is reflective of the time in which this book was published. In reissuing this book, no offence is intended by the Publishers to any reader.

Class, race and gold

A study of class relations and racial discrimination in South Africa

Frederick A. Johnstone

Routledge & Kegan Paul
London, Henley and Boston

*First published in 1976
by Routledge & Kegan Paul Ltd
39 Store Street,
London WC1E 7DD,
Broadway House,
Newtown Road,
Henley-on-Thames, Oxon RG9 1EN
and 9 Park Street,
Boston, Mass. 02108, USA
Manuscript typed by Reba Lawless
Printed in Great Britain
by Redwood Burn Limited
Trowbridge & Esher
© Frederick A. Johnstone 1976
No part of this book may be reproduced in
any form without permission from the
publisher, except for the quotation of
brief passages in criticism*

ISBN 0 7100 8276 2

To my mother, my father and Bonnie

Contents

Acknowledgments   xi

Abbreviations   xiii

Introduction   1

Part one   **Class structure, class interests and racial discrimination**   11

1. The system of racial discrimination as a product of the class structure and as a system of class instruments: class colour bars   13

    (A)   The mining companies and the system of racial discrimination   13

    1. The class position of the mining companies   13

    2. The class colour bars of the mining companies: the exploitation colour bars   26

    (B)   The white workers and the system of racial discrimination   49

    1. The class position of the white workers   49

    2. The class colour bars of the white workers: the employment colour bars   64

2. The system of racial discrimination as a projection and mediation of class contradictions   76

Summary of part one — 89

Part two Class relations, class conflict and racial discrimination — 91

3 Class colour bars and class conflict: the mining companies and the white workers — 93
1. *The post-war profitability crisis* — 93
2. *The offensive of the mining companies against the white workers* — 119
3. *The counter-attack of the white workers* — 150

4 Class colour bars and class conflict: the African workers — 168
1. *Unrest, conflict and repression* — 168
2. *The African workers and the class colour bars: structural grievances* — 184

Summary of part two — 201

Conclusions — 203

Notes — 219

Bibliography — 261

Index — 290

Tables

1. Rates of pay, African workers, Witwatersrand gold mines — 42
2. Estimated effects on profitability of employment of white workers in unskilled labour in the gold mines — 83
3. Costs, output and profits, Witwatersrand gold mines, 1915–21 — 94
4. Costs and output, Witwatersrand gold mines, 1914 and 1921 — 95
5. Principal gains secured by the white workers in the Witwatersrand gold mines during the First World War — 98
6. Costs and output of labour, Witwatersrand gold mines, 1914 and 1920 — 100
7. Wages (per shift) of white workers, Witwatersrand gold mines, June 1921 and May 1922 — 137
8. Labour substitution and the displacement of white workers in semi-skilled work after 1922 — 139
9. Operating figures, Witwatersrand gold mines, before and after 1922 — 145
10. Average earnings per shift, African workers, Witwatersrand gold mines, 1911–19 — 181

Acknowledgments

I would like to thank the Canada Council for its financial support, both in Doctoral Fellowships for my studies at St Antony's College, Oxford, and in a travel grant for research in South Africa. For many stimulating discussions, notably in the London and Oxford seminars, I would like to thank Ernesto Laclau, Martin Legassick, Shula Marks, John Rex, Stanley Trapido and Harold Wolpe. I would like to express my gratitude to Kenneth Kirkwood, and to Arthur Keppel-Jones, for their unfailing assistance. I would like to thank the various archivists and librarians in Pretoria, Johannesburg, Cape Town, Oxford, London, Geneva and elsewhere who were of help. I would like to thank friends in South Africa, who shall remain nameless. I would like to thank Bonnie.

This work, which was my doctoral dissertation for Oxford University, was finished in March 1972, and, with the exception of the Introduction and the last section of the Conclusions, reflects my knowledge and insights as of that time.

Abbreviations

Archs	Archives
ARTCM	Annual Report of the Transvaal Chamber of Mines
Nat. Archs	National Archives (South African State Archives), Pretoria
NRC	Native Recruiting Corporation
OFS	Orange Free State
SAEDFA	South African Engine Drivers' and Firemen's Association
SAIF	South African Industrial Federation
SAMWU	South African Mine Workers' Union
SAP	South African Police
SARWA	South African Reduction Workers' Association
TUCSA	Trade Union Council of South Africa
Tvl Ch. of Mines	Transvaal Chamber of Mines
Tvl Nat. Cong.	Transvaal Native Congress
WNLA	Witwatersrand Native Labour Association

And under his feet the strong, obstinate strokes of the picks kept on. His comrades were all there, he could hear them following his every stride. Wasn't La Maheude there under that patch of beets, her back aching, her breath rising so hoarsely along with the noise from her ventilator? To left and right and farther on he thought he recognized others under the wheat, the greening hedges, the young trees. Now well up in the sky the April sun was shining in its glory, warming the earth as she brought forth. From her fostering side life was springing, buds were bursting into green leaf, the fields were atremble with the upward thrust of grass. Everywhere seeds were swelling, reaching out, breaking up through the plain in their need for warmth and light. A flood of sap poured out with whispering voices, the sound of the seeds spread in a great kiss. Still, still, more and more clearly, as if they were rising to the surface, his comrades were tapping. Under the sun's fiery rays on this morning of youth, it was with the sound they made that the countryside was pregnant. Men were coming up, a black, avenging army, slowly germinating in the furrows, growing for the harvests of the century to come. Soon their germination would shatter the earth.

Émile Zola,
'Germinal'
(Willard Trask translation, Bantam Books)

Introduction

1

Over the last few centuries a system of extreme social inequality has developed in South Africa. Its most prominent feature has been a system of racial domination, in which a relatively small group of whites has increasingly subordinated a large population of non-whites.
In a world increasingly intolerant of racial discrimination, let alone social inequality in general, this system has become one of the major political issues and social problems of our epoch. Whatever the rights and wrongs of the situation, the past development and present nature of this system need to be understood in all their depth and complexity, and they present us with difficult problems of explanation. This book is a study of class and race relations in South Africa which hopes to deepen such understanding and to help to resolve some of these problems.
Generally speaking, such explanation has not been taken very far. This cannot simply be put down to insufficient inquiry, of which, on the contrary, there has been some abundance; it must also be said to reflect deficiencies of approach.
Much of this inquiry has expressed, albeit often only implicitly, a particular school of thought, which blends the traditional preoccupations of race relations research (attitudes and ideology) with a strong dose of neoclassical economics. According to this approach, the system of racial domination in modern South Africa is seen and explained as a 'dysfunctional' intrusion upon the capitalist economic system, stemming from non-material factors outside it such as prejudice, racism, nationalism and 'social and cultural pluralism', but doomed over the long term to destruction by the inexorable imperatives of

rational industrialism and 'colour blind' capitalism.

This perspective has predominated, and continues to do so, and is the root cause, I would argue, of the inadequacy of much accepted and attempted explanation. This study proceeds in terms of an alternative approach, a Marxist structuralist approach, which sees and explains the system of racial domination as a product of the system of production of which it formed a part, and as determined in its specific forms, functions and nature by this system.

This work is an in-depth sociological and historical study of social relations, racial discrimination and historical developments in a core sector of South Africa - the gold mining industry, during a very important historical period - the early twentieth century, notably during and following the First World War.

The gold mining industry stood at the centre of the structure and evolution of the modern South African social formation. Its rise and consolidation in the late nineteenth and early twentieth centuries transformed South Africa, ushering in an important new socio-economic system. The industry became the mainspring of industrialisation and of the modern economy in South Africa. Its economic importance in this and other regards is well known. What has been less recognised, but is more important from a sociological point of view, is the specific nature of the socio-economic structure and system which it constituted.

The gold mining industry was a capitalist system of production based upon a capitalist social structure. And it was the first really large-scale capitalist industry in South Africa. Its social structure comprised two classes differentially related to the means of production: a class of owners of means of production (notably in the form of financial and industrial capital) and a class of workers who, not owning means of production, were thereby compelled to subsist through selling their labour power to the owners in exchange for wages. And these two classes were concentrated and engaged together in a capitalist system of production: a form of production in which the capitalist class used its privately-owned means of production as an instrument for its self-enrichment by appropriating for itself as profit the surplus part of the value of the output produced by workers but not returned to or secured by them for their own subsistence and reproduction (the worker's wage not being equal to the value of his output; were it so, the capitalist would hardly be inclined to invest his capital). Politically, the industry was further characterised by a divided working class, with a small group of politically free workers and a large group of politically unfree workers, all working together in the same industry but subject to fundamentally different and unequal political relations with the capitalist class employing them.

The gold mining industry is also of great sociological significance because it was here that occurred the first and most extensive industrial institutionalisation of racial discrimination in South Africa. The industry was made up of members not just of two classes but also of two different pigmentation or 'racial' groups (light and dark, and referred to in the situation as 'whites' and 'non-whites'), related together in a dominational system of racial differentiation, operated by the 'whites' over the 'non-whites'. (1) The 'whites' comprised the employers and one group of workers, the politically free workers, and the rest of the workers, the politically unfree workers, were 'non-white'. It is with the understanding and explanation of this racial system, and specifically with the elucidation of its relationship to the economic system, that this study is chiefly concerned.

The specific historical period and developments on which this study is focused are also most significant. The early decades of the twentieth century were a very important, formative time in the development of modern South Africa. It was a period of far-reaching economic and social change, a period of emergent capitalism, of industrialisation and urbanisation, of proletarianisation and class formation, and of class conflict. This class conflict reached a notable peak in the upheaval of 1922, with the strike of the white mine workers and ensuing warfare on the Witwatersrand (the 'Rand' or 'Reef' of gold bearing ore, in the area in and around Johannesburg). This was the largest explosion of class conflict within the white group in South Africa. Yet this was only the tip of the iceberg, merely one of many significant developments of class relations and class conflict within the white group and between whites and non-whites at this time. The fact that this and other tensions and events were centred on the gold mines is symptomatic of the extent to which the industry was at the heart of the general socio-economic developments which were changing the face of South Africa. It was around the time of the First World War, notably during and following the war, that these developments came to a head in a critical conjuncture, and it is with this period in particular that this study is concerned.

Such, then, are the book's specific subject and scope. Its main purpose is to develop a valid account and explanation of the system of racial discrimination in the gold mines, and of historical developments concerning this system during and following the war. Its general thesis is that this racial system may most adequately be explained as a class system - as a system of class instruments (which are referred to as 'class colour bars')- generated, and determined in its specific forms and its specific nature and functions, by the specific system of production and class structure of which it formed a part; and that these historical developments may most adequately be explained in terms of this explanation, and tend to confirm, as historical manifestations, the class nature of this system and thus the validity of this explanation.

The study progresses through two major stages. Part 1 develops an explanation and description of the system of racial discrimination, through a Marxist class analysis of its genesis, nature and dynamics. Part 2 goes on, in the light of this, to examine and explain the course of historical developments.

It is an inter-disciplinary study, a work both of sociology and of history. Part 1 is more explicitly sociological, more concerned with the systematic elucidation of the specific nature of a social system, a form of historical sociology. Part 2 is more historiographical, concerned with a particular historical episode, but a sociologically structured and focused historiography, concerned with social system questions.

The study thus converges from two directions on to the class nature of the social realities it is investigating - from a class analysis of a social system, and from a class analysis of historical events. And its general thesis thus comprises, it may be noted, two philosophically distinct kinds of proposition, concerning the bearing of some theory on some reality, and the bearing of some reality on some theory. On the one hand, it is argued that a particular approach (Marxist theory and analysis, as creatively applied in the situation under investigation) enables us to go some way towards explaining a particular social system (the racial system) and historical events associated with it. On the other hand, it is held that these particular historical developments (the war-time and post-war relations and conflict between the mining capitalists, the white workers and the non-white workers, notably the dramatic events of 1922) are a very clear historical manifestation and confirmation of the class nature of the system of racial discrimination, and thus of the validity of the specific class analysis and theoretical approach in terms of which that nature is here elucidated.

2

I should like now to go on to situate this book in its more general context, with some observations about the field of 'race relations' and current approaches in it. In the first place, underlying this book's approach is a theoretical rejection of the concept of 'race relations', and of the field of inquiry designated by it, and a redefinition of the field in Marxist terms. Thus while this study might simply be seen and labelled as a work on 'race relations', which in a certain literal sense it is, this would be deceptive and unsatisfactory, because of the theoretical deficiency of that concept and its field.

Since there is nothing intrinsically problematical, of a provable nature, about race, and since 'race relations' inquiry is often concerned with 'race relations situations' that do not involve race at all, there is clearly no theoretical justification for the designation of a field of inquiry by the term 'race relations'. Adding 'ethnic' does not resolve the problem. The concept of 'minority groups' is better, but questionable in its conventional usage, which tends towards the reification of biological and ethnic forms of social inequality. Is the working class in capitalist society a minority group? If not, why not? Is it not a distinct group, subject to subordinate treatment of an ascriptive nature? It is indeed all of these things, and the degree to which working class life in capitalist society is ascriptively determined in a negative way is not sufficiently recognised. However by focusing on ascriptive differentiation involving biological and ethnic distinctiveness, the concept acquires a certain theoretical usefulness, the degree of which depends on the way it is used.

A valid procedure is simply to conceive of social inequality as a general object of inquiry, which includes within its field, among other things, any phenomena of social inequality associated with such terms as race relations and minority groups, and which leaves any other such phenomena (e.g. race, ethnicity) to other inquiry, notably anthropology and ethnology. The study of social inequality of biological and ethnic forms, and the study of race and ethnicity, are distinctly different and intrinsically unrelated fields of inquiry, and study of the former may be subsumed within the general study of social inequality.

Social inequalities of biological and ethnic forms do, however, present certain specific problems for inquiry, as regards their specific nature and their relationship to the total social system of which they form a part. We are faced in them with the problem of mystification to an extreme degree.

This problem (with which both Marxist and Freudian social science have been systematically concerned, to their credit) refers to the fact that things do not often seem what they are; more specifically, to the fact that the specific form of a social reality, its specific outward appearance and manifestation, is often not a clear picture of, a clear window on to, its specific nature - its reality - as it is actually, as opposed to apparently, constituted and determined. Inquiry is consequently faced with the task of penetrating behind the mask of specific form and appearance to specific nature, of un-masking and de-mystifying and thus elucidating specific nature.

The problem of mystification is a fairly general one, an integral feature of most past and present societies, and often having to do with religious ideology. But it is always and notably present in an extreme form in minority group types of social inequality. In cases of biologically based inequality, such as the racial system in South Africa, the specific form of inequality is an absolute mystification of its specific nature, telling us nothing whatsoever about its specific nature, because of the intrinsic insignificance of race and sex as causal determinants of the social inequality so often formally constituted in terms of them. And while ethnicity, as a cultural and ideological factor, could in principle be such a determinant, it should not uncritically be assumed to be, and historically systems of ethnic inequality tend to be closely bound up, in a dependent way, with other forms of social inequality, notably class inequality, but this connection is greatly mystified by the ethnic factor (just as it also is by cultural factors constituted around biological factors, such as the ideologies of racism and sexism). Minority group forms of social inequality thus present us with extreme non-correspondence of specific form with specific nature.

In some cases of social inequality, appearance and reality coincide. In the ancient world, in feudal Europe, in Victorian England, to take just a few examples, many things seemed to be about class and actually were about class. These class realities were ideologically legitimised in various ways. But the dominant form of social relations and inequality was simply socio-economic (various classes differentially related to the means of production), bluntly reflecting the specific socio-economic, class nature of the social inequality.

But in other cases, everything seems to be, for example, about race, and in fact is, in people's experience, 'about race'. Yet how can that be, what does this mean, since race does not in itself have anything to do with social inequality? Clearly, such a race system, and similar minority group forms of inequality, must be some disguised form of something else. Just what that something else is, is a matter for inquiry, and merits specific investigation within the general study of social inequality. Sometimes it is simply the class structure itself, in disguise. As often as not, however, racial, sexual and ethnic forms of stratification have an asymmetrical relationship to the class structure, so that certain groups, such as the white workers in South Africa, are incongruously positioned. In all cases, the genesis, functions and specific nature of such forms of social inequality have to be brought to light and specified. Such deciphering, such un-masking, is a basic goal of this study.

This brings us to the second general issue, that of approaches, attempts at explanation or at deciphering. In its concern with minority group forms of inequality, and the question of social inequality generally, this study is ultimately involved in two different debates in social science.

In the first place, and less importantly, there is the argument between non-environmental determinism, notably genetic determinism (which sees and explains social inequality as solely or significantly determined by non-environmental factors, such as genes, 'race', instinct, sex, 'human nature', etc.), and environmental determinism (which explains social inequality in terms of factors in the social environment). It is the resurgence of the former approach, notably in such work as that of Jensen and Eysenck (not to mention the growing spate of social-darwinist ethology, e.g. Ardrey), which perforce involves us in a kind of argument, particularly over racial inequalities, that had, for good reasons, died away. (2) I hope that this study, in its environmentalist approach, helps to demonstrate the validity of this approach - one which, it should be noted, does not claim that non-environmental factors do not in any way determine human life, only that such factors have not been shown to explain systematic social inequality, while socio-environmental factors have.

If one holds an environmentalist position, then the significant area of argument over explanatory approaches is within the environmentalist camp. Generally speaking, explanation in the 'race relations' area has not been taken as far as the amount of inquiry in it might have promised. And this undoubtedly in part reflects problems and deficiencies in the specific environmentalist approaches which have predominated. When we try to identify these approaches, when we elucidate the theoretical roots or 'deep structures' of much of this inquiry, what we find, above all, are two major philosophical tendencies, that of idealism and that of empiricism. This is not altogether surprising, since these underlie so much past and present social science.

Idealism refers to a tendency of seeing and explaining social realities solely or essentially in terms of mental and psychological factors, such as attitudes, ideas, beliefs, values and ideology. Empiricism refers to a tendency to proceed in inquiry on an 'ad hoc' basis, of attempting to understand and explain things merely by 'describing what is', of equating reality with its specific form, with the picture of reality immediately apparent to the investigator and to those in the situation under investigation, and of treating all kinds of dependent and derivative factors as 'given'.

How do these deep tendencies manifest themselves? The idealist tendency shows itself in the conventional preoccupation with attitudes and prejudice (such as race prejudice), and with ideology (such as racism), both descriptively and for purposes of explanation. The empiricist tendency is evident in a heavily descriptive orientation, and in much unprincipled description of apparent reality. The two tendencies are closely related theoretically, since 'apparent reality' overlaps so extensively with 'reality as it is perceived in the consciousness of those in the situation under investigation'.

These approaches are weak, both intrinsically and in the degree to which they are relied upon. An empiricist approach is clearly deficient in the fundamental respect that the specific nature of any given social reality is not always clearly apparent in its specific outward form, and its elucidation must of necessity involve some kind of dynamic theoretical framework, the absence of which is the distinctive feature of empiricism. The basic problem with the idealist tendency, as far as explanation is concerned, is its neglect, or inadequate recognition, of the material determination of social reality. Of course the factors with which it is concerned are very significant, and may be important causal determinants in their own right. But what may be questioned is the relative importance it invariably attributes to such factors. It is certainly necessary to try to show, in specific cases, such as this study, the inadequacy of the tendency to explain racial discrimination solely or essentially in terms of prejudice and racism.

The basic issue is not whether conventional inquiry, in its idealism and empiricism, has yielded anything of value. Quite obviously it has. And let us at all costs avoid vulgar, mechanistic materialism, and always recognise the crucial importance of values and ideology in social life. And let us have 'a healthy respect for the facts'. The basic issue here is the relative scientific value of any approach, in relation to the particular object of inquiry. If the Marxist approach seems superior to idealist and empiricist approaches, especially for the kind of things this study is concerned with, it is not in any arrogantly absolute sense but in relative ways, by virtue of the fact that it avoids the real pitfalls of empiricism and idealism, but does not, if handled with care, replace them with other deficiencies of equal weight.

The nature of this approach may be left to speak for itself in this study, but a few general observations are in order here. The philosophical and theoretical specificity of Marxist science resides in its dialectical materialism and historical materialism - in its general theory and conception of the nature and social significance of the system of production in any given social formation, and in its specific materialist analysis of specific historical systems and developments. And what basically differentiates Marxist class analysis from other so-called class analysis is that it is an integral part of this more general theoretical framework, from which it derives whatever explanatory power it has.

Class analysis has come to mean various things, but Marxist class analysis means something quite specific, and its specificity must be recognised. It is obviously completely distinct from idealist class analysis (in which class is defined in terms of such things as status) of the kind evident in American sociology. And, more importantly, it does not mean, and is quite distinct from, empiricist-materialist class analysis (which merely involves an empiricist 'attention to economic factors' and selection of 'class variables', such as income and occupation, and the correlation of such factors with others in an empiricist study of 'social stratification', without forming part of any general social theory with explanatory power, and tending to lead only to re-description rather than substantial explanation of social inequality). What it means, above all, is the systematic elucidation of the differential relationships of individuals and social groups to means of production in historically and structurally specific systems of production and social formations, and the elucidation of the various ramifications of these structural differentiations, within a general theory about these systems and formations, from which it acquires its explanatory power.

As far as environmentalist approaches are concerned, therefore, this study argues in favour of a Marxist approach, and is a Marxist class analysis of a so-called 'race relations situation'.

This study is thus involved with certain general issues. Its approach to the study of phenomena associated with such concepts as 'race relations' involves a rejection of the conventional reification of such phenomena, and a subsuming of them into the general study of social inequality in its various forms and natures. And in the explanation of such phenomena, it reflects a rejection of both non-environmental determinism and of idealist and empiricist environmentalism in favour of dialectical and historical materialism.

I hope that it may contribute something of value to sociology and history, notably in the areas of South African, Marxist and so-called 'race relations' studies. Concerning the latter, there has been relatively little systematic scholarly work on South Africa, and in the 'race relations' area generally, taking a Marxist approach. Historically, the work is based on research into much important and original primary data (a note about which will be found in the bibliography), which has permitted a fairly informed and in-depth study of a vital historical period, which may hopefully shed some light on the historical development of social relations and racial domination in South Africa. As regards sociology, I hope in particular that my analysis of the system of racial discrimination, notably the conceptualisation of racial discrimination in terms of 'class colour bars', and the analysis of these class colour bars as a system of class instruments, extending and mediating class contradictions, may be useful. (3)

In attempting to shed more light in these various areas there is, of course, no question of searching for, or of claiming to have found, any perfect explanation or final account of things. All that can be hoped for is to travel some small distance along the difficult road of understanding.

part one

Class structure, class interests and racial discrimination

The first part of this study is concerned with developing an explanation and description of the system of racial discrimination which arose in the South African gold mining industry, by means of a Marxist analysis of its relationship to the economic system and social formation of which it formed a part.

1 The system of racial discrimination as a product of the class structure and as a system of class instruments: class colour bars

This racial system was operated by two groups of light skinned ('white') people (capitalists and white workers) over a group of dark skinned ('non-white') people (notably non-white workers). The basic purpose of this part is to elucidate the specific nature of the involvement of the two 'operator' groups in racial discrimination, and the specific nature and dynamics of the system of discrimination.

(A) THE MINING COMPANIES AND THE SYSTEM OF RACIAL DISCRIMINATION

1. THE CLASS POSITION OF THE MINING COMPANIES

1 The organisation of the mining companies

After the discovery of the gold fields of the Witwatersrand in 1886, it was not long before they became the site of the largest gold mining industry in the world. The rapid growth of this industry owed much to the recent development of the Kimberley diamond mines, which meant that by the time of the gold discovery there were already established in South Africa groups of entrepreneurs with good connections in the international capital markets, and a supply of investible capital. With the discovery of gold on the Rand, the capitalists who had enriched themselves in the diamond industry were quick to buy up and amalgamate claims, to float companies, and to invest capital in gold mining - out of which arose what was to be South Africa's key industry. (1)
    The structure of ownership of the gold mines came to be characterised, like that of the diamond mines, by a high

degree of centralisation. The geological nature of the gold fields made this imperative from the very beginning. Unlike the original diamond deposits, which were easily available on the surface to individual claim holders, the reef of gold-bearing ore (the 'banket', as it was called) sloped downwards deep underground, and the average grade of gold in the ore was very low. This meant that the extraction of gold necessitated large-scale mining operations - deep level mining and large and complex reduction works - which required very large capital outlays, beyond the resources of the kind of small claim holders who had opened up the diamond mines. From the start, therefore, the ownership of the gold mines came to be concentrated in the hands of a few groups of capitalists, which at that time and place were the only groups of people with the capital resources necessary to exploit and develop the new mineral discoveries. And the geology and size of the gold fields meant that

> in contrast to the diamond industry, which had flooded South Africa with relatively easily won wealth, the development of gold mining in the Rand implied the establishment in the interior of the country of a highly organised large-scale modern industry dependent on large supplies of capital and labour. (2)

But the different market conditions of gold compared with those of diamonds - specifically the different relationship between price and output - determined that the structure of ownership of the gold mines was to be less monopolistic than that of the diamond industry. The price of diamonds was determined by the supply, which led the most powerful group of diamond capitalists, that of Cecil Rhodes, to establish complete control over production and output through the monopolisation of ownership, so as to control price and profit. But this kind of control was not necessary in the gold industry, because the price of gold was internationally fixed. What developed in the gold mining industry was an oligopolist but highly centralised structure of ownership and control. The absence of any need to restrict output, and the large size of the gold fields, combined to produce a distribution of ownership between several large corporations. But these corporations, or Groups, as they were called, came to establish common central organisations and to implement common measures in order to eliminate competition between the mining companies for factors of production, especially labour, and to rationalise the process of production.

The seat of power in the gold mining industry lay in the Groups, which controlled the mining companies and the various central organisations. The mining companies comprised the actual productive enterprises. During the early decades of the twentieth century, they numbered about fifty. They were owned by share-holders, and effectively controlled by the Groups through majority shareholding. As a government Commission reported: 'It is found in practice that the real power is vested in the hands of that Group which has a sufficiently large shareholding to permit of its assuming control of the company.' (3) These Groups, which were six in number, were companies 'formed for the purpose of financing, directing and controlling mining companies'. (4)

The Groups played various important roles. Foremost among these was the provision of capital and the stabilisation of capital investment. Capital investment in the gold mines derived from two sources - the working profits secured from the operation of the gold mines, and new investment from outside the industry. The Groups were both investment companies and issue houses. They invested the bulk of their investment capital in the gold mines, and were able to provide amounts of capital and a continuity of investment which would have been beyond the resources of the average single gold mining company. And most of the private listed foreign capital investment in the gold mines was raised by the issue of equity shares by the Groups. Given such factors as the Groups' large assets, their extensive involvement in the industry in terms of both investment and production, and their established position in international capital markets, these shares were easily dealt with in these markets and on the Johannesburg Stock Exchange. (5)

The Group system also served to stabilise capital investment in the gold mines. With the large amount of pre-profit development work, high overhead costs and geological uncertainties involved in gold mining on the Rand, investment in the gold mines was fraught with risks. The Groups exerted a stabilising influence by pooling these risks within a framework of extensive capital and technological resources, so that, as one inquiry has observed, 'there is an improved chance that poor areas will be offset by good, and that even development will be maintained'. (6) The Groups also exerted such an influence by providing the industry with a source of capital which, while drawing on foreign capital markets, was not dependent on them, and was able to ensure continuity of investment - especially important for development work - at times (such as during the First World War) when foreign capital was in short supply. (7)

The system of Group control also served to rationalise the process of production, through the pooling of various

technical and administrative services for member companies, and through the restructuring of productive enterprises along more profitable lines through company amalgamations, which the Groups were able to implement as they wished since they controlled the companies. Such amalgamations were frequent; and as a mining executive explained:
> The actuating principle underlying these amalgamations is in most cases thoroughly sound. The advantages of greatly reduced cost of production obtained by consolidating a number of units into one large concern, with a centralised crushing plant, are obvious. . . . In addition to these, the enlarged scope of operations . . . is also the means of equalizing the output of gold and preventing violent fluctuations in the price of the company's shares. (8)

The Group system thus constituted 'a growing centralisation at a high level of the provision of finance and of technical and administrative services'. (9) The benefits to be derived from centralisation were further secured through the establishment of collective organisations which represented the common interests of the mining companies as a whole. Foremost among these was the Transvaal Chamber of Mines, founded in 1887. The Chamber became the central organisation of the gold mining industry, which served to represent and secure the common interests and policies of the Groups and companies in all areas, and to provide the companies with a wide range of services. (10) The Chamber was an instrument of its members, the mining companies, and was ultimately controlled by the Groups, who controlled the production companies. (11)

Other central organisations of more specific purpose were also established, the most important of which were two labour recruiting agencies - one for African labour from outside British South Africa (the Witwatersrand Native Labour Association, founded in 1896), and one for African labour within British South Africa (the Native Recruiting Corporation, set up in 1912). An essential function of these agencies, as we shall see, was to eliminate costly competition between the mining companies for African labour.

The ownership of the gold mines of the Rand thus rested in the hands of capitalist companies; and the company structure of the gold mining industry thus comprised a three-tier formation of controlling companies, production companies and central organisations serving the companies, the whole formation being under the hegemony of the controlling companies - the Groups. This was a modern structure of capitalist enterprise. As an economist was led to observe:

Chapter 1

The gold mining industry may claim to provide a working model of a 'rationalised' industry. Through the Group system of control of the separate mining companies, and the close cooperation of the whole industry through the Chamber of Mines and its subsidiary services, it has substituted for the blind selection by competition of the fittest to survive, a conscious and deliberate choice of methods, equipment, areas and personnel on the basis of an extremely detailed comparative study of results. (12)

2 The cost structure and profit accumulation problems and imperatives of gold mining on the Rand

The mining companies which owned and operated the gold mines were capitalist companies: that is, enterprises owned by private owners of property in the means of production for the purpose of accumulating surplus capital, or profit, through the investment of capital in the productive employment of the labour power of a class of workers separated from ownership of such property and compelled thereby to sell their labour power to the owners of the means of production on terms favourable to the latter. The system of production which they established to mine the gold of the Rand was such a system of profit accumulation - a capitalist system of production. And the fundamental class interest - the driving interest - of the mining companies was the accumulation of profit through the investment of capital in, and the operation of, this system of production.

The realisation of this class interest - such accumulation of profit through the mining of gold on the Rand - was circumscribed by a unique cost structure, which was determined by certain important geological and economic factors, and which in turn determined the specific profit accumulation problems and imperatives of the mining companies. These factors comprised the low average grade of gold, the internationally fixed price of gold, and the high level of development and overhead costs.

Geologically, the gold-bearing reef on the Witwatersrand was distinguished by the very low average grade of its gold. The gold was very thinly - and uniformly thinly - distributed in the ore in comparison with gold fields elsewhere. As the Chamber of Mines observed: 'Taken over its whole area . . . the Rand is, relatively speaking, a low-grade gold field; in other words, a field in which the average value of the gold content is no more than $6\frac{1}{2}$ dwts. to the ton.' (13) And as the Chamber pointed out:

The grade of ore worked on the Witwatersrand is much
lower than is considered profitable in other parts of
the world. For example, in Western Australia, the
average grade of ore worked is 12.91 dwts. per ton;
and in the Hollinger Mine in Canada, the grade is 10.28
dwts. per ton. The average on the Witwatersrand is
6.537 dwts. (14)
The grade varied to some degree, and mines had blocks of
higher and lower grades of ore. But the average grade was
very low.

The second major determinant of the industry's cost
structure was the fact that the price of gold, unlike the
price of other commodities, was internationally fixed, independently of the producers, and for most of the time remained stationary. As an economist has observed:

> The differentiating issue for the gold mining industry
> is not the relationship between the price of its pro-
> duct and the general level of costs with which it has
> to contend; in this respect, it differs in no way from
> other industries. What does differentiate it is that
> for long periods of time the price of its product has
> remained constant, though the cost level may have gone
> up. (15)

The fixed and stationary price of gold had two significant
consequences for the industry. On the one hand, it meant
that the mining companies were unable to transfer increases in production costs to consumers in the form of
price increases. This made the industry extremely vulnerable to cost inflation. As the Chamber of Mines pointed
out:

> The gold mining industry is affected by an increase in
> working costs in an entirely different way to an indus-
> try which can pass on increases in cost to the con-
> sumers of its products. Sheltered trades, such as the
> printing and building industries, add increases in
> working costs to the price of their product, and thus
> pass on such increases to the community. The gold
> mining industry obviously cannot do so. (16)

But it also meant that the gold mining industry was not
subject to crises of over-production, and that output
could be maximised indefinitely without jeopardising
profits.

The third major factor was the high level of development and overhead costs attendant upon deep-level gold
mining. This meant that profits could not be secured
without very substantial, on-going capital outlays and
without a high minimum level of output. This problem was
clearly depicted by the President of the Chamber of Mines:

> Every mine has to meet large standing charges, such as

administration, pumping, lighting, maintenance, depreciation, claim licences, phthisis charges and many other items, and these charges continue irrespective of the tonnage broken during any particular period. It follows that the whole product of the mine, up to a certain point, is swallowed up in defraying the cost, not only of recovering that amount of product, but also of these standing charges. That point varies in different mines: a rich mine may attain it by mining, say, 50 per cent of its normal tonnage, while a struggling mine may barely do so when it attains the full 100 per cent of its normal output.

Every mine has thus a critical percentage of its normal output which has to be attained before any profit can be made. Where that percentage approaches 100, any falling off from the normal means, not only no profit, but an actual loss; and even where the critical percentage is low, the loss of profit from a reduced output far exceeds the proportion of output lost, since all the profit arises only from that part of the output exceeding the critical percentage. Thus, in the case of a mine whose critical percentage is 80 per cent, a reduction of 10 per cent in tonnage means a loss not of a tenth but of a half of its profit. (17)

In addition to substantial constant standing costs, development costs were also very high - the cost both of development work within producing mines and of opening new mines - and these added to overhead costs. This high level of overhead and development costs in deep-level mining on the Rand exerted strong downward pressure on profit margins, in the manner described by the President of the Chamber.

The specific cost structure comprised by these three factors - the low grade, the fixed price and the high overheads - determined the specific problems and imperatives of profitable gold mining. It meant that profits could only be secured through a very low level of costs and a high level of output. It determined that the two fundamental imperatives of profitable gold mining were the minimisation of costs and the maximisation of output (and, by the same token, that the two great dangers were cost inflation and falling output). The most important of these was cost minimisation, since this affected profitability and output far more than output maximisation affected profitability and costs.

But how were costs to be minimised? And how was output to be maximised? The main components of production costs were the cost of labour and the cost of materials. The mining companies had very little ability to minimise the cost of materials, and labour costs thus became the crucial area of cost minimisation. And the industry's specific cost structure meant that gold could only be acquired profitably through extremely low labour costs. The imperative of cost minimisation thus led in the direction of the ultra-minimisation of labour costs. The imperative of output maximisation led, in turn, in two directions: the maximisation of the supply of low cost labour, and the maximisation of the productivity of the labour force (through such means as technological innovation and work extension). And both of these general imperatives were to propel the companies in a fourth direction: that of making the most profitable possible utilisation of labour (through not only raising labour productivity, but also substituting ultra-cheap for more expensive labour and generally seeking to secure the most productive possible employment of ultra-cheap labour), which served both to minimise costs and to maximise output.

The two general imperatives of cost minimisation and output maximisation thus became four specific imperatives: the ultra-minimisation of labour costs, the maximisation of the supply of ultra-cheap labour, the maximisation of labour productivity, and the most profitable possible utilisation of labour.

These specific imperatives were all of importance in their own way to the profitability of the mining companies, but in varying degrees. By far the most important, in this regard, was the ultra-minimisation of labour costs. Those concerning labour productivity and labour utilisation were by no means unimportant; and, as we shall see in Part 2, in the specific configuration of conditions which came to prevail during and following the First World War, the realisation of these particular imperatives was to become of great historical significance, and what their realisation involved we shall then observe. However, of far more importance to the profitability of the mining companies - of critical importance to the very existence of the gold mining industry - was the ultra-minimisation of labour costs. And how the mining companies came to realise this imperative is what we have now to consider.

3 The ultra-exploitability of non-white labour in South Africa

The mining companies were to find the general solution to their labour cost problem within the specific social formation prevailing in South Africa. For in the part of the world in which the gold fields were situated, and in which the mining companies had to operate, there existed a social formation in which the extreme exploitation of labour could take place.

What was coming to prevail in South Africa by the time of the gold discovery, and was continuing to develop thereafter, was an ultra-exploitative system of production: a system of production in which a group of white property owners privately and exclusively owning property in the means of production, productively employed, and appropriated the surplus of, the labour of a class of non-white workers separated from ownership of such property and subject to extreme extra-economic compulsion and domination.

The economic basis of this system of production was the private and exclusive ownership of property in the means of production by white property owners for the purpose of accumulating the surplus product of the labour of a class of workers separated from ownership of such property and thereby compelled to provide labour to the owners of such property in exchange for subsistence.

On the basis largely of superior military technology and economic power, white property owners were able to transform the structure of ownership of means of production in South Africa to their advantage, steadily extending their private ownership of such property - notably land - at the expense of the African inhabitants. The latter became increasingly deprived of free access to land and thereby increasingly compelled to enter into new relations of production as workers dependent upon and in the employment of the new white owners of the means of production. As De Kiewiet pointed out, the wars between the whites and the Africans in South Africa were concerned, unlike for instance those between the whites and the Indians in North America, not only with land but also with labour, not only with the appropriation of means of production but also with the integration of the conquered as workers into a new system of production.

> Actually the native wars were a process which gave the white community more than possession of the bulk of the best land. It gave them a considerable measure of control over the services of the natives. The land wars were also labour wars. In other words, the natives lost free access to the land, but were permitted to draw sustenance from it as labourers, herdsmen, tenants or renters. (18)

The typical form of the economic relationship which emerged between the new private owners of the means of production and the economically dependent masses was that: 'In return for residence, the right to cultivate a piece of land and graze a few animals, the landowner usually received the services of the tenant in the field and of his women in the household.' (19) The specific form of labour, remuneration and surplus appropriation varied considerably, as one inquiry observed:

As vacant or subjugated land was taken up by the European immigrants, dispossessed or fugitive natives or remnants of scattered tribes remained or penetrated for protection into the areas of European occupation, and were allowed to settle upon their farms, generally on a tenure of service. These natives are usually called 'squatters'. There is no statutory definition of this word, which is or has been made use of in many different connotations. Whether a native lives on an occupied or unoccupied farm, whether he pays rent or gives his own service or that of his family, whether or no wages are paid, whether the service is casual labour at call or seasonal or for specified periods, whether he cultivates for a share of produce - in all these cases he is called a squatter. The term therefore covers undefined leasehold, metayage, labour tenancy, part time service and, in fine, every condition of settlement except fixed leasehold and full time wage service. (20)

But these various specific forms of the economic relationship rested upon a common economic base - the private and exclusive ownership of the means of production by a group of property owners, the increasing economic dependence of the rest of the population, and the compulsion exerted by these conditions upon the latter to provide labour for the new owners of the means of production in exchange for subsistence.

The system of production established by the white property owners was further constituted and determined at political, juridical and ideological levels by a system of domination, which, by perpetuating the new structure of ownership of means of production and by establishing highly coercive relations of production through various forms of extra-economic compulsion, served both to reinforce and reproduce the economic basis of this system of production and to secure the ultra-exploitability of labour, so as to permit its ultra-exploitation.

As will have been noted, the people forming the new dominant class of property owners were of light skin pigmentation - 'white' - while the rest of the inhabitants, who, as a result of the transformation of the structure of ownership of the means of production were becoming a class of workers employed by these property owners, were 'non-white'. This was a circumstance that was to be fully exploited by the white property owners, who developed their system of class domination as one of racial domination, which, by restricting the property ownership and property rights of non-whites, and by restricting the political rights of non-whites and subjecting non-whites to various forms of extra-economic compulsion and domination, served specifically to perpetuate the economic dependence of the non-white population and to secure the ultra-exploitability of their labour.

The system of class domination erected by the white property owners thus assumed the specific form of a system of racial domination. This system consisted of various measures of racial discrimination and a racist ideology: measures of racial discrimination serving to maintain non-whites in a position of economic dependence; measures of racial discrimination serving to subject non-whites to various forms of extra-economic compulsion; and a racist ideology serving to legitimise and mystify the system of class domination and exploitation.

The economic basis of the system of production was sanctioned and reinforced by racially discriminatory property laws instituted by the white property owners, laws which served to perpetuate the economic dependence of the non-white population by restricting the property rights of non-whites. The de facto distribution of land ownership was reinforced and given de jure legitimation by the Native Land Act of 1913, which defined the great bulk of the territory of South Africa as 'white areas' in which Africans were prohibited from the right to purchase or otherwise acquire land. (21) With the discovery of minerals, the whites also instituted laws to exclude non-whites from property and trading rights in mining areas. Non-whites were barred from the right to acquire mining licences; (22) from the right to trade in minerals; (23) from the right to reside on proclaimed ground; (24) and from the right to establish shops on such ground. (25) The Gold Law of the Transvaal prescribed that: 'No coloured person may be a licence holder, or in any way be connected with the working of the gold mines, except as a working man in the service of whites.' (26) Through such discriminatory legislation, the whites ensured that the only class position in which non-whites were legally permitted access to mines and minerals was that of workers in the employment of white property owners.

Other measures of racial discrimination were deployed by the white property owners to subject non-whites to various forms of extra-economic compulsion. These comprised, on the one hand, measures to reinforce the compulsion exerted upon non-whites by separation from ownership of means of production to labour for white property owners - notably taxation and squatting laws. Taxation measures forced Africans to seek such employment by compelling them to acquire money to pay taxes. (27) And laws were instituted to prohibit independent squatting by Africans, and to regulate and limit the number of African squatters per white land-owner, so as to equalise the distribution of African labour to white employers. (28) On the other hand, there were measures serving to secure the extreme powerlessness of non-whites and the extreme exploitability of non-white workers. Foremost among these were the Master and Servant Laws (29) and the Pass Laws, (30) which subjected non-whites generally and non-white workers in particular to various forms of extra-economic coercion, such as criminal penalties for breach of contract and coercive regimentation, which placed them in a position of extreme powerlessness and exploitability in relation to their employers. A racially discriminatory political franchise and system of government, depriving non-whites of rights of government, also served to secure their extreme powerlessness and the ultra-exploitability of their labour. (31)

In addition to instituting these various kinds of measures of racial discrimination, the whites propagated a racist ideology, which defined 'white' pigmentation as a sign of membership of an innately superior racial group, and 'non-white' pigmentation as a sign of membership of an innately inferior racial group. By so defining non-whites, and by thus attributing the respective class positions of white property owners and non-white workers to membership of innately unequal racial groups, this ideology served to legitimise and to mystify the system of class domination, racial discrimination and labour exploitation established by the white property owners.

The system of class domination thus assumed the specific form of a system of racial domination, which, by thoroughly restricting the property and political rights of non-whites, and ideologically attributing this system of domination to innate racial differences, served to perpetuate the economic dependence of the non-white population and to secure and maintain the ultra-exploitability of non-white labour.

Such a situation was just what the gold mining companies needed. Their most imperative requirement was a large supply of ultra-cheap labour. And the ultra-exploitability of non-white labour in the system of production established by the white property owners in South Africa provided the companies with the means of realising this requirement.

It was in consequence of this state of affairs that the great bulk of the labour force of the gold mining industry was to be made up of non-white workers. However, the industry's labour force was not to be drawn entirely from this source. Deep-level and large-scale mining work required the use of many different and complex skills. The mining companies thus required, in addition to a large supply of unskilled labour, a number of skilled industrial mine workers. But there were hardly any such workers in South Africa at the time of the discovery and initial development of the Rand gold fields. Such workers were to be found in Europe and in such European-settled areas as North America and Australia, and after the gold discovery such workers migrated from these areas to take up skilled employment in the Rand gold mines.

These workers were not ultra-exploitable. They enjoyed considerable economic and political power, because of the scarcity of skilled labour, and because as whites they were not subject to the same system of class domination to which non-white workers were subject through the system of racial domination - they were politically free in the specific sense that they could assert themselves in relation to the employers through such means as trade unions and the vote. These factors placed them in a strong bargaining position in relation to the employers, enabling them to command high wages and making white labour far more expensive than non-white labour.

The labour force of the gold mines thus came to comprise a large sector of unskilled, ultra-cheap, forced (non-white) labour, and a small sector (about one-tenth of the labour force) of skilled, expensive, free (white) labour. The composition and situation of the mining labour force and of the South African working class generally will be considered more fully later on. What needs to be noted at this stage is that the presence of a sector of expensive and politically free labour intensified the importance of the ultra-cheapness of the rest of the labour force to the profitability of the mining companies.

The system of production established and being consolidated by white property owners in South Africa was thus highly beneficial for capitalist gold mining on the Rand. The ultra-exploitability of non-white labour provided the mining companies with the general solution to their labour cost problem, and the economic dependence of the non-white population provided them with a fruitful source of ultra-exploitable labour. What we have now to consider is how the mining companies came to insert themselves into this system of production and to operate and shape it for their own class ends.

2. THE CLASS COLOUR BARS OF THE MINING COMPANIES: THE EXPLOITATION COLOUR BARS

The crucial imperative of profitable gold mining was thus the ultra-minimisation of labour costs (the mining companies required ultra-cheap labour); the ultra-exploitability of non-white labour in South Africa provided the general means of realising this imperative, and this condition was rendered all the more important by the presence of a sector of expensive, politically free workers; and, given the large size of the gold fields and the imperative of output maximisation, the companies required a large supply of non-white labour. It therefore became a critical class interest of the mining companies to acquire such a supply and to secure and maintain the ultra-cheapness of this labour. We have now to examine the specific ways in which the companies came to secure this interest and to realise these imperatives.

1 Securing the supply of non-white labour

The President of the Chamber of Mines was not exaggerating when he declared that:
> As far as the mining industry is concerned, it is a platitude to say that we must have labour. The mining industry without labour is as bricks would be without straw, or as it would be to imagine you could get milk without cows. (32)

In their requirement of a large supply of non-white labour, the mining companies were confronted with three basic problems: a continuing measure of economic independence among Africans, competition between employers for African labour in South Africa, and a consequent 'shortage' of non-white labour in South Africa. The companies were to meet these problems in three general ways: through increasing the compulsion upon Africans to work for white property owners, through the monopsonisation of labour recruiting, and through the importation of non-white labour from outside South Africa.

(a) The mobilisation of African labour As we noted, the transformation of the structure of ownership of means of production by the white property owners had the effect of considerably reducing the economic independence of the African population. But the communal system of production of the African tribes was not completely destroyed. It persisted in the areas not settled by the whites, and its continuation constituted something of a problem for employers, especially for the mining companies because of their large labour requirement.

The problem was that, through collective ownership of land and production for use and direct consumption, this system of production, where it still prevailed, provided Africans with a considerable measure of economic independence, enabling them to subsist without having to render labour or sell their labour power to private owners of means of production and without needing to accumulate money. This state of affairs was not a cause of rejoicing among the mining companies. As the President of the Chamber of Mines complained:

> The tendency of the native is to be an agriculturist, who reluctantly offers himself or one of his family as an industrial worker for just so long as the hut tax can be earned, and expects the industrial demand to expand to give him work when his crops are bad. He cares nothing if industries pine for want of labour when his crops and home-brewed drink are plentiful. (33)

The white property owners, we noted, did institute measures to intensify the economic dependence of the non-white population, and to mobilise Africans into labour for them by reinforcing the compulsion to labour exerted on many Africans by the changed structure of ownership of means of production with such measures as taxation and squatting laws. These measures helped to secure labour for the mines, and were supported by the mining companies. As the President of the Chamber declared:

> What is wanted is surely a policy that would establish once for all that outside special reserves, the ownership of land must be in the hands of the white race, and that the surplus of young men, instead of squatting on the land in idleness and spreading out over unlimited areas, must earn their living by working for a wage, as every white man who is not a land-owner has to do. (34)

And the Chamber wanted the government to 'do everything to encourage the native to be a wage-earner by extending the policy of splitting up into family holdings land now held in native reserves under tribal tenure.' (35) The 'pull' factors instituted by the whites were reinforced by certain 'push' factors, such as population growth, crop failure, stock decimation, soil erosion and the desire to acquire the means of purchasing guns and cattle.

But the existing labour mobilisation mechanisms together with these 'push' factors were not sufficient in themselves to produce the quantity of African workers sought by the mining companies. The companies therefore developed their own system of mobilising Africans into mine labour - a system of loan advancement and debt inducement. The companies employed recruiting agents in different areas, through whom they paid a capitation fee of 25s. to traders and others in different districts and locations for every African they secured for labour in the mines; given the incentive of the capitation fee, traders then sought to procure Africans for the mines by inducing indebtedness among Africans through credit advances and loans.

According to the President of the Chamber, it was ónly through
> paying out large sums to recruiters, who in turn endeavour to induce the natives to come to work by offers of loans and the wherewithal to pay their taxes and their debts to the local traders who have given them credit, that we have been able to keep up the supply of labour to what it is today. (36)

What happened, according to an African leader, was that:
> The native is induced and encouraged to take as much in the way of goods as he likes although he has no cash to pay for them. Then his crop fails and he finds he cannot pay, and the trader comes along and says 'If you do not join for the mines I will run you in and you will have to pay all the costs. I will take out a Civil Action and annex your cattle'. (37)

According to another: 'It is a very great temptation to a trader to keep a man constantly in debt to him to have a pull on him, and we think that that is a vicious thing.' (38) In his district, 'so far as I am aware, almost every native is in debt for some money or other'. (39) As another African explained:
> The trader is able to exert an undue influence over the natives. He allows a native to get into his debt for goods that he does not need and cannot pay for, and then he compels him to join up and go to work on the mines and for these natives recruited in this way he receives a certain fee as well as getting paid for his goods. (40)

Africans brought to the mines in this way could not, he went on, be regarded as free agents: the system of deliberately producing indebtedness was a form of economic compulsion to labour. (41)

The problem of the continuing economic independence of part of the African population was thus met in part by the general labour mobilisation measures, and to these the mining companies added their own system of labour mobilisation - that of debt inducement. The capitation fee provided an incentive to traders to induce indebtedness among Africans and to procure such Africans specifically for the mines. This indebtedness served further to reduce the economic independence of Africans, and to increase the compulsion upon them to go to work for wages. And this compulsion to labour was of particular importance for the mining companies, since the industry's specific cost structure meant that to have attracted labour by higher wages would have been self-defeating. As a mining official affirmed:

As far as the British South African native is concerned, is there any way short of compulsion to make him go to a mine? - Not one that I know of.

He would have to be compelled? - We might achieve it by paying a very high rate, but that would not help us in our difficulties. It would defeat the object we have in view. (42)

(b) The monopsonisation of labour recruiting   Increasing the compulsion upon Africans to provide labour helped to solve the labour supply problem of employers by dealing with the problem of continuing economic independence among Africans. But this was far from the end of the matter. For there was not an infinite supply of African labour. Another major problem, therefore, was that of competition between employers for African labour.

In their drive to secure their own supply of African labour, the gold mining companies found themselves in competition both amongst themselves and with other groups of employers. While a state of competition between the mining companies did not prevail in relation to the selling of their product, it did in relation to the procurement of African labour. In addition, the companies were in competition with other groups of employers, both within and without South Africa. Within South Africa, they faced competition from the farmers, the diamond and coal mines, and, increasingly, from the secondary and tertiary sectors; outside British South Africa, they had to compete with sugar planters, cocoa planters and other interests. (43) As the President of the Chamber of Mines observed: 'We have to compete in our quest with the farmer, the merchant, the railways, harbours and the general requirements of the towns.' (44)

The fundamental problem arising out of this competition was that it exerted upward pressure on labour costs and wage rates. One response of the mining companies to this problem, as we shall see, was to import non-white labour from outside South Africa. And it was in this direction that the first step was taken towards the centralisation of recruiting, with the formation of the Witwatersrand Native Labour Association (founded in 1896, and coming into full operation after the South African War), which centralised recruitment of African labour for the mines from outside British South Africa. And after the South African War, the problem was temporarily offset by the importation of Chinese workers to the mines in 1904.

But this problem became particularly acute for the mining companies by the time of Union, by which time these Chinese workers had been repatriated, consequent upon the British government's prohibition of their continued presence. This repatriation meant that the mining companies had been forced, as the President of the Chamber put it, into 'scouring' the Union for African labour, and 'had led to unseemly competition amongst all employers of labour for the services of the natives'. (45) 'The most serious aspect of the labour supply of the gold mines', he declared, 'is the ever increasing cost of recruiting, and an increase in the wages of natives.' (46) Since the repatriation of the Chinese, the cost of recruiting Africans from the Union for work in the gold mines had risen by 7d. per shift worked. (47) At a shareholders' meeting in London in 1911, a mining magnate

> affirmed that the gold mining industry might have avoided the disastrous increased costs on mines arising from mad competition to secure labour. He deprecated the unbusinesslike methods of bringing natives' wages to the present level, and said that most of the disappointments of the year were due to this competition. (48)

More 'businesslike' methods were not long in the coming. 'It should go out to the world', the President of the Chamber announced early in 1912, 'that a change is coming over the industry. The spirit of cooperation has dawned in every department.' (49) And in that year:

> In order to obviate competition in the recruitment of natives within the Union by the various mining groups, an agreement was arrived at amongst all the mining companies . . . by which all recruiting of natives within the Union was placed under the management of the Native Recruiting Corporation, which was formed for the purpose of procuring and organising the supply of native labour from within the Union to the mines. (50)

The fundamental purpose of the new agency was to eliminate the cost-maximising competition between the mining companies for African labour. As a Chamber official explained: 'One object of the formation of the Native Recruiting Corporation was to stop this competition. They were paying higher capitation fees and wages, so that only the rich mines would have been able to survive.' (51) If companies continued to recruit independently, the President of the Chamber explained, 'the competition that would ensue in the scramble for available labour would be so keen that recruiting methods and labour conditions generally would become in the highest degree unsatisfactory.' Such competition tended to raise costs and thus to undermine profitability, and 'this was the real consideration that induced the majority of the industry to combine and form the Native Recruiting Corporation'. (52)

Because this centralisation of labour recruiting comprised a monopoly of buying - the combination of the buyers of a particular commodity in a common purchasing organisation - it constituted a monopsony, which was, in this case, a labour recruiting monopsony. The structural significance of this monopsonisation of labour recruiting was that it greatly increased the control of the mining companies over the cost and supply of African labour. One of the main functions of the Native Recruiting Corporation was that of minimising African wages, a function which will be considered further on. Its other vital functions were those of reducing the cost of recruitment of African labour and of rationalising the distribution of the African labour supply.

Through the benefits of centralisation - improved organisation, the elimination of competition and duplication, the reduction of capital overheads - the monopsonisation of recruiting had the desired effect of lowering recruitment costs. Between 1913 and 1924, the cost of recruiting Africans for work in the gold mines fell by about 20 per cent. (53)

At the same time, the distribution of the African labour supply to the mines was rationalised and equalised by a system of labour rationing introduced by the Corporation. A technical committee was set up in 1914 to calculate the labour requirements of each mine. This 'complements committee', as it was known, studied the productive capacity of each mine, in the light of various factors, such as pending development, ratio of men to machines, and average efficiency in different areas of production (conditions, such as hardness of rock, varied from mine to mine). It then estimated the optimum number of African workers required by each mine, which constituted its African labour 'complement'. (54) The calculation of these complements was completed by 1915, and the complements were then adjusted every quarter of the year. (55) The African workers recruited by the agencies were then distributed to the mines in such a way as to provide each mine with the same proportion of its complement. (56)

The costly problem of competition within the gold mining industry for African labour was thus resolved by the monopsonisation of recruiting. The President of the Chamber of Mines concluded that:

The result of this centralisation of the previously existing numerous individual native recruiting departments of the different Groups can hardly be sufficiently appreciated, and it cannot fail to be of the greatest benefit to the mines. The cut-throat competition obtaining in the past, which continually increased the cost of our native labour . . . (has) been practically put an end to. (57)

(c) The importation of non-white labour from outside South Africa The monopsonisation of labour recruiting dealt only with competition for African labour within the gold mining industry. Competition for this labour between different groups of employers in South Africa remained, and intensified as time went by.

The gold mining companies were not in a strong position in this competition, because mine work was the least popular form of work among Union Africans, and because the industry's specific cost structure made an inelastically ultra-low non-white wage level more imperative than for other enterprises. How, therefore, could the mining companies secure and maintain the large supply of non-white labour which they required, given the finiteness of the South African supply, the increasing demand for it, and the preference of Union Africans for other work? The answer of the mining companies to this problem was the importation of non-white labour from outside South Africa. Other sources of labour, as the Chairman of the Native Recruiting Corporation put it, had to be 'tapped':

With reference to the competition for labour from industries other than the mining industry, there is no doubt that many natives who would otherwise come to the mines of the Transvaal are being attracted to more congenial work on the surface, such as sugar estates, railway and road construction. As other industries spring up and become developed, this competition will no doubt increase, and . . . other sources of native labour must be tapped, as British South Africa cannot provide a sufficient supply of native labour for the mining, farming and other industries. (58)

The mining companies left few stones unturned in their search for non-white labour, which, outside of the Union, Basutoland, Bechuanaland and Swaziland, they obtained from Portuguese East Africa, Northern Rhodesia, Southern Rhodesia, Nyasaland, South West Africa, and parts of tropical Africa (north of latitude 22 degrees south). And from China. The most notorious episode in their procurement of foreign non-white labour was their importation of indentured Chinese workers after the South African War. At the end of this war, the mining companies found themselves with a serious shortage of non-white labour, due to various factors, notably a reduction of African wages by the companies, increased demand for African labour by other employers, and difficulties in securing African labour from Portuguese East Africa. Thus in 1904 they imported about 60,000 indentured labourers from China. These workers were soon repatriated, however, in consequence of mounting opposition to, and the eventual prohibition of, their continued employment.

But the most important foreign source of non-white labour for the gold mines was, and has remained, Portuguese East Africa. Every year, the mining companies imported more workers from Portuguese East Africa than the total brought from China during the importation of Chinese. By the time of Union, half of the industry's African labour force was made up of 'East Coast natives' (as Africans from this area were called), and the President of the Chamber of Mines could refer to them as 'the mainstay of the industry'. (59)

The explanation for the industry's importation of foreign non-white labour is to be found not only in factors of necessity - such as the finiteness of the South African supply, growing demand, the unpopularity of mine work, and the high economic and political costs attendant upon the employment of unskilled white labour - but also in factors of expediency. For the mining companies secured important economic and political benefits from the employment of foreign - and particularly of East Coast - labour.

Economically, one effect of such labour importation was to exert downward pressure on African wage rates in South Africa - an aspect that will be considered later. Another important economic advantage in the employment of Portuguese Africans was the longer minimum period of their labour contracts. Whereas the minimum period for Union Africans was six months (until 1924, when it was raised to nine), with an average stay of eight months, the minimum contract for Portuguese Africans was twelve months, and their average stay was eighteen months. (60) In the Chamber's view, this difference, which reflected the more competitive labour market within South Africa, 'greatly increases the value to the mining industry of the East Coast native'. (61) In the first place, the longer contract stabilised the African labour supply and raised the average level of competence of the African labour force. Second, it served to reduce recruiting costs. For the fact that Portuguese Africans stayed on the mines for twice as long as Union Africans meant that to maintain 100,000 Portuguese Africans on the mines, only 66,000 had to be recruited annually, whereas to maintain 100,000 Union Africans on the mines would have meant recruiting 132,000 of them annually. (62) Another economic advantage of the Portuguese Africans was that they could be used to even out the quotas of African labour distributed to the mines by the recruiting agencies. Some of the Union Africans would choose the mines they wanted to work on, or try to avoid the most unpopular mines, and consequently 'the East Coast native is used to even up, and he largely goes to the more unpopular mines'. (63)

This employment of foreign migrant labour was also politically advantageous to the mining companies. As has been pointed out, the employment of such labour produces 'a basic modification in the social and political structure of the indigenous population', fragmenting the working class and weakening its bargaining power. 'In a word, it achieves the "de-nationalisation" of decisive sectors of the working class, by replacing the indigenous proletariat with an imported proletariat, which leads a marginal . . . existence deprived of political, trade union and civil rights.' (64) Nowhere was this truer than in South Africa - and in the gold mines in particular - where the working class was already extremely fragmented economically, politically and culturally, and became more so with the large-scale employment of foreign workers.

The importation of non-white labour from outside South Africa, especially from Portuguese East Africa, was thus of considerable importance to the mining companies, in counteracting the problem of competition for such labour within South Africa, and in various other ways. Indeed, the Chamber of Mines was disturbed that 'many people do not realise how essential the East Coast native is, and always has been, to the success of the mining industry in the Transvaal', declaring that without this labour supply, 'the opening up of the gold fields and the development of South Africa would have been very greatly retarded'. (65)

2 Securing the ultra-cheapness of non-white labour

The imperative of acquiring a large supply of non-white labour was thus realised by various means. But the crucial imperative was the ultra-minimisation of labour costs. The critical requirement of the mining companies was to secure and maintain the extreme cheapness of this labour. This they came to achieve in various ways: generally, through the subjection of African workers to extreme extra-economic compulsion, and to certain pressures serving to weaken their market position, and specifically, through a system of wage minimisation.

(a) Extra-economic compulsion: the contract system, the pass system and the compound system As we noted, the system of class domination established by the white property owners in South Africa included measures of racial discrimination serving to secure the extreme powerlessness of non-whites and the extreme exploitability of non-white workers by subjecting non-whites to various forms of extra-economic compulsion. In securing the extreme subordination of non-white workers, the most important of these were the coercive contract system of the Master and Servant Laws and the coercive regimentation system of the Pass Laws. To these, the mining companies added their own institution of forced labour - the mine compound system. By securing the ultra-exploitability of non-white workers, these measures of extra-economic compulsion played the key role in securing the ultra-exploitation of non-white labour.

One of the first things which white property owners had done, as they integrated non-whites as workers into the new system of production which they were establishing, was to institute legislation restricting the contractual rights of non-white workers. These rights were defined and restricted by a body of laws known as the Master and Servant Laws. These laws, which were closely modelled on the first such law, that of the Cape of 1856, regulated the formation, duration and termination of contracts, and the duties and obligations of servants and masters under labour contracts. The central and essential feature of this legislation was that it made breach of contract by non-white workers a criminal offence, carrying penalties of imprisonment (and various other acts by servants, such as insubordination and making a disturbance on the master's property, were also defined as criminal offences). (66) And the breach of contract provisions of the Master and Servant Laws were made specifically applicable to all African workers in the gold mines by the Native Labour Regulation Act of 1911. (67)

The Director of Native Labour expressed the prevailing attitude of employers and government officials about the contractual rights of African workers when he stated that:

> I regard the average native labourer much as I should regard the European youngster apprenticed to a trade. . . . He enters into a contract at random and breaks it at random . . . and there is no civil remedy that can be satisfactorily enforced against him. . . . To make him an entirely free agent as a labourer . . . would certainly cause industrial dislocation and jeopardise the economic prosperity of the country. (68)

The subjection of non-white workers to penal sanctions for breach of contract was one of the important differences between their position and that of white workers, who were only subject to civil penalties. As the leader of the South African Labour Party put it, the difference was that:
> If I make a contract to labour for you and I refuse to carry out that contract, your only remedy is to sue me in the courts. If a native enters into a contract to labour for me and does not carry out his contract, it is a crime against the State for which he can be punished with imprisonment. That distinguishes the free system and the quasi-feudal system. (69)

The contractual position of African mine workers was distinguished not only by penal sanctions for breach of contract but also by long term minimum-time contracts. All Africans taking up work in the gold mines had to enter into long term contracts, during which they could not legally seek or take up employment anywhere else. The minimum contract period was six months, which applied to Africans from British South Africa, until 1924, when the mining companies extended it to nine months; (70) and the minimum contract period for Portuguese and other foreign Africans was twelve months.

These penal sanctions for breach of contract and these long term contracts played an important role in restricting the power and freedom of African mine workers. The penal sanctions made any strike action or other insubordination by African workers illegal. As will be seen, it was to these sanctions that the employers made recourse in their repression of the unrest which developed among African workers on the Rand during and following the First World War. And the long term contracts instituted by the mining companies further restricted the freedom and mobility of African mine workers.

Another major concern of white property owners in South Africa, in addition to that of establishing a coercive contractual relationship with non-white workers, was that of controlling and directing the movement of non-whites. This concern found concrete expression in a system known as the pass system, which was instituted in a body of laws known as the Pass Laws, laws which, like the Master and Servant Laws, were initiated in the nineteenth century and consolidated over time.

The pass system was a system of movement control and labour regimentation, serving to strengthen the hold of white property owners over non-white workers, by controlling and directing the movement of non-whites generally and of non-white workers in particular. Before they could leave their place of residence to seek employment elsewhere, travel from one labour district to another, seek employment in an urban area, take up employment, or leave the boundary of a mine, Africans had to obtain a pass, within which details about them were registered, and which in certain cases cost 1s.; and Africans residing within urban areas were subject to a night curfew, prohibiting them from being in any public place between 9 p.m. and 4 a.m. without a written pass from their employer. As in the case of the Master and Servant Laws, infringement of the Pass Laws was a criminal offence, carrying penalties of imprisonment. All African mine workers (many of whom came from outside South Africa) were made subject to the Pass Laws by the Native Labour Regulation Act of 1911. (71)

The essential purpose of this system was to reinforce the hold of employers over African workers - in particular, to check breach of contract and desertion by these workers, and to weaken the position of these workers in the labour market. Having coercive labour contracts was not much good to employers if African workers could not be kept to their labour contracts. Something had to be done to discourage and check desertion, a problem with which all employers, not least the mining companies, were faced. 'The industry has hitherto suffered materially', the President of the Chamber of Mines complained, 'in consequence of the frequent desertion of native labourers during the currency of their contracts.' (72) There was a considerable tendency among African mine workers to desert from their jobs and escape from the mines. By the time of Union, in 1910, the annual desertion rate was about 15 per cent - about 30,000 out of about 180,000. (73)

The pass system was designed to keep African workers in their labour contracts. It provided, a government report observed, 'a means of enforcing contractual obligations between natives and Europeans and of detecting deserters'. (74)

> Some measure of control was considered necessary for the maintenance of contracts, and the force of control lay in the administration of the pass laws. . . . One of the principal objects of the pass system was to secure the fulfilment of contracts entered into by natives and the fear that any relaxation of the control it aimed at securing would result in wholesale desertion. (75)

The system served to enforce labour contracts and to check desertion through its movement controls and as an identification and reference system. The system prevented Africans from moving about freely, subjecting them to various checks, and the passes contained details of their employment position (as well as information about any offences committed by the pass-holder, and a 'character' column in which employers gave their opinions about the pass-holder), which provided a means of inhibiting desertion and generally rationalising the movement of Africans to suit white property owners.

The pass system also served to weaken the pre-employment bargaining position of African workers in the labour market, by forcing them to take up employment within a short space of time. Within twenty-four hours of arrival in a labour district, the African worker had to report to a pass office to obtain a six-day pass. If he had not become employed within six days, he was liable to fines, imprisonment and expulsion from the labour district. This enabled employers to offer negligible wages, knowing that African workers had to accept them or face arrest.

This coercive regimentation system constituted by the pass system thus complemented the coercive contract system in securing the ultra-exploitability of non-white workers. To these two institutions of forced labour, the mining companies added a third one of their own specifications, that of the compound system. This was a system, first developed in the Kimberley diamond mines and then implemented on a large scale in the gold mines, of accommodating African mine workers in concentration-camp-like compounds on the grounds of the mines. It constituted an important form of labour control, from which the mining companies derived economic and political benefits.

Economically, the system helped to reduce costs and to stabilise the African labour supply. The standardised mass feeding and housing of African workers permitted economies of scale, and established living standards at a level of subsistence and cost chosen by the mining companies. And the compounding of workers served to inhibit absenteeism and desertion.

But the most important advantages were of a more political nature. The system served both to maximise the control of the companies over the behaviour of African workers, and to isolate these workers from the society around them. The fragmentation, isolation and concentration of the African labour force in separate, dependent and prison-like compounds was of great advantage to the companies in the management of unrest and insubordination among African workers. This system enabled them to deal with such unrest - as will be seen - by sending in police and troops to surround and enter the compounds, to bring compounds under control one at a time, to prevent communication between compounds, to tell workers in one compound that all other workers had returned to work, and so on. The compounds were physically constructed so as to be virtual prisons once enclosed from the outside. The model compound, in the view of the police, was that of the City Deep mine. 'It is surrounded first of all by a high galvanised iron fence. It has barbed wire on the top which prevents anybody getting in or out.' (76) And it had a special construction that permitted goods to be hauled in and out without the gates being opened. An efficient compound was defined as one which could adequately 'contain' African workers, and which had a reliable guard, a sufficient supply of arms and ammunition in the manager's office and strict supervision over entry and exit. (77) The Director of Native Labour was concerned that new compound plans should be checked to see 'if their defences needed strengthening'. (78) The compound system also served the political interests of the companies by isolating African mine workers from other workers and Africans and life generally on the Rand. This isolation was not total; African workers could and did leave the compounds - for which they had to obtain a pass. But their general life and work situation in the mine compounds was artificially removed from the society around them.

Employing nearly 200,000 African workers, who were concentrated together in a relatively small area, the mining companies were concerned to secure the maximum possible degree of coercive control over this enormous industrial labour force. The compound system served this purpose. And the combination of these various systems of coercive labour control - the contract system, the pass system and the compound system - served to secure and maintain the extreme exploitability of African mine workers.

(b) The system of wage minimisation With the ultra-exploitability of African labour thus assured, the mining companies were in a position to engage in the ultra-exploitation of African labour. What this involved specifically was a system of wage minimisation which served to secure the extreme minimisation of African wages through the elimination of competitive wage determination and through the collective standardisation of African wages at an extremely low level.

(i) The elimination of competitive wage determination As an essential first step towards the ultra-minimisation of African wages, the mining companies came to eliminate competitive determination of African wages. Such wage determination within the gold mining industry was terminated by the formation of the Native Recruiting Corporation in

1912, which fully monopsonised labour recruiting and introduced a new system of uniform African wage rates. And the pressure on wage rates that might have resulted from competition between different industries and employers for non-white labour in South Africa was neutralised by the mining companies by the importation of non-white labour from outside South Africa.

As we noted, the fundamental purpose of the monopsonisation of labour recruiting with the formation of the Native Recruiting Corporation was the minimisation of African labour costs. This partly involved the reduction of recruiting costs and the introduction of a new system of labour distribution. What it also involved was the elimination of competitive wage determination, and the introduction of a new system of wage fixation. An important effect of competition between the mining companies for African labour, we noted, was to exert upward pressure on African wages. As an economist observed:

> In particular centres such as the Rand, until agreement was reached among the mine-owners for wage fixation, conditions approximated towards equilibrium of supply and demand, and as the supply of workers usually lagged behind demand, there tended to be sharp competition for labour among the mine managers, resulting in wage rates being driven above what was regarded as a desirable maximum. (79)

The principal function of the Native Recruiting Corporation was to eliminate any such competitive wage determination within the gold mining industry, and to replace it with a system of wage fixation which, as we shall see, standardised African wages at an extremely low level.

It was this monopsonistic organisation of recruiting and wage determination that lay behind the phenomenon reported by the Economic and Wage Commission, in regard to the gold mining industry, that: 'Everywhere we were informed that there was a shortage of native labour, yet the ordinary result of such a shortage - a rise in wages sufficient to reduce the demand to equality with the supply - does not take place.' (80) But this was no 'ordinary' situation, since the 'law' of supply and demand had been suppressed by the recruiting monopsony. As an economist pointed out:

> The pricing system as a rationing device, and one which, moreover, tends to ensure that scarce labour will be used for more productive rather than for less productive purposes (the more productive mines could outbid the less productive mines if they were free to do so), has thus been superseded. Mine labour . . . is distributed between employers in an arbitrary manner. (81)

It may have seemed 'arbitrary', but for the gold mining companies it was a rational solution to a serious problem.
While the problem of competitive wage determination within the gold mining industry was dealt with by the monopsonisation of labour recruiting, there was still the danger that competition between different groups of employers for non-white labour in South Africa might exert upward pressure on wages. This problem the mining companies resolved through the importation of non-white labour from outside South Africa. This served to neutralise such pressure - and thus to benefit all employers and not just the mining companies - by raising the total supply of non-white labour and thus reducing competitiveness in demand.

Such labour importation thus weakened the market position of African workers in South Africa. Without 'the natural compensating factor, namely, the surplus Mozambique native', the President of the Chamber of Mines pointed out, the mining companies and other employers would be threatened by labour shortage, which would exert upward pressure on wages. (82) And it was precisely for this reason that Union Africans objected to this 'compensating factor'. 'We say', an African leader declared, 'that the natives in the Union are not in a position to ask for better pay, because the mines have an immense gang of cheaper labour elsewhere outside the Union.' (83) 'The resort to tropical natives', in the view of the Transvaal Native Congress, 'is an effort to obtain cheap labour and to avoid paying a decent wage to natives within the Union.' (84) 'The industries of the Union', the Congress stated, 'must (and they can) be made to develop on the resources of the country from within', and employers could elicit more labour from within South Africa with better wages and less coercive labour conditions. (85) Union Africans, an African leader affirmed, felt that the more the mines were flooded with non-Union labour, the more 'this would take the bread out of their mouths'. (86) 'We are in the same position as the white workers in this case,' an African mine worker observed. 'The white workers think that we are gradually ousting them, and we think those people will oust us.' (87)

(ii) Wage fixation, the maximum average system and the loafer ticket system   The elimination of competitive determination of African wages, through the monopsonisation of recruiting and the importation of foreign non-white labour, thus also provided - in addition to the system of extra-economic coercion - a general foundation for the ultra-exploitation of African workers. Such exploitation was then specifically secured by the mining companies through a system of wage minimisation, which worked through the establishment of ultra-low time and piece rates, through a system of minimising piece work earnings, and through a system of unpaid and extra-contractual labour.

This system was one of the innovations implemented by the mining companies with the formation of the Native Recruiting Corporation. Through a new wage system introduced and administered by the Corporation, the companies standardised the remuneration of all African workers employed in the gold mines, and standardised it at an extremely low level, in three basic ways. In the first place, the Corporation fixed all time work and piece work wage rates of African workers at an ultra-low level, which averaged about 2s. per shift (day's work). The standard rates fixed for the main occupations in which African workers were employed are shown in Table 1.

TABLE 1 Rates of pay, African workers, Witwatersrand gold mines

Type of work	Rate per shift s. d.
Shovelling	1 6
Tramming	1 8
Machine helping Spanners Handles	1 9 2 0
Hand drilling (hammer boys) Up to 2 hours shovelling and less than 6 inches drilled Up to 2 hours shovelling and between 6 and 36 inches drilled	- 9d.-2s. 6d.

NRC Ltd, Schedule of rates of pay, 'Report of the Mining Industry Board' (Cape Town: 1922, UG 39/22), pp.46-51.

In the second place, it introduced a system known as the maximum average system to restrict the earnings of African workers engaged in piece work. The Corporation included in its schedule of rates of pay for African workers a provision that the average wage paid to African workers employed in piece work could not exceed a maximum of 2s. 3d. per shift, and that any company which allowed the average to exceed this maximum was liable to the penalty of a fine. (88) This system was rendered more flexible at the end of the First World War, when a sliding scale maximum average was introduced, in which the permissible maximum average fluctuated between 2s. 3d. and 2. 9d. per shift according to the percentage of Africans in piece work (the higher the percentage, the higher the maximum), and a company's average would have to exceed the maximum for two consecutive months before the company became liable to penalisation. (89) But the system remained in its essentials, restricting the maximum permissible average earnings of African workers engaged in piece work (which was mainly hand drilling) to well below 3s. per shift. The Corporation also provided that no company could pay more than 3 per cent of its total underground complement of African labour as high as 3s. per shift. (90)

A third way was through the 'loafer ticket' system - a system of unpaid and extra-contractual labour. African workers engaged in drilling work were paid at piece rates, which varied according to the number of inches drilled. But it was the practice of the companies - a practice incorporated into the Corporation's schedule of rates of pay - to employ these African workers for several hours before their drilling work in shovelling and lashing work, which was not specified in their contracts, and for which they were not paid. Then if, as was often the case, these workers, after doing this other work, failed to drill a certain minimum number of inches, they were subjected to a double penalty: they received no payment (later a token payment) for that shift, and that shift was not counted as a contract shift - the African received a 'loafer ticket' for such a shift, and had to work an additional shift for every such shift to complete his contract. At first, the system fixed by the companies (in 1909) was no payment for less than 30 inches drilled. (91) But following the reports of the Native Grievances Inquiry (1914) and of the Economic Commission (1914), this was changed to no payment for less than 6 inches, and a token payment (of 1s.) for less than 24 inches. (92) And in all cases, the shift was not counted as a contract shift. As the Corporation's pay schedule prescribed:

> Any shift during which a native employed in hand drilling fails to do sufficient shovelling . . . to clear the face after the preceding blast and in addition to drill 24 inches, shall be deemed to be an incomplete shift, and shall not count against the period of service. (93)

This system - which, as we shall see, constituted a particularly acute grievance of African mine workers - thus served both to minimise labour costs and to intensify the rate of exploitation through the non-payment of part of the labour performed in all African drilling shifts, and through the non-payment, and later negligible payment, of entire 'loafer ticket' shifts; and to maximise the labour supply, since such shifts were not recognised as contract shifts, and every such shift meant an additional shift.

The system instituted by the mining companies to minimise the remuneration of African workers thus secured the ultra-cheapness of African labour in various ways. (94) This system, particularly the maximum average system, was an interesting form of capitalist collectivism, which inhibited the profit maximisation of certain individual companies for the sake of maximising the profitability of all of the companies. Thus the introduction of the maximum average system had the effect of restricting the productivity and profits of the most profitable companies, whose average piece work rates were higher than the new maximum average. On certain mines, the new system brought about a fall in the average from about 4s. to about 2s., and the scheme was opposed by certain mine managers. (95) The maximum average system thus had all the appearance of being 'dysfunctional', since, as a Commission of Inquiry reported, it operated in such a way that 'whenever the general run of natives on this work becomes more efficient, the management is compelled to reduce the rate, thus actually penalising efficient work'. (96)

But such was only appearance. Like the recruiting monopsony, the maximum average system was a rational product of the pursuit of profitability. The specific function of the system, as of the whole wage minimisation system, was to minimise African wages in such a way as to prevent the profitability of the less profitable companies from being jeopardised by the establishment of wage rates that could only be profitable to the most profitable companies. As this Commission continued: 'The purpose of this clause is of course to prevent the mines outbidding each other for piece work labour, just as the prescribed rates prevent them with respect to day's pay labour.' (97) 'Our great idea', the Chairman of the Native Recruiting Corporation explained, 'was to break down the continual competition for labour which was raising everything.' (98) As another Corporation official stated: 'It was only done . . . to prevent the richer mines from paying a higher wage to their natives than the poorer mines, and thereby attracting labour to themselves and leaving the poor ones to languish; that was the reason.' (99) In short, as the Chairman put it, the wage fixation system 'serves the useful purpose of keeping things within limits'. (100)

But why was this specific function of the wage

minimisation system 'functional'? What was the general significance of this system? In other words, why did capitalists not invest their capital and determine the system of production solely or primarily in terms of the rate of profit of specific companies?

The answer is that in the capitalist gold mining industry of the Rand, the mass of profit that could be accumulated from the operation of the largest possible number of companies that could operate profitably, albeit at a lower average rate of profit than certain highly profitable companies, was far greater than the mass of profit that could be accumulated from a few companies operating at a high rate of profit. And this formula, which might have been potentially the case in other industries but not realised in practice owing to a competitive structure of ownership and control, in fact became a dominant principle of organisation and practice in the Rand gold mining industry, because this industry, as we noted earlier, was a kind of oligopoly, in which the individual producing companies were not autonomous enterprises but were owned and controlled by a few groups of capitalists, whose investment in gold mining was an investment in a group of companies, and whose profit comprised the total profit accumulated by the group of companies.

Specifically, what this meant was that wage rates were to be determined not in the interest of the maximisation of the rate of profit of the most profitable companies, but at such a level as to secure the widest possible extension of the margin of profitability, in the interest of the maximisation of the total volume of profit accumulated by the collective operation of all of the companies that could operate profitably. This was the general function of the maximum average system, as of the whole system of wage minimisation.

3 The involvement of the mining companies in racial discrimination

The preceding analysis has sought to show why and how the mining companies came to be involved in racial discrimination, an involvement the nature and significance of which we may now review and discuss. This involvement, we saw, served to secure the class interests of the mining capitalists, interests which derived from their specific position in the class structure and system of production of which they formed a part.

The driving interest of the class of private owners of capital which owned and operated the mining companies was the accumulation of profit; the accumulation of profit through the mining of gold on the Rand was critically dependent on the ultra-minimisation of labour costs; the resolution of this problem was made possible by the ultra-exploitability of non-white labour in the system of production established by white property owners in South Africa, a system of production which included a racially discriminatory system of class domination and forced labour, which served to secure the extreme powerlessness of non-whites generally and of non-white workers in particular, and thus to permit the ultra-exploitation of non-white labour; the profitability of the mining companies came to be secured through the operation of various specific forms of racial discrimination, which served to secure and maintain the ultra-exploitability and ultra-exploitation of non-white labour. For the mining companies, therefore, racial discrimination served as a means of securing profit.

Measures of racial discrimination serving to secure class interests and to resolve class problems will be referred to in this study as 'class colour bars'. The class colour bars of the mining companies were those measures of racial discrimination through which the companies secured the ultra-exploitability and ultra-exploitation of non-white labour. These will be referred to as the 'exploitation colour bars'. The exploitation colour bars essentially comprised the contract system, the pass system, the compound system, and the wage minimisation system.

The exploitation colour bars included but were not synonymous with the system of forced labour. The latter chiefly comprised the contract system, the pass system and the compound system (while also including such discriminatory measures as the discriminatory political franchise and system of government), which served to secure and maintain the ultra-exploitability of non-white labour. But the exploitation colour bars also included the discriminatory system of wage minimisation which, through the ultra-minimisation of time rates, and of piece rates (the maximum average system), and the loafer ticket system of unpaid and extra-contractual labour, served to secure the ultra-exploitation of non-white labour.

The involvement of the mining companies in racial discrimination was partly an involvement in exploitation colour bars already in operation, already instituted by property owners in South Africa - such as the contract system, the pass system and the compound system. And it was partly an adaptation and extension of this discrimination to meet their own specific interests - in such forms as the institution of minimum long term contracts, the consolidation and large-scale implementation of the compound system, and the system of wage minimisation.

It may be noted in passing that the term 'colour bar' has not usually been used in relation to the exploitation of labour. The tendency, in the study of the socio-economic aspects of race relations in South Africa and elsewhere, has been for the term to refer merely to one particular type of racial discrimination - discrimination in access to employment. The 'colour bar' has usually meant the 'job colour bar' (of the white workers). The reasons and significance of this usage aside - they will be discussed later on - it is clearly unjustified. For racial discrimination (and other forms of discrimination) in the socio-economic sphere may be and has been of other types, such as measures securing the ultra-exploitability of workers belonging to the discriminated-against group, and measures securing and maintaining the proletarian condition of its members. And such other types of discrimination may play and have played a very important role in the exploitation and ultra-exploitation of labour, as did the measures of racial discrimination wielded by property owners in South Africa. (101)

The exploitation colour bars thus served to secure profit for property owners through the ultra-exploitation of non-white labour. For no group of owners was this of more vital importance than for the gold mining companies. This was because, as we saw, the specific economic and geological conditions of the Rand gold mining industry, notably the fixed price and the low grade, made imperative the ultra-minimisation of labour costs, and rendered the profitability of the mining companies critically dependent on the ultra-exploitation of non-white labour. While all owners benefited from the exploitation colour bars in the form of profit maximisation, for the mining companies they were the sine qua non of profitability.

This critical dependence of the mining companies was an undisputed fact, and the companies were themselves the first to acknowledge it. 'It was not so much the richness of these fields that attracted the necessary capital', the Chamber of Mines declared (in something of an understatement, in view of the very poor grade of the ore), 'as it was their apparent continuity and the fact that they could be worked efficiently by cheap native labour.' (102) The Chamber did not tire of emphasising that: 'There is no factor in the industrial fabric of the mines of greater importance than the native labour supply.' (103) 'Without the native', the 'South African Mining Journal' observed, 'the Witwatersrand gold mining industry would not exist, or, if it did exist, then only on a very small scale.'

(104) As a mining engineer pointed out: 'As a mining proposition, the Rand is known all over the world as a low grade proposition, and you would not be able to work it unless you did have very cheap labour.' (105) And as an economist concluded: 'What made the Rand possible was the fact that the Kaffir worker would be employed for not over £50 per year . . . It is indisputable that the mines were saved by the services of a non-competing group of black workers.' (106) The profitability of the mining companies depended on the minimisation of the wages of the ultra-exploitable 90 per cent of their labour force to an average of 2s. per shift (in comparison with the average of 20s. per shift of the politically free 10 per cent of the labour force). Higher wages for 90 per cent of the labour force would have been quite incompatible with profitability.

> A shilling a day to the boys [as a wage increase] would wipe out practically half the dividends paid by the Rand? - Yes, and it would be a great deal more than that; it would wipe out the bulk of the Rand except a very few mines. (107)

And this was just a question of a 1s. increase. The cost of politically free labour would have been far more than 3s. a shift. Without the exploitation colour bars and the ultra-exploitation of non-white labour, few if any of the mining companies would have been able to operate profitably. (108)

In the preceding sections, we looked at all of the ways in which the mining companies came to maximise the supply and minimise the cost of non-white labour. As was evident, some of these, such as the recruiting monopsony, the system of debt inducement, and the importation of labour, did not constitute measures of racial discrimination. It was not the case that every instrument of profit maximisation operated by the companies was a measure of racial discrimination. What was the case was that the profitability of the companies was critically dependent on the system of racial discrimination constituted by the exploitation colour bars, which secured and maintained the ultra-exploitability (subjection to a system of forced labour) and ultra-exploitation (appropriation of profit from the labour of ultra-exploitable workers) of non-white workers.

Our concern here has been to elucidate the specific nature of the involvement of the mining companies in racial discrimination. This involvement was seen and explained as a means of securing the driving class interest of the companies: the accumulation of profit. This involvement in racial discrimination for the purpose of profit accumulation took the specific form of measures of racial discrimination serving to secure and maintain the ultra-exploitability and ultra-exploitation of non-white workers - referred to as exploitation colour bars. The exploitation colour bars were the profit-maximising part of what were referred to as the class colour bars - racially discriminatory class instruments serving to secure class interests - of the property-owning class (the other part being the property colour bars, serving to secure and maintain the separation of non-whites from ownership of property in the means of production), adapted and extended by specific groups of property owners, like the mining companies, to meet their own specific profit accumulation requirements. And, because of the specific conditions of the gold mining industry, the profitability of the mining companies was critically dependent on the exploitation colour bars.

(B) THE WHITE WORKERS AND THE SYSTEM OF RACIAL DISCRIMINATION

In seeking to elucidate the involvement of one of the groups which operated the system of racial discrimination - the mining capitalists - in this system, we considered the specific class position, problems and interests of this group, and the way in which these determined its specific involvement in racial discrimination. Following the same analytical procedure, we shall now be concerned to elucidate the involvement in racial discrimination of the other group which operated the system - the white workers.

1. THE CLASS POSITION OF THE WHITE WORKERS

The first questions in an examination of the white workers must be, why speak of a group of white workers? What is the analytical meaning, for this study, of the term 'white workers'? Of course an answer to the first question could simply be found in the observed fact that one of the groups operating the system of racial discrimination which this study is concerned to explain was a group of white workers, which merits particular attention for that reason. But there is a more important and more fundamental answer to these questions, which concerns the South African social formation and the respective political positions of white and non-white workers, and which needs to be made clear at this stage.

As was earlier observed, in the system of production which they established in South Africa, white property owners instituted particular relations of production with a particular group of workers - highly coercive relations of production with non-white workers. They established a racially discriminatory system of class domination, the main function of which was to secure the ultra-exploitability of non-white workers, by securing, through various forms of extra-economic compulsion and domination, the extreme powerlessness of non-whites generally and of non-white workers in particular (its other function being to reproduce and consolidate the economic base of the system of production by increasing and perpetuating the separation of non-whites from ownership of or free access to property in the means of production).

It came to pass, however, for reasons which we shall observe, that another group of workers came into being in South Africa - workers who shared with non-white workers the general class condition of separation from ownership of or free access to property in the means of production, but who were members of the white pigmentation group, and were, as such, not subject to the highly coercive system of class domination operated by the property owning class over non-white workers. Unlike the non-white workers, these white workers were politically free, in this specific sense of not being subject to the system of forced labour, of being free from extra-economic restrictions on mobility in the labour market, and free to organise and act collectively through such means as trade unions and strikes, and political parties and the vote.

The South African working class thus came to be made up of two groups of workers subject to quite different relations of production with the property owning class - a group of ultra-exploitable (non-white) workers and a group of politically free (white) workers, a sector of forced (non-white) labour and a sector of free (white) labour. And the analytical meaning, for this study, of the term 'white workers' is thus 'politically free workers', in the sense defined above, just as the analytical meaning of the term 'non-white workers' is thus 'ultra-exploitable workers' - that is, workers subject to a system of forced labour. Moreover, not only were the white workers not subject to the racially discriminatory system of forced labour; they themselves came, for reasons and in ways which we shall observe, to institute and operate racial discrimination. We may now take a closer look at this group of workers.

Chapter 1

1 Class formation and class situation

(a) The genesis of the white working class   The formation of a group of white workers in South Africa stemmed essentially from two factors: the immigration of white skilled industrial workers to the Rand consequent upon the absence of such workers in South Africa at the time of the gold discovery, and the proletarianisation of part of the white group in South Africa.

As was earlier observed, the mining of gold on the Rand came to comprise large scale and complex industrial production, both in the deep-level mining operations necessary to reach and mine the low-lying, downward sloping reef of ore, and in the complex reduction operations necessary to extract the gold from the very low grade ore (as also did the industrial infra-structure which arose on the Rand to service the gold mining industry). While the bulk of labour could be performed by unskilled workers, this industrial production required a considerable number of skilled industrial workers. But there were virtually no such workers in South Africa at the time of the discovery and initial development of the gold fields. Such workers were to be found in Europe and European-settled areas. Skilled industrial - and white - workers migrated from these areas to the Rand, and provided the skilled labour force of the gold mining industry, which will be examined shortly.

But far more important than the scarcity of skilled labour as a cause of the genesis of a group of white workers was the capitalist system of production evolving in South Africa, particularly the system of property ownership which constituted its economic base. The operation of this system of property ownership and this system of production had the effect of proletarianising an increasing number of whites - that is, of separating an increasing number of whites from ownership of or free access to property in the means of production, and thereby compelling them to subsist through selling their labour power in exchange for wages as workers in the employment of the owners of such property. While the skilled labour scarcity reflected particular labour market conditions, which might have been different (and not produced a group of white workers), this process of class formation within the white group in South Africa was an inexorable and necessary internal development of the specific system of production arising in South Africa.

This process of proletarianisation involved two related developments: the separation of certain whites from ownership of or free access to land, and the movement of these landless whites from the land into wage employment or unemployment in the urban areas.

The first of these developments stemmed from the operation of the capitalist system of property ownership in a situation of increasing land scarcity. The class consequences of this system, and of the system of production of which it formed the economic base, had been held in abeyance by the availability of new land. But by the end of the nineteenth century, most of the appropriable land in South Africa had been taken by white property owners. The system of private ownership of property for the purpose of profit maximisation then had the effect of excluding and separating numbers of whites from ownership of and free access to land - whites who did not possess sufficient capital to buy land or to remain economically viable on land which they owned. This effect was accentuated by the Roman-Dutch law of property rights, in force in the Boer Republics, whereby every son was entitled to a legitimate share of his father's land. This led to an increasing sub-division of farms, to the point where land which was acquired was often economically unviable. (1)

It thus transpired that, as De Kiewiet observed, 'rural society began to separate into classes of landed and landless men'. (2) Though deprived of land ownership, many of these landless whites initially remained on the land, as tenant farmers. These whites were known as 'bywoners'. In exchange for their labour, they generally received a house, grazing rights and some payment in kind or money. The position of the bywoner was not legally defined. There were no written contracts, no standard rate or form of remuneration, and no clear definition of duties. (3)

However, this quasi-feudal situation was only an intermediary stage in the process of class formation, which was superseded as the bywoners were propelled off the land altogether, into wage employment in the urban areas. This second phase of the process - the urbanisation of landless whites - also stemmed from the internal development of the capitalist system of production, in this case, from the capitalist restructuring of farm production, in conjunction with certain contingent historical factors.

As the wealthier property owners extended their land ownership at the expense of poorer owners and non-owners, they came to restructure farm production along more profitable lines, away from small-scale and extensively subsistence production, towards large-scale commercial production utilising the cheapest, most exploitable (nonwhite) labour. This led to the eviction of the bywoners, whose continuing economic independence and political freedom stood in the way of such a capitalist rationalisation of the system of farm production. (4)

This structural generation of urbanisation of landless whites was reinforced by certain historical events. While the rise of the gold mining industry provided some relief to such whites by creating a demand for transport riders, the completion of the railways to the Rand in the 1890s put the transport riders out of business. (5) Then a severe rinderpest epidemic in 1896 'forced into the towns a large number of those who had returned to the land as bywoners after the transport riding to the Rand had ceased'. (6) Then the South African War 'had the result of intensifying all the causes making for distress among the rural population', destroying many farms and much livestock, and pushing more whites off the land. (7) At the end of this war, about 10,000 rural whites who had been placed in British concentration camps were unable to find employment on the land. (8)

Forced off the land, the landless whites moved into the urban areas. And while this urbanisation was certainly due to a variety of factors, one must agree with De Kiewiet's conclusion that 'most of them went to the towns for the same reason that water flows uphill when driven by machinery'. (9) This urbanisation was concentrated in the Transvaal, where the relative and absolute number of whites in urban areas swelled dramatically, as these landless whites moved into the industrial complex emerging in and around the gold mining industry of the Witwatersrand.

Between 1904 and 1921, the proportion of the total South African population living in urban areas rose by 55 per cent. (10) Between 1891 and 1926, the proportion of the white population living in urban areas rose from 35 per cent to 58 per cent. (11) But the proportion of the white population of the Transvaal living in urban areas had reached 55 per cent in 1904, and rose to 60 per cent in 1911 and 64 per cent in 1921. (12) Between 1904 and 1911, while the urban population of South Africa as a whole rose by 14 per cent, the urban population of the Transvaal rose by 58 per cent. (13) Similarly, while the number of whites living in urban areas in South Africa rose by 7 per cent between 1904 and 1911, the number of whites in urban areas in the Transvaal rose by 42 per cent (70,000). (14)

The magnet at the centre of this urbanisation in the Transvaal was the Witwatersrand. The number of whites living in the Witwatersrand area had reached 123,000 by 1904, and rose to 196,400 in 1911, and 250,400 in 1921. (15) Between 1891 and 1926, the white population of Johannesburg increased from 10,000 to 168,000. (16) The population of the mining suburbs around Johannesburg on

the Rand also mushroomed during this period. (17)   The
total population of the Witwatersrand was 278,000 in 1904,
rising to 608,000 in 1921. (18)

Thus arose an indigenous group of white workers within the
white group in South Africa. It was thus a case first of
separation from ownership, then of complete dispossession
and proletarianisation, of eviction and urbanisation.
Just as in the opening up of the diamond mines, individual
small claimholders had been dispossessed by the large
capitalist groups, so too on the land did the richer property owners come 'to purchase holdings of their neighbours which were too small for economic exploitation or
independent holdings'. (19)   Separated from land ownership, but initially remaining on the land, landless whites
were then forced off the land altogether, to make way for
more profitable production. 'With the progressive abandonment of subsistence farming', De Kiewiet observed, 'the
semi-feudal relations of bywoner and labour tenant began
to give way little by little to relations more fitted to a
cash economy.' (20)   Began to give way, in other words, to
the more systematic exploitation of non-white labour and
the complete proletarianisation of white labour. 'Merely
human relationships are giving way, as they did in Europe
in the sixteenth century', MacMillan noted, 'to a cash
nexus', (21) and he concluded that:
> Underlying subdivision, locusts, and even drought,
> there is a fundamental cause, so widely prevalent in
> the de-populated areas as to be all but general. It is
> that South Africa is going the way of old Rome or of
> Tudor England. If the small man is disappearing, it is
> because he is being bought and pushed out more than is
> necessary for the big men, or safe for the country as a
> whole. (22)

And with this process of proletarianisation, the problems
of this group of whites were only just beginning.

(b) The white labour force of the gold mining industry
A group of white workers thus came into being in South
Africa, and the distinctive specific feature of the class
position of this group was its political freedom, in the
specific sense of its non-subjection to the system of
forced labour operating over non-white workers. But while
the members of this group shared a common general class
position, the group was internally differentiated in certain important respects, notably in respect of skills and
position in the occupational structure. For instance, it
was far from being the case that all white workers were
skilled workers, as we shall have occasion to observe.
What we have now to consider is the composition and

situation of the specific group of white workers with which this study is concerned - the white labour force of the gold mining industry.

The white mine workers occupied something of an elite position within the South African working class, enjoying a position of considerable strength in relation to the capitalist class. This strong position reflected various factors: their possession of scarce and highly required skills, together with the economic importance of the industry in which these skills were employed; their control, through trade unions, over the distribution of these skills to workers and of the supply of skilled labour to employers; and their general political freedom. This strong class position enabled the white mine workers to secure substantial wages and benefits. With this class position, and the conditions of employment following from it, the white labour force of the gold mines constituted a sort of labour aristocracy.

In the gold mines, the white labour force constituted the skilled labour force. All skilled workers were white workers, and all skilled and most semi-skilled jobs were held by whites (and, as will be seen, restricted to whites). The white workers in the gold mines fell into three main categories: the miners (employed in actual rock breaking - in stoping, shaft-sinking, development and reclamation); the artisans and mechanics (including banksmen, boiler makers and platers, brick layers, carpenters, drill sharpeners, electricians, fitters, erectors, machinists, masons, millwrights, moulders, painters, pattern makers, plumbers, pipe fitters, pumpmen, riggers, sawyers, smiths, skilled forge workers, splicers, stationary and locomotive engine drivers, winch drivers, skipmen, trammers, turners and various skilled workers in the reduction works, such as amalgamators and cyanide workers); and semi-skilled workers (employed in less skilled work in such areas as waste packing, pipe fitting, drill sharpening and track laying). During the period with which this study is concerned, there were about 18,000 whites employed in the gold mines, of whom about 17,000 were non-professional and non-salaried workers. Of these 17,000, about one-third were miners, about one-third were workers engaged in other skilled work, and about one-third were workers employed in less skilled work. (23)

The white mine workers were organised in various trade unions. Unions had been formed at an early stage in the development of the Rand, with the formation of the Amalgamated Society of Carpenters and Joiners in 1881, of the Amalgamated Engineering Union in 1886, of the Witwatersrand Mine Employees and Mechanics Union in 1892, of the

Iron Moulders' Society in 1896, and of the South African Engine Drivers' Association in 1898 (the first two of these being branches of British unions). By the early twentieth century, the white mine workers were organised in several craft unions and one quasi-industrial union. Various groups of skilled workers were represented by various craft unions, the main ones being the South African Engine Drivers' and Firemens' Association, the South African Reduction Workers' Association, the Amalgamated Engineering Union and the Amalgamated Society of Woodworkers (previously the Amalgamated Society of Carpenters and Joiners). The boiler makers, iron moulders and building workers also had their own unions. The largest were the Engineering Union (with about 3,000 members in 1913), and the Engine Drivers' Association (with about 1,000). (24) The miners were organised in the Transvaal Miners' Association, formed in 1902. But this union, which in 1913 became the South African Mine Workers' Union, gradually became something of an industrial union, representing not only the miners but also many of the other white workers employed underground. It was the largest union, with a membership of about 6,000 in 1913 and 7,000 in 1922. (25) The white workers also came to be served at the level of collective union bodies and political parties, with the formation, in 1902, of the Witwatersrand Trades and Labour Council (which, among other things, ran candidates for political elections); in 1909 of the South African Labour Party (which was committed to improving the position of the white workers); and in 1911 of the Transvaal Federation of Trades, which in 1914 became the South African Industrial Federation (which came to play an active role on the industrial front).

The strong class position of the white mine workers - a position which, as we shall see, they perpetuated and reinforced by controlling, in various ways, the supply and utilisation of skilled labour - gave them considerable bargaining power with the employers, and enabled them to obtain substantial wages and benefits. It enabled them to secure an average wage of about 20s. per day (about 25s. per day for skilled workers and about 15s. per day for semi-skilled workers), compared with the average African wage of about 2s. per day; and various benefits, such as phthisis and accident compensation, paid holidays, overtime rates and reductions in working hours, all of which raised the cost of white labour to the mining companies.

The group of white workers which came into being in the gold mining industry thus provided the industry's skilled labour force, and constituted a group of politically free, relatively expensive workers. The labour force of the gold mining industry thus came to comprise a large group of unskilled, ultra-exploitable (non-white), ultra-cheap workers, and a small group of skilled, politically free (white), relatively expensive workers. This was the general pattern. However, as time went by, the specific composition and distribution of this labour force was to change in certain important respects, the nature and significance of which will become apparent in Part 2.

2 The structural insecurity of the white workers

What we have so far observed of the class position of the white workers, and of the South African class structure and the system of production of which it formed a part, may be seen to indicate that the white workers were placed, by their specific position in this specific structure and system, in a position of great insecurity. This structural insecurity of the white workers, which we shall now go on to consider more closely, stemmed from the combination of two structural conditions: that of proletarianisation, and that of the forced labour system securing the ultra-exploitability of the majority of workers in South Africa. (26)

(a) Proletarianisation The structural insecurity of the white workers stemmed, in the first place, from the condition of proletarianisation. The condition of being separated from ownership of property in the means of production meant dependence for livelihood upon employment by the owners of such property, whose interest in such ownership was that of profit maximisation. This particular condition of economic dependence was a condition of fundamental insecurity.

It may be noted that the proletarian condition of the white workers differed from that of many African workers. The white workers were completely proletarianised. But this was not the case with many African workers, who retained some means of subsistence and some measure of economic independence in the areas, both within and without the Union of South Africa, not appropriated by white property owners, and who only periodically entered the labour market, and periodically left it, as migrant workers.

The white workers, however, could not periodically return to the land in this way. They lacked any means of subsistence besides that of selling their labour power to the owners of the means of production. As a trade union leader observed:

There is no question about it that the native is not so

divorced from other means of livelihood as the white man is. Many whites have only one means of living. The native can ... go back to the native territories and live there. (27)
And as a mining official put it, 'the native, who has somewhat peculiar circumstances, manages to keep himself and his family by working [outside the 'native territories'] only six months in the year, while a white man has to work twelve months.' (28) While the economic independence of the African population was being steadily and systematically reduced, a measure of such independence remained, and it was the case that the white workers, in their complete proletarianisation, were structurally more economically dependent than many African workers.

(b) *The differential exploitability of labour: the white workers and the ultra-exploitability of non-white labour* The structural insecurity of the white workers was greatly increased by the ultra-exploitability of the rest of the workers in South Africa. As we have observed, the South African working class came to be composed of two groups of workers subjected to radically different relations of production with the property-owning class: a group of ultra-exploitable (non-white) workers, whose ultra-exploitability was secured by a racially discriminatory system of class domination and forced labour, which served to secure the extreme powerlessness of non-whites generally and of non-white workers in particular; and a group of politically free, less exploitable (white) workers, who were not subject to the system of forced labour operating over non-white workers. This differential exploitability of white and non-white labour was reflected in a corresponding differentiation in the wages, and total cost to employers, of such labour: non-white labour was ultra-cheap, and white labour was relatively expensive.

The ultra-exploitability and ultra-cheapness of non-white labour greatly extended the structural insecurity of the white workers. For it constituted a very great incentive to employers to maximise profit by maximising the utilisation of non-white labour and minimising the utilisation of white labour.

The white workers were affected by this specific condition of insecurity in different ways. For the skilled white workers, it posed the threat of displacement from employment, while for the unskilled white workers it meant the restriction of employment opportunities.

(i) *The skilled white workers and the ultra-exploitability of non-white labour* By virtue of their skills, the skilled white workers enjoyed a more secure position than the unskilled. But the possession of skills was not in itself an immunisation against the problem of displacement by ultra-exploitable, ultra-cheap labour. If non-white workers acquired skills, and if employers were free to employ such workers in more skilled work, the security of the skilled white workers would be seriously undermined. There was no economic reason why, if non-white workers acquired skills, such workers could not be used in place of white workers; there was no economic reason why in the gold mining industry non-white workers could only be used for unskilled labour. And there certainly was an economic reason for the employers to seek to employ ultra-cheap (non-white) labour in more skilled work in place of relatively expensive (white) labour. The white mine workers were thus faced with the potential threat of undercutting and displacement by ultra-exploitable, ultra-cheap (non-white) labour, and this was to lead them to take measures to protect themselves against this threat.

And it was during the historical period upon which this study is focused - the period during and following the First World War - that this potential threat to the white mine workers became increasingly actual, for reasons and in ways and with consequences which we shall be examining in Part 2. This, we may note briefly, reflected various developments: the exodus of a number of white mine workers from their jobs to the war, and the inflow of a number of less skilled white workers; the acquisition of skills by a number of non-white workers, and their employment in certain semi-skilled jobs; and a serious profitability crisis of the mining companies, the resolution of which was to involve the displacement of white workers by non-white workers. Since these and other related developments will be considered in detail later on, they will not be pursued any further here.

(ii) The unskilled white workers and the ultra-exploitability of non-white labour: the 'poor white problem' As we observed earlier, a group of whites within the white group in South Africa became proletarianised. A significant feature of these workers was that, unlike the white workers who had migrated from outside South Africa to the Rand, most of them did not possess industrial skills, and had to seek employment in unskilled labour. But, given the availability of a large supply of ultra-exploitable and ultra-cheap (non-white) unskilled workers, employers preferred, for obvious reasons, to employ such workers in unskilled labour, and most unskilled labour in South Africa was thus done by non-white workers, at ultra-low wages. Unequipped to take up skilled work, unskilled white workers thus also found themselves unable to take up employment in the only work for which they were qualified. Thus ensued what became known as the 'poor white problem'.

For unskilled white workers, the structural insecurity deriving from the ultra-exploitability of non-white labour thus took the form of a barrier to employment opportunities. This barrier stemmed from the differential exploitability of white and non-white labour, and was reinforced on the ideological level.

The basis of this barrier was the ultra-exploitability of non-white labour, and the presence in the labour market of a large supply of unskilled non-white labour - conditions which provided employers with a great incentive, both in terms of labour cost and of control over labour, to employ non-white rather than white workers in unskilled labour. These conditions permitted, and explain, the extreme minimisation of wages in unskilled labour - the average being about 2s. per day, a level which was completely inadequate to meet the minimum, let alone average, living standards of the white workers. 'The scale of native wages', the Transvaal Indigency Commission reported, 'is considerably below what the white man has been in the habit of regarding as the minimum amount upon which he can live.' (29) And as an incentive to employers, the ultra-exploitability of non-white labour also served to close off employment opportunities for unskilled whites by ensuring the continuity over time of this ultra-cheapness of labour, and by providing employers with workers who could be treated far more coercively than politically free workers. Had white workers been extensively employed in unskilled labour, they could have acted to raise wages; and when white workers were employed in unskilled labour, a Commission observed, they were more assertive than non-white workers, more likely to 'work in a slovenly manner or behave uncivilly to employers'; not surprisingly, employers shared the opinion expressed by one employer to this Commission, about the employment of 'natives' in 'native's work': 'I myself prefer getting a native to do native's work, because I have less trouble with him.'(30) 'The Kaffir is so much more amenable to certain demands than the white man would be,' another Inquiry was told. 'There is not the least doubt about that. You can deal with the Kaffir very much as you like, but you cannot deal with the white man as you like.' (31)

This basis of the barrier to employment opportunities in unskilled labour for unskilled whites was compounded, on the ideological level, by the taboo status which had come to be accorded, within the ideology and status system of the white group in South Africa, to the performance of

unskilled manual labour by whites. A most important cause of the 'poor white problem', the Transvaal Indigency Commission reported, was 'the attitude of the people towards manual labour'. 'Many people', it observed of this attitude, 'do not appear to realise its strength and the real effect it has in preventing white men from doing unskilled work.' (32) The Inspector of White Labour reported that:
> No opportunity is ever lost by the Department of placing a boy in a satisfactory billet when occasion arises; but it is a difficult task, as so many of the boys do not realise that hard work is essential at the start and consider that manual labour should be performed by Kaffirs while they act as overseers only. (33)

The employment prospects of the unskilled whites were thus further restricted by the prevailing characterisation of unskilled labour as 'native's work'; by the fact that whites had been conditioned 'to regard any form of labouring as "Kaffir work" and hence as beneath the white man's dignity'. (34) It may be noted, moreover, that by leaving unskilled labour in the hands of non-white workers, this aversion to and rejection of unskilled labour by whites also served, in the long run, to threaten the security of the skilled white workers. As the Government Mining Engineer observed - an observation that was certainly true of the gold mining industry -
> The refusal of the white man to do what is called Kaffir work accelerates his own displacement. By letting the native do the work he also lets the native get the training, and when he is sufficiently trained, the temptation to the employer to put him in the place of the more expensive white man becomes irresistible. (35)

Out of these conditions thus arose what became known as the 'poor white problem'. For the new group of unskilled white workers, the initial traumatic experience of dispossession and proletarianisation - of being 'suddenly dragged from Arcadia into the glare and the roar of Birmingham, faced with the necessity to earn their bread in competition with the trained sons of a modern city' (36) - was accompanied by the equally traumatic experience of finding the only employment for which they were qualified virtually closed to them.

The 'poor whites' were defined by the Transvaal Indigency Commission as those able-bodied whites who were unskilled and unemployed and 'unable to obtain employment in rough manual labour in competition with the native'. (37) It was estimated that by 1920, the minimum number of 'poor whites' was between 100,000 and 120,000 - about 8 per cent of the white population. (38) The total number, however, was estimated to be much greater - about 15 per cent. (39) One report calculated that already in 1916 there were 37,000 whites without visible means of support, and 106,000 without adequate subsistence - figures which were considered to be 'undoubtedly gravely disquieting in a country which is not over-crowded, which should be able to produce sufficient food for itself and to spare, and which has been favoured by nature in the provision of vast mineral resources'. (40) And the deprivations normally accompanying such poverty were widespread. Thus a quarter of school-age white children, the report calculated, were without schooling because of poverty. (41) Between 1916 and 1920, while the white population of South Africa rose at an annual rate of 5.1 per cent, the annual rate of increase in the number of 'poor whites' was 11.6 per cent. (42) The 'poor whites' were made up almost entirely of those whites, mostly Afrikaners, who had recently been dispossessed and proletarianised in South Africa; hardly any of the immigrant, English-speaking white workers fell into this category. (43) And the bulk of the increase in the white population of the urban areas, especially of the Witwatersrand, noted earlier on, was made up of these 'poor whites'. (44)

The presence of this group of 'poor whites' was to be of considerable significance in the historical course of group relations in South Africa, in the 1920s in particular, as will be seen. That the 'poor white problem' did constitute a phenomenon of particular sociological significance was recognised by the many investigations which came to inquire into it, investigations which, in dealing with it, came to grapple - with varying degrees of success - with the problem of analysing and explaining the South African social structure and the situation of group relations emerging in South Africa. The Transvaal Indigency Commission considered that 'the poor whites are the peculiar product of countries in which there is a large coloured labouring population', and that:

> It is evident that the experience of America confirms the experience of South Africa as to the effect of the presence of the native on social and economic conditions. Where the white man directs and the coloured does the work, the relatively incapable white man is bound to be unable to maintain his position as an aristocrat in the economic world and must either merge with the coloured population or become a parasite on the white community. (45)

In the view of the Carnegie Commission on the Poor Whites, The term 'poor white' could hardly have come into common usage except in a country inhabited by an inferior non-European population as well as by Europeans. The term 'poor white' itself implies that traditionally the European inhabitants have a higher standard of living. (46)

The Unemployment Commission alleged that 'in a homogeneous nation individuals rise and fall according to their capacity, and find occupations suitable to it', but that

> when society is divided by an impassable racial distinction, those members of the superior race who would naturally occupy the lower stratum of society, and there be provided for, are debarred from earning a living by the sentiment against mixing with the inferior races. (47)

The problem was said to be caused by

> the presence in the country of two races at different levels of civilisation which do not mix. . . . The native, owing to his living on a lower scale of civilisation, and being physically as capable as the white, is able in unskilled work to sell his labour at a price at which the white man cannot live. (48)

Another Commission reported that:

> It may seem a paradox that there should be unemployment and poverty in a country where there is in the mines a wealthy industry employing hundreds of thousands of workmen, skilled and unskilled, and always crying out for labour. The answer to this and similar questions must be looked for in the social and economic conditions of this country, where there is a vast supply of efficient, and not unintelligent, labourers content to work at a lower wage than Europeans, and whose employment on similar work, side by side with them, is contrary to the feeling of the community. (49)

While these and other inquiries did at least focus on social and economic conditions, they begged as many questions as they answered. What were the specific structural determinants of these 'social and economic conditions'? Could the 'poor white problem' really be explained as 'the effect of the presence of the native on social and economic conditions', as 'the peculiar product of countries in which there is a large coloured labouring population'? Or was it not the effect of something else? Did the problem really stem from certain whites allegedly being 'incapable' and 'natural occupants of the lower stratum of society'? Or did the position and predicament of the 'poor whites' not stem from something else, which had nothing to do with 'natural incapacity'? Was it really a question of one group of workers being 'content' to work for negligible wages, and 'able' to because of low living standards, a 'low scale of civilisation'? Or did these wages and living standards not reflect something else, which had nothing to do with voluntary and preferential choice? Could the explanation of the problem be at all advanced by reference to such factors as 'the superior race' and 'the presence of an inferior race'? If 'an impassable racial distinction' lay at the root of the problem, why was there such a distinction, and, its specific form aside, what was its specific nature? And what was the structural basis of the 'sentiment against mixing with the inferior races', of the 'feeling of the community' against a certain kind of employment?

What was generally missing from such contemporary - as well as from later - accounts of the 'poor white problem', was a recognition and systematic analysis of its class nature and class basis. As the preceding analysis has suggested, in the all-too-brief space at its disposal, this problem may be explained as a particular type of class problem, deriving from and determined by a specific system of production and class structure. Within this system and structure, all white workers were placed in a position of extreme structural insecurity by the combination of their proletarian condition within a system of production in which the means of production were privately owned and used for the purpose of the maximisation and private accumulation of profit, and the ultra-exploitability of the majority of the workers in this system of production in which they, politically free workers, were dependent for their livelihood on employment. And for unskilled white workers, the effect of these conditions, and the specific form of this insecurity, was that of a bar to employment, unemployment, and poverty. The 'poor whites' were thus also victims - in addition to, though not in the same way and degree as, the non-whites - of the system of class domination, forced labour and ultra-exploitation of labour operated by the property-owning class over non-white workers.

2. THE CLASS COLOUR BARS OF THE WHITE WORKERS: THE EMPLOYMENT COLOUR BARS

We have observed the specific class position of the white workers, and we have observed how, in this position, this group was placed in a situation of extreme structural insecurity. This was to lead them to take measures to protect themselves against this insecurity. And the specific nature and form of these measures were to reflect and be determined by the specific nature and form of this insecurity.

This insecurity stemmed, we noted, from the proletarian condition of this group of whites, and the ultra-exploitability of the rest of the workers within the capitalist system of production in South Africa. The white workers were dependent for their livelihood on employment by private owners of the means of production, whose interest in such ownership and in labour was that of profit maximisation. And their access to and conditions of employment were seriously jeopardised by the ultra-exploitability of the majority of workers in South Africa.

In response to these conditions, the white workers came to take measures to secure and improve their access to and conditions of employment. Just as these conditions affected the security of skilled and unskilled white workers in different ways, so too did the achievement of this end mean different things for these two groups of workers. For the skilled white workers, it meant the control and restriction of the supply and distribution of skilled labour. For the unskilled white workers, it meant the creation and improvement of employment opportunities in unskilled work. The specific nature of the measures taken by the white workers in response to their structural insecurity was thus to be the pursuit of this end, in these different ways.

The specific form of these measures was to reflect the specific form of this insecurity. For protection against competition for employment from ultra-exploitable workers, the politically free (white) workers were to seek to restrict the employability of ultra-exploitable workers. As we have seen, the ultra-exploitable workers in South Africa were non-white workers, the ultra-exploitability of non-white labour being secured by a racially discriminatory system of class domination and forced labour, established by the property-owning class over the non-white population to secure the extreme powerlessness of non-whites generally and of non-white workers in particular, thereby permitting the ultra-exploitation of non-white labour. The restriction of the employability of ultra-exploitable workers thus meant the restriction of the employability of non-white workers. Certain of the measures taken by the white workers to secure and improve access to and conditions of employment were thus to assume the specific form of racial discrimination.

Thus did the white workers come to be involved in racial discrimination and to institute measures of racial discrimination. In the case of the skilled white workers, this racial discrimination was to assume the specific form of a job colour bar in skilled work, which served to restrict the employability of non-white workers in skilled work, by restricting all skilled work to whites. In the case of the unskilled white workers, this racial discrimination was to assume the specific form of a system, known as the 'white labour policy', of providing and restricting certain unskilled employment to white workers, at higher than prevailing unskilled wages.

The protectionist measures of the white workers were thus to take the specific form of employment colour bars. These were the class colour bars of the white workers, which we may now go on to examine. Given the particular focus of this study, attention will be focused on the job colour bar in the gold mining industry.

1 The employment colour bars

(a) The job colour bar in the gold mining industry

The white workers in the gold mining industry came to establish a comprehensive job colour bar - the most systematic and entrenched job colour bar in South Africa. Skills and skilled employment had originally been confined to white workers, the only skilled mine workers and industrial workers in the South African labour market being white. But in response to the conditions which we have just been examining, the white mine workers came to perpetuate this racial demarcation, to formalise and legalise the exclusion of ultra-exploitable (non-white) workers from skilled work. Gradually but steadily, a job colour bar restricting skilled work to white workers became entrenched in law.

There were two general spheres of skilled work in the mines - actual mining work, and the supervision and operation of machinery. In the latter sphere, discrimination first became incorporated into law in the 1890s, in the Boilers and Machinery Law of the South African Republic (the Transvaal), which provided 'that every person having charge of a winding engine used for raising and lowering persons shall be the holder of an engine driver's certificate of competency. No coloured person may hold an engine driver's certificate of competency.' (50) The mining legislation of the Crown Colony of the Transvaal retained this discrimination and extended it to include locomotive engine driving underground. 'No coloured person', it prescribed, 'shall be permitted to drive such engines.' (51) The draft Mining Regulations drawn up by the Mining Regulations Commission of 1907-10, which formed the basis of the Union's Regulations, proposed the generalisation of this colour bar to all supervision and operation of machinery: 'Boilers, engines and all machinery shall be in

charge or under supervision of competent white persons.'
(52) This was incorporated into the Mining Regulations of
the Union of South Africa.
As regards actual mining work, and related work, the
Mining Regulations Law of the South African Republic in
the 1890s only restricted the work of blasting to holders
of a blasting certificate of competency. But, as the
Government Mining Engineer later pointed out, 'the practice generally was the same as at present, namely, the
competent man was always a white man'. (53) The Crown
Colony's mining legislation repeated the Republic's provisions about blasting. (54) But the Mining Regulations
Commission included the draft Regulation that 'no person
other than a white man shall conduct blasting operations
in or about a mine'. (55) This was incorporated into the
Union's Regulations. As regards related work, jobs such
as those of gangers, banksmen, onsetters, mine overseers,
shiftbosses and surface foremen were also confined to
white workers on a de facto basis, 'there being at the
time no skilled coloured persons who could do the work'.
(56) But the Mining Regulations Law of 1896 restricted
the jobs of banksmen and onsetters to whites, and the
Regulations of Ordinance 54 of 1903 extended this discrimination by restricting the jobs of shiftbosses, surface
foremen and mine overseers to whites. This was continued
in the draft Regulations of the Regulations Commission,
and in the Union's Regulations.
The job colour bar was also legally entrenched at the
time of the importation of indentured Chinese workers by
the mining companies after the South African War. The law
governing the introduction and employment of these workers
- the Transvaal Labour Importation Ordinance of 1904 - included a provision restricting about 55 specific occupations and trades to whites. The Ordinance prescribed
that:
> So long as the labourer remains in this Colony he shall
> be employed only on unskilled labour . . . and in particular shall not be employed in any of the trades or
> occupations specified in Schedule I to this Ordinance
> except for unskilled labour therein. (57)

And it defined unskilled labour as 'such labour as is
usually performed in mines in the Witwatersrand District
by persons belonging to the aboriginal races or tribes of
Africa south of the equator'. (58) The Ordinance was repealed a few years later, with the repatriation of the
Chinese; but it set a precedent for the extension of the
job colour bar in coming years.
The job colour bar was incorporated into, and consolidated and extended by, the Mining Regulations of the newly

68 Chapter 1

formed Union of South Africa. The Union's mining legislation and regulations were embodied in a Mines and Works Act, and Mining Regulations, that were closely based on the draft Act and Regulations drawn up by the Mining Regulations Commission, appointed in 1907 by the Transvaal government to consolidate mining legislation and regulations. As we noted, the Commission's draft Regulations retained and extended the job colour bar. The Commission also introduced the term 'white' in place of 'European', the former being considered 'the more precise of the two'.

(59)
> Chairman: . . . I think the way in which it is suggested is alright. 'Every elevator shall be in charge of a competent and reliable European person'. Say European or white person, and leave European out?
> Fergusson: 'European' is defined as being a person of European extraction.
> Witness: Is not the word 'European' used throughout the Regulations, where white is meant?
> Chairman: I should say 'white person'. . . .
> Fergusson: You have got to exclude coloured persons then.
> Secretary: There are twenty two definitions by law of coloured persons.
> Dr Porter: If you say a person of European extraction, a Cape boy might be that too. . . .
> Chairman: If a Colonial is only a little tinged and you know that he is reliable, you can pass him. But you do not want a real coloured person, a black.
> . . .
> Fergusson: I think 'white person' would do.
> Chairman: I should change it all through.
> Dr Heyman: Excluding Japanese?
> Chairman: And Chinese and Indians.
> Witness: We had Japanese at our college.
> Chairman: The policy of the South African is to keep this as much as possible a white man's country. Both parties are agreed on that point. We do not want Japanese here if we can help it, nor Chinese.
> . . .
> Fergusson: If we put 'white' instead of 'European', we might have an albino Kaffir.
> Chairman: He is not a white. He is white coloured. We can discuss it further if necessary.
> Price: But we will take that as recommended there.

(60)
The term 'white' thus made its way into the Regulations. The Mines and Works Act was enacted by Parliament in

1911, and the new Mining Regulations were promulgated in 1911. (61) It was in the Regulations that the job colour bar was prescribed. The Union Regulations incorporated the job colour bar recommended by the Commission, and extended it. Many specific jobs were restricted to white workers, the most skilled jobs - such as those of mechanical and electrical engineer, winding engine driver, locomotive engine driver, boiler attendant, and miner entitled to blast - were specifically restricted to holders of certificates of competency, and a sweeping new discriminatory provision, Regulation 285, ruled that: 'Certificates shall not be granted to any coloured person in the Transvaal and Orange Free State, and certificates granted to any coloured person in any other Province shall not be available outside such Province.' (62)

Racial discrimination was established in the Regulations but not in the Act itself. The Act empowered the government to make Regulations about various matters, but not to make racially discriminatory Regulations. This was no innovation; it was the prevailing practice in the mining legislation since 1903, a practice which could be said to stem from a concern to avoid making such discrimination any more overt than necessary. (63) But this was to have political consequences at a later date, as will be seen, since technically it meant that the discriminatory Regulations were illegal for being ultra vires the enabling Act. This was common knowledge, recognised by both the Chamber of Mines and the mining unions. (64) But, for reasons which will become apparent, this was not to be tested in the courts until 1923, when the Supreme Court was to rule that these Regulations were ultra vires. As a result of this, the Mines and Works Act was to be amended by the 'Colour Bar Act' of 1926, which introduced racial discrimination into the enabling Act itself.

The incorporation and extension of the job colour bar in the Union's Mining Regulations reflected demands made by the white mine workers through their unions. The extension of the job colour bar in the draft Regulations of the Regulations Commission expressed these demands. (65) So did the extension of the job colour bar in the Union's Regulations. Thus the generalised discrimination of Regulation 285, concerning certificates of competency, was an implementation of a demand made by the Engine Drivers' Association. (66) And as a result of further representations from the unions, immediately after the promulgation of the Regulations, certain Regulations were amended so as further to strengthen the position of the white workers. (67) The implementation of the demands of the white mine workers reflected the considerable bargaining power of their unions, notably of the Engine Drivers' Association, whose members occupied a key position in the industry, and which played a leading role in the representation of these demands. A bargaining power which moved the Chamber of Mines to complain to the Department of Mines that:

> At the present time the gold mining industry is at the mercy of a very small number of men, namely, the Council of the South African Engine Drivers' and Firemen's Association, to an extent which the gold mining industry believes is unprecedented in the history of mining. (68)

By the time of the First World War, skilled work in the mines had thus become officially restricted to white workers by a job colour bar in the Mining Regulations. This legal job colour bar covered about two-thirds of the white mine workers, in about 35 skilled occupations. However, the one-third of these workers who were employed in semi-skilled work, in about 20 less skilled occupations, were not protected by these discriminatory Regulations, only by de facto discrimination. As the least skilled of the white mine workers, these workers were to be the most vulnerable to displacement. And during the First World War, the mining companies were to introduce a number of non-white workers into semi-skilled work. This was to lead to an extension of the job colour bar, in the Status Quo Agreement of 1918, to protect white workers employed in semi-skilled work. This was to be followed by an acute conflict between the mining companies and the white workers over the relative scope of the job colour bar, as the companies sought to resolve a profitability crisis through the more profitable utilisation of labour. With these and related developments we shall be concerned in Part 2.

(b) The White Labour Policy in unskilled work While the protectionist response of the skilled white workers to the structural insecurity deriving from the ultra-exploitability of non-white labour took the specific form of a job colour bar, restricting skilled work to white workers (in response to the specific threat of displacement from employment), protection for the unskilled white workers took the specific form of employment-creating racial discrimination in the sphere of unskilled work (in response to the specific problem of the extensive restriction of employment opportunities). This was known as the White Labour Policy.

The White Labour Policy was a policy pursued by the State as an employer, of giving preferential treatment in the public sector, notably the railways, harbours and postal services, to unskilled white workers, by providing and restricting certain unskilled employment to such workers, at higher than prevailing unskilled wages. This policy was pursued first by provincial governments shortly before the formation of the Union in 1910, and then by the Union government, in response to the rise of a group of unskilled white workers and of the 'poor white problem'. But it came into prominence in the 1920s, after the formation, following the 1924 election, of a Nationalist-Labour government, which pursued this policy more extensively and systematically than before, as the Civilised Labour Policy.

As a policy of the State qua employer in the public sector, as well as for various other reasons, notably that of extreme incompatibility with profit maximisation, the White Labour Policy was not applied to, and did not operate in, the gold mining industry; though certain calls were made for its application to the mines, something to which the mining companies were greatly opposed, as will be seen. The employment colour bar with which a study of the gold mining industry is concerned is thus the job colour bar in skilled work. All that is intended here is to take note of the White Labour Policy as a second form of racial discrimination in employment.

2 The involvement of the white workers in racial discrimination

The white mine workers thus came to institute and operate a system of racial discrimination in the form of a job colour bar in skilled work - an involvement in racial discrimination which we set out to explain. This specific involvement in racial discrimination was seen and explained, just as was the specific involvement of the mining companies in such discrimination, as a response to a specific class problem, and as a product of the specific system of production and class structure from which that class problem derived.

The specific class problem to which the job colour bar was a response was the extreme structural insecurity of the white workers, consequent upon the presence, in the labour market of the system of production in which they were dependent for their livelihood on employment, of a large group of ultra-exploitable workers, and which for the skilled white workers took the specific form of a threat of displacement from employment. The problem was, as we noted, that the ultra-exploitability of non-white labour constituted an enormous incentive to employers, in terms both of labour cost and of control over labour, to employ non-white rather than white (politically free) labour in all levels of work. Most importantly, it meant that non-white labour was very much cheaper, and could be kept ultra-cheap over time. 'The native is cheaper', the Mine Workers' Union pointed out, 'and he is employed for that reason throughout the country, because he is cheaper, and because his labour will remain cheaper.' (69) 'It is obvious that it is unfair competition as far as the whites are concerned,' an industrialist recognised. 'One man gets 3s., and the employer says that he is doing as good for 3s. as the white man for 20s. He will obviously take the 3s. man.' (70)

It was this problem which immediately underlay the job colour bar. As a leader of the Mine Workers' Union declared: 'What we are up against is the unfair economic competition we have to contend against. We realise that if we have to compete with the native at the native's standard it will be hopeless.' (71) The job colour bar served to protect the white mine workers from this problem, by restricting the employability of ultra-exploitable (non-white) workers in skilled work, by restricting skilled work to white workers. 'The real object of the white worker', declared another union representative, 'is to protect himself. He feels that if the colour bar is removed there will be unfair competition, and he has to do something to protect himself.' (72)

But, we noted, as a response to this condition of structural insecurity, the job colour bar was a product of the specific system of production and class structure of which that condition was itself a product: the capitalist system of production and the proletarian position of the white workers in it, and the ultra-exploitability of most of the workers in that system of production in which the white workers were dependent on employment. And since the ultra-exploitability of non-white labour was secured by the exploitation colour bars of the employers, embodied in the racially discriminatory system of class domination and forced labour established and operated by the property-owning class over non-white workers, the job colour bar may be said to have been a product specifically of the exploitation colour bars. It was the exploitation colour bars of the employers which, by extending the exploitability of non-white workers, extended the structural insecurity of the white workers, creating the need for a system of employment protection, and determining that it should take the specific form of a colour bar.

The white workers were thus specifically concerned, it is interesting to note, to identify the forced labour system operated by the employers over non-white workers as a system of colour bars, and as the factor responsible for the job colour bar. They were concerned, in the first place, to make it clear - in opposition to the habit of employers and others of referring to the job colour bar simply as 'the colour bar', as if it were the only form of racial discrimination in the mines - that those measures through which non-white workers were 'deprived in the interest of the companies, of any power to better their position or resist a ring of the companies which . . . does in fact exist to keep down their wages', were as much colour bars as the job colour bar. (73) The coercive contract system, which was 'the foundation upon which the whole of the system of recruiting cheap indentured native labour is built up', was 'one big colour bar'. (74) The employers wielded discriminatory labour controls 'expressly designed to enable the labour of the native to be obtained at the lowest figure which the ring of big employers can manage to keep it down to'. (75) The African worker

> during his term of service . . . is governed by laws which forbid, under criminal penalties, any attempt on his part to insist on improvement in his pay and conditions, and he is under a legal control by his employer during his term of service which makes him in effect something more like a serf than a labourer as the term is now understood in civilised countries. (76)

And it was this racially discriminatory system of forced labour, this system of 'indentured native labour', the white workers were concerned to stress, which, by securing the extreme exploitability of non-white workers and thus extending the insecurity of the white (politically free) workers, necessitated the job colour bar. As the Mine Workers' Union declared:

> The existing colour bar, whether it is justifiable on general grounds or not . . . has always been looked upon by the European worker of these fields as a protection set up by law against the tendency of the system of indentured native labour to encroach upon his sphere of livelihood. (77)

'The colour bar', a union leader stated, was 'our only safeguard against being eventually swamped by cheap indentured black labour'. (78) The job colour bar was seen as a necessary concomitant of the forced labour system. As the leader of the Labour Party told the President of the Chamber of Mines: 'I look upon this restriction as being complimentary to your indentured labour system. The native is here under the indentured labour system - he is not here under a free system.' (79) So long as the employers secured the ultra-exploitability of non-white workers the white workers had to protect themselves, they declared, against 'a system which tends unfairly to squeeze out the more civilised European worker'. (80)

It follows that any proposals we have to make to resist that tendency must be open to the criticism that they are artificial protection to the European worker and unfair to a certain proportion of native workers. Our reply to this criticism is that we are not responsible for the policy which makes the employers continually less dependent on our aid and leads to our position being constantly assailed; and that in the circumstances as they exist, we are entitled to such temporary protection as can be devised, however imperfect. . . . We therefore submit . . . that so long as the present policy holds by which the mine owners are helped by the operation of special laws to fill their labour requirements with masses of cheap indentured labour, we, as part of the European working population, are entitled to measures of protection for our means of livelihood. (81)

By the same token, the white workers considered that, as far as they were concerned, the reduction or abolition of the job colour bar would have to be contingent upon the reduction or abolition of the forced labour system. As the Mine Workers' Union declared:

We feel that if any partial or whole abolition of the colour bar took place the industries could not expect to have their cake and eat it. If they abolish the colour bar then they must abolish the indentured labour system and give every man full facilities to earn the full amount. (82)

Dissolution of the job colour bar would not be acceptable to the white workers 'until the aids to the employment of native labour are abolished'. (83)

The job colour bar may thus be explained as a response to a specific class problem, produced by the specific system of production and class structure from which that problem itself derived. The extension of the exploitability of the majority of workers, by the racially discriminatory forced labour system of the employers, extended the structural insecurity of the proletarianised but politically free and less exploitable (white) group of workers, leading the latter to institute an extensive system of employment protection, and determining that it, too, should take the specific form of racial discrimination. It was thus a case of one system of class colour bars - the exploitation colour bars of the dominant (owning) class - generating another - the employment colour bars of the politically free section of the economically dependent (working) class, including the job colour bar of the white mine workers. It was the involvement of the employers - notably the mining capitalists - in racial discrimination which generated the involvement of the white workers - notably the white mine workers - in racial discrimination.

2 The system of racial discrimination as a projection and mediation of class contradictions

We have observed why and how the mining companies, and the white workers, became involved in racial discrimination, and a system of racial discrimination came to be operating in the gold mining industry. We have observed the class basis and class nature of this system. What we have now to consider is what significance this system had for relations between the groups operating it. What was the significance of the job colour bar of the white workers for the mining companies? What was the significance of the exploitation colour bars of the mining companies for the white workers?

The system of racial discrimination affected the relations between these groups in two different ways. On the one hand, and most importantly, it constituted a projection of contradictions within the system of production and class structure from which, as the preceding analysis sought to show, it derived. At the same time, however, it had the effect of mediating - of bearing upon in such a way as to neutralise or offset the effects of - these contradictions. In these different respects, the system was both to provoke historical conflict between the groups operating it, and to circumscribe the scope of this conflict.

The system of racial discrimination was more than just a product of a specific system of production and class structure. It was, at the same time, a projection of contradictions within this system and structure, between the groups operating it - between private capital and politically free labour. These groups occupied not just different, but contradictory, class positions, from which derived contradictory class interests and imperatives. Profit maximisation by owners of means of production through the exploitation of labour was a contradiction of the security of workers. Resistance to and curtailment of such

Chapter 2

exploitation by workers was a contradiction of profit maximisation by owners. The system of racial discrimination embodied these structural contradictions. It was a system not just of different class colour bars but of contradictory class colour bars. The job colour bar was a contradiction of profit maximisation by the mining companies. And the exploitation colour bars were a contradiction of the security of the white workers. These structural contradictions, thus projected and embodied in the system of racial discrimination, were, during a specific configuration of historical conditions - with which we shall be concerned in the second part of the study - to generate historical conflict between the operators of the system over the operation of the system. But at the same time, the system was to have the effect of mediating these contradictions, with the job colour bar and the exploitation colour bars having positive as well as negative effects for the mining companies and the white workers respectively. This was to circumscribe the scope of this historical conflict.

1. THE MINING COMPANIES AND THE JOB COLOUR BAR

What were the effects and significance of the job colour bar for the mining companies, and what were the structural determinants of the historical behaviour of the companies towards the job colour bar? Into what pattern did these conditions tend to shape this behaviour?

The answer to these questions is complex, for the effects were mixed, and were compounded by certain other factors, also leading in opposite directions. The most important effect was a negative one - the job colour bar's contradiction of profit maximisation. This was to lead the mining companies to oppose it, an opposition which, in relation to another factor - the reduction of grievances among non-white workers - was to be politically expedient as well as economically necessary, and an opposition which, during a specific conjunction of conditions, was to lead to acute class conflict. But the job colour bar also served the interests of the companies; and it expressed certain realities of power which they could not ignore. These factors were to circumscribe the opposition of the companies to it, and to give them good reason to accommodate it.

As was noted earlier, the two fundamental profitability imperatives for the gold mining companies were the minimisation of costs and the maximisation of output. The job colour bar constituted a contradiction of profit maximisation by contradicting both of these imperatives. By extensively restricting the freedom of the companies to employ ultra-exploitable, ultra-cheap (non-white) workers in anything but unskilled work, by reserving skilled work to less exploitable, relatively expensive (white) workers, the job colour bar obstructed the minimisation of labour costs. And by confining specific work and responsibilities to white workers, and restricting the work and responsibility of white workers, the job colour bar obstructed the maximisation of labour productivity and the minimisation of unit costs.

This contradiction contained the seeds of conflict, and was to provoke the opposition of the mining companies to the job colour bar. It was not synonymous with conflict, however, for, as will be noted, this effect of the job colour bar was offset by various factors, which made it far from incompatible with profitability and far from intolerable to the mining companies. But during a particular period - the period during and following the First World War - this contradiction was to become of great historical importance, for a combination of reasons, notably: the extension of the job colour bar in the Status Quo Agreement of 1918, the development of an acute profitability crisis, and the inability of the mining companies to resolve this crisis other than by taking action against the job colour bar. The first of these was to intensify the contradiction, the second was to intensify the relative importance of any such contradiction for the mining companies and the third was to intensify the importance specifically of the job colour bar as such a contradiction. Since this aspect of the job colour bar, and these developments, are closely examined in Part 2, they will not be pursued further here.

The job colour bar thus constituted a contradiction of profit maximisation, and the mining companies were to come to oppose and attack it for this reason. This opposition was to be reinforced by other factors. The job colour bar was also a source of grievance to African workers; it was in the interest of the companies to reduce grievances within their enormous African labour force; and while the major grievances of these workers, as we shall see, concerned not the job colour bar but ultra-low wages and the forced labour system - upon which the profitability of the companies depended and the elimination of which would have meant the end of the companies - the job colour bar was a source of grievance the removal of which, far from being incompatible with the ultra-exploitation of non-white labour, was a means of maximising it.

Opposition to and reduction of the job colour bar were thus to be politically expedient for the companies as well as economically imperative, signifying not only the more profitable utilisation of labour, but also the containment of unrest among African workers, as a kind of 'safety valve'.

Supposing no safety valve is provided and the amount and class of work the native is allowed to do is no more and no less than it is now, in spite of additional aspirations and ambitions and additional wants which he may acquire, what is your position as to the position which will arise? - I have not the least doubt that there will be trouble later on.

The natives will not sit down to it? - No, I do not think so. . . .

You must provide some species of safety valve or attempt to send them to some corner of the country and say you must stay there. Is that sort of policy possible? . . . Having them here, do you think it is a matter of practical politics to suggest segregating them? - No, I do not.

So you are driven to the position of having to provide some safety valve as they advance? - Yes. (1)

Reduction of the job colour bar was seen as a good 'precaution', which might 'stave off' unwanted developments.

Do you think the best precaution to take is to give the natives more opportunities of rising in their sphere of labour, to reduce the number of white men to look after them and get a better class of white men to do it. It is not a programme easy to carry out? - No, it is not, it cannot be done in a day. Were this goal aimed at, we should be doing a great deal in staving off any likely combination on the part of these natives. (2)

These views of the Chamber of Mines, the Compound Managers' Association and the Native Recruiting Corporation about the 'safety valve' value of a reduction of the job colour bar were echoed in the strongest terms by the Director of Native Labour, in 1919. It was, he warned, 'futile to attempt any longer to confine to their present sphere of labour by repressive legislation some 200,000 industrious and generally efficient labourers', and if no remedial action was taken, 'the time is not far off when a standing army will not keep at work a mass of workers who have little to lose and all to gain by concerted action in the direction of overthrowing a system which actually prohibits their advancement'.

To tinker with the matter at the present time is only to postpone the evil day. The choice of one of two alternatives presents itself: either to continue to

sit on a volcano with the day of eruption drawing
nearer each day, or to treat an admittedly grave situation in a big and statesmanlike way by eliminating the
colour bar and thereby going to the root of the inefficiency alleged to be throttling the low grade
mines, as well as taking out of the hands of the natives one of the most powerful political and industrial
levers that can be exerted against the government and
the white community generally. (3)

While it was to be this factor of profitability, complimented by this factor of the 'safety valve', which were to
underlie and motivate the opposition of the mining companies to the job colour bar, the companies were to be inclined to picture this opposition as an expression of concern for social justice, human rights and the immorality
of racial discrimination - a picture which was not, however, to gain much credibility, in view of their own extensive and persistent involvement in social injustice and
racial discrimination. Their perpetuation of the ultra-
exploitation and ultra-exploitability of non-white workers
was to suggest that the place of 'universal moral principles' in their behaviour was at the level of justification rather than that of motivation.

As a contradiction of profit maximisation, the job
colour bar was thus to meet with opposition from the
mining companies. But various factors were to mediate
this contradiction, to limit this opposition, and to determine the general strategy of the mining companies towards the white workers and the job colour bar. Certain
factors served to offset the effect of this contradiction,
most importantly the ultra-exploitability - and consequent
ultra-cheapness - of non-white labour. This rendered
tolerable to the mining companies the cost of white labour
and of the job colour bar, a cost which would otherwise
have been highly incompatible with profitability. This
was complimented by such factors as technological innovation and the maximisation of the supply of non-white
labour.

While such factors offset the effect of the contradiction, there was another important factor which was to determine the response of the mining companies to it, and to
restrict their opposition to the job colour bar: the
power of the white mine workers. As was noted earlier,
these workers occupied a particularly powerful position in
relation to their employers, by virtue not only of their
political freedom as white workers (their non-subjection
to the racially discriminatory system of forced labour
operated by employers over non-white workers), but also of
their possession of scarce and necessary skills and their

control over the availability and utilisation of skilled labour. This power could not be ignored by the mining companies, and the job colour bar was an expression of this power. It meant that the job colour bar could not be dealt with by the companies with impunity, that this particular contradiction of profit maximisation was not one to be easily eliminated.

What this factor was to mean was that the cardinal issue for the mining companies was to be not the acceptability of the presence of a group of politically free workers and of a job colour bar in the industry, but the relative size of this group and the relative scope of this bar. What the companies were to seek was the minimisation of both - the minimisation, not the expulsion, of the group of politically free workers, and the minimisation, not the elimination, of the job colour bar. Their general policy towards the white workers and the job colour bar was to be one of accepting but restricting them, a policy of encouraging the restriction of the position of white workers in the industry to that of a small 'labour aristocracy' and of accommodating the job colour bar in skilled work to this end, while maintaining the restriction of unskilled work to non-white workers and resisting the White Labour Policy, which sought to extend the employment of white workers to unskilled work. And in the context of this general policy, the job colour bar was by no means wholly disadvantageous to the companies. For it served to maintain and reinforce the prevailing division of labour in the industry, and the prevailing division of the working class generally, the restriction of unskilled work to non-whites and the lack of solidarity between white and non-white workers - conditions which were of advantage to the companies. The last thing the companies wanted was an end to these divisions, for instance by white workers incorporating non-white workers into the ranks of unionised labour or extending the employment of white workers to unskilled work. By alleviating the problems of the white workers - thus discouraging more radical steps on their part, and by formalising and perpetuating the prevailing divisions between workers and their spheres of employment, the job colour bar served the interests of the companies.

On the one hand, therefore, the mining companies were to go along with the job colour bar. Their opposition to it was to be limited, and concerned merely with its relative scope (though not unexplosive in its consequences for being so). Their general policy towards the job colour bar was to be one of peaceful coexistence and accommodation.

This was to be apparent time and again. We see this at

the time of the Chinese labour importation. The Chamber of Mines saw no benefit to be gained from 'the introduction of unskilled Europeans'. (4) And as a quid pro quo for the importation of Chinese labourers, the companies were happy to have job protection secured for the white workers. If white unskilled workers were imported, a mining magnate declared in a speech to white mine workers, extolling the benefits to the latter from the employment of non-white unskilled workers in the mines, 'what would be the inevitable result? Why, that this unskilled labour would very soon become skilled labour, and compete against you.' Consent to legislation governing the introduction and employment of Chinese workers would not be given, he promised, unless it included a provision prohibiting the employment of such workers in anything but unskilled work. (5) The Transvaal Labour Importation Ordinance of 1904 duly contained such a provision, as we noted. And the President of the Chamber considered that: 'In agreeing to import Chinamen here . . . we were really the best friends the skilled artisan of this country ever had.' (6)

Then again, at the time of Union, we see the Chamber of Mines manifesting noticeably little concern over the incorporation and extension of the job colour bar in the Union's Mining Regulations. The Chamber made detailed and forceful representations to the government over the Mines and Works Bill and Regulations on the issues of the prohibition of Sunday milling, the employment of juveniles underground, and the introduction of an eight-hour day for underground workers, but it showed no such concern over the job colour bar. (7) It did point out that the discriminatory Regulations appeared to be ultra vires. (8) And the President of the Chamber warned the government 'against legislation tending to militate against healthy competition amongst white workers'. (9) But it did not seriously contest the consolidation of the job colour bar in the Union's Regulations. And later on, as will be seen, this accommodationist disposition of the Chamber towards the job colour bar was also to be evident in its cooperation with the white workers over the Status Quo Agreement of 1918, in the relatively limited nature of its opposition to the job colour bar in the post-war conflict, and in its failure to take significant advantage of the Supreme Court judgment of 1923 ruling the job colour bar in the Regulations to be illegal.

Complimentary to this accommodation of the job colour bar in skilled work was a determination to restrict unskilled work to non-white workers. Few things filled the companies with greater alarm than the White Labour Policy. The reason was straightforward: the employment of politically free workers rather than ultra-exploitable workers in unskilled labour, in which about 90 per cent of the labour force was employed, would have had a disastrous effect on profitability. Some idea of this effect may be gained from Table 2.

TABLE 2 Estimated effects on profitability of employment of white workers in unskilled labour in the gold mines

	Wages per shift			
	7s. 6d.	10s.	12s. 6d.	15s.
Number of mines that would cease to make a profit	16	26	35	41
Number of mines that could continue working at a greatly reduced profit	36	26	17	11

Figures prepared by the Transvaal Chamber of Mines for the Select Committee of the House of Assembly on European Employment and Labour Conditions, of 1913, based on the 1913 operating figures of 52 mines ('South African Mining Journal', 26 July 1913, p.571). It will be noted that this Table illustrates the critical importance of the profitability of the mining companies of the ultra-exploitation of non-white labour, the lowest wage in the Table - 7s. 6d. - being itself nearly four times greater than the average wage of non-white workers.

As we have observed, the profitable operation of the gold mines required the ultra-exploitation of the mass of workers, and white workers, unlike non-white workers, were not ultra-exploitable - they were not subject to the racially discriminatory system of forced labour operated by the employers, they were able to resist and curtail the exploitation of their labour, they were able to improve their conditions and to raise the cost of their labour to employers. This is what underlay the fears of the mining companies over the White Labour Policy (and this is what is taken for granted in Table 2, with wages beginning at 7s. 6d.). As a company director explained to the leading advocate of the policy:

With reference to your trial of white labour . . . on the mines . . . I have consulted the Consolidated Gold Fields people, and one of the other members of the Board . . . has consulted Messrs. Wernher Beit & Co., and the feeling seems to be one of fear that if a large

number of white men are employed on the Rand in the
position of labourers, the same troubles will arise as
are now prevalent in the Australian colonies, i.e. that
the combination of the labouring classes will become so
strong as to be able to more or less dictate, not only
on questions of wages, but also on political questions,
by the power of their votes. (10)

The mining companies were thus to be uncompromisingly
opposed to the White Labour Policy.

While the White Labour Policy was to be a public sector
policy, its proponents did not automatically exclude the
gold mining industry from their sights, and in fact it was
in the industry that it was first advocated and experimentally applied. At the turn of the century, its leading
advocate - Frederick Creswell (then a mine manager, and
later to become leader of the Labour Party and a Minister
in the Pact government), experimentally employed white
workers in unskilled labour in the mines. Creswell's experiments provoked considerable debate and controversy,
and their results were to be interpreted in various ways.
There was no doubt, however, that they signified an increase in costs. A detailed study of them found that,
when all factors were taken into account, the substitution
of white for non-white workers in unskilled work had
raised average working costs by the very high figure of
5s. 8d. per ton mined - an increase which, if generalised
to the industry as a whole, would have eliminated the profitability of most companies. (11) The only other notable
assertion of the White Labour Policy in the direction of
the gold mines was the report of the Mining Industry Commission of 1907-8, which attacked the extreme dependence
of the gold mining industry on non-white labour and
favoured the increasing use of white labour, and recommended limitations on the importation of non-Union Africans,
the eventual ending of such importation and the abolition
of the special powers wielded by employers over non-white
workers in South Africa. (12)

While Creswell's experiment was virtually the only
attempt to apply the White Labour Policy to the gold
mines, and while none of the many other Commissions of Inquiry into the industry were to share the Mining Industry
Commission's support for it, these were enough to arouse
the anxiety of the mining companies and to lead them to
denounce it in uncompromising terms. Creswell was constantly dismissed as 'a faddist and a fanatic'. (13) The
Commission's views were considered to be 'visionary and
destructive' and merely 'building a castle in the air'.
(14) Before the First World War, when white unemployment
on the Rand began to rise as unskilled whites arrived from

rural areas, efforts were made to find employment for such whites in unskilled work. While co-operating to some extent, the Chamber of Mines opposed such efforts in principle. The solution, the President of the Chamber declared, was that white workers should form a superior group of workers, occupying the upper grades of work, supported by a large mass of unskilled non-white workers. (15) And the Chamber asked the government to post notices in rural areas discouraging the migration of unskilled whites to the Rand. (16) The Chamber's ideology about labour was perhaps most clearly expressed by the President during the Chinese labour episode:

> The white man will not, he cannot and should not, do unskilled labour side by side with the Kaffir. (Hear, hear.) In this country, so long as you have the black man working here - and I believe he will be here always - it is necessary to maintain a broad division between the scale upon which he lives and the scale upon which the white man lives, and I hope that plane - that difference in the way in which they live - will always be maintained. (17)

Twenty years later, the President of the Chamber was to be reiterating this basic principle. Pursuing the White Labour Policy, he declared, was like trying 'to encourage tropical agriculture in the Arctic regions'. For, 'The whole industrial basis of the country . . . is, and always has been, that the heavy physical labour should be performed by natives while the European confines his energies to skilled work and supervision.' (18) 'The superior intelligence of the white man', declared the 'South African Mining Journal' (the leading managerial publication, which shared and propagated the views of the mining companies), 'very seldom counter-balances the muscular cum fatigue-resisting qualities of the African native', who 'has become a sturdy and muscular machine'. In its view,

> The fact must be plain to all unbiased students of industrial and political economy in this country that the basis of industry and of most things else south of the line is the essential Kaffir. We do not believe that the white man ever has been or ever will be able to compete with him as a hewer of wood, a shifter of earth, or as a labouring machine in any branch of industry. (19)

The connection between this concern of the mining companies to restrict unskilled work to non-white workers, and their accommodation of the job colour bar in skilled work, was that the latter helped to maintain the former. Without the protection of the job colour bar, the white workers might have been inclined to take more radical protectionist measures, to act towards eliminating the enormous differential between the wages and cost of white and non-white labour. But the job colour bar reduced the likelihood of this, thereby serving to stabilise the labour status quo. This served the interests of the companies.

The significance of the job colour bar for the mining companies was thus complex. On the one hand, it was a contradiction of profit maximisation, and, as such, it was to provoke the hostility of the companies, and was to be a source - during a particular set of circumstances - of acute conflict. But certain factors served to mediate this contradiction and to limit the scope of this opposition and conflict: the ultra-exploitation of non-white workers, the power of the white workers, and the beneficial effect of the job colour bar for the companies. The actual cost of the contradiction was offset by the ultra-minimisation of non-white labour costs, the potential cost of removing it (the power of the white workers), and the actual benefit of the job colour bar to the companies, as a stabiliser of the labour status quo. The latter made the cost of the job colour bar to the companies not only necessary but worthwhile. These mediating factors were to determine the general policy of the companies towards the white workers and the job colour bar - a policy of accommodating but minimising the white 'labour aristocracy' and the job colour bar in skilled work, while maintaining and maximising the sphere of employment of non-white workers; and these factors were to determine that opposition to and conflict over the job colour bar were to be concerned not with the job colour bar per se, but with the relative scope of protection afforded by it to the white workers.

2. THE WHITE WORKERS AND THE EXPLOITATION COLOUR BARS

The significance of the exploitation colour bars of the employers for the white mine workers was also complex. On the one hand, they contradicted the security of the white workers, by extending their structural insecurity; in response to this, they instituted the job colour bar. This we have already observed.

But at the same time, the exploitation colour bars had an altogether opposite kind of effect for the white mine workers. The profitability and existence of the gold mining industry were, we saw, critically dependent on the ultra-exploitation of the mass of its workers - non-white workers, and the ultra-exploitability and ultra-exploitation of non-white workers were secured by the exploitation colour bars. By the same token, this meant that the employment of the industry's white labour force, at the level of wages and benefits which it enjoyed, was also dependent on the ultra-exploitation of non-white labour. While posing the threat of displacement to the white mine workers, the exploitation colour bars thus also formed the foundation stone of their employment.

This important factor goes far towards explaining the historical response that the white mine workers were to take towards the contradiction of their security, the general policy that they were to pursue towards the employers and the non-white workers. This policy was to be a conservative and 'economistic' policy of maximising benefits from the status quo and of alleviating the effects rather than eliminating the causes of their class problems, of protecting themselves against the effects of structural insecurity without acting to end the causes of this insecurity. And this policy is largely to be explained by the economic benefits deriving to the white workers from the status quo and the ultra-exploitation of non-white labour.

This factor goes far towards answering the following question: 'Granted that the job colour bar may be explained as a form of protection generated by a specific class problem, the question still arises as to why the response of the threatened group of workers to this problem was - and, more importantly, remained - of this nature. Why, if the extension of insecurity stemmed from the differential exploitability of labour, did the less exploitable group of workers not seek to eliminate the cause of this specific problem by eliminating or reducing the ultra-exploitability of non-white labour?' The fact was, that while such a radical policy might well have ended this problem, it would also have ended the employment of the white mine workers. For them, it meant the replacement of one problem by a far greater problem.

This factor was to be of particular importance for the white workers in the gold mines, because of the industry's exceptional degree of dependence - given its specific cost and profitability structure - on the ultra-exploitation of non-white labour. But it was to underlie the conservatism of the white workers in general, who were to come increasingly to benefit economically from the status quo - something which the employers had a cardinal interest in ensuring.

Conservatism among the white workers in relation to the non-white workers and the exploitation colour bars was also to be determined by various other factors, notably the prevailing racist ideology and status system, which served to reinforce the division of the working class constituted by the differential exploitability of white and non-white workers, by conditioning white workers to see themselves as members of a superior race, of an 'aristocracy of colour'. Afrikaner nationalism was also to be an important influence in this direction. But underlying all such factors were to be the economic benefits deriving to the white workers from the status quo.

Paradoxically, therefore, the exploitation colour bars of the employers both contradicted and ensured the security of the white mine workers. On the one hand, the maximisation of profit through the ultra-exploitation of non-white labour threatened the white workers with displacement; this generated the job colour bar, and was, like the job colour bar, to be a source of conflict between the mining companies and the white workers. But the effect of this contradiction was greatly offset by the economic benefit secured by the white mine workers from the ultra-exploitability and ultra-exploitation of non-white labour. This was to incline them towards a conservative policy of maximising benefits within the status quo and of protecting themselves against the effects of problems rather than of seeking to eliminate their causes.

Summary of part one

The first part of the study has examined and attempted to explain the system of racial discrimination in the gold mining industry, by reference to the wider economic system and social formation in which it was situated.

Its first and major concern has been to elucidate the specific nature of the involvement in racial discrimination of the two white groups operating the system, and the specific nature of the system. It sought to show how this involvement, and the specific forms and functions of racial discrimination, were generated and determined by the specific class problems and interests of these groups, deriving from their specific positions in the capitalist system of production and class structure of which they formed a part. And the system was seen and explained as a system of class instruments, referred to as class colour bars, which were measures of racial discrimination which served to resolve the class problems and secure the interests of these groups. These class colour bars were the property colour bars and exploitation colour bars of the employers (which served to maximise the economic dependence and the exploitability of non-whites generally and non-white workers in particular), and the employment colour bars (which served to restrict the employability of ultra-exploitable workers).

It then also went on to analyse the structural significance of the system for relations between the groups operating it. We observed how the system both embodied and mediated certain class contradictions, with the job colour bar contradicting profit maximisation and the exploitation colour bars contradicting the security and livelihood of the white workers, but with both having some beneficial effects for the other group, so that the system was a structural source of both conflict and accommodation between the two operator groups.

part two

Class relations, class conflict and racial discrimination

From the preceding class analysis of the structure and dynamics of the racial system, and in the light of it, we turn now to an examination and explanation of some important historical developments concerning this system and the groups involved in it. During and following the First World War, this system became a crucial issue for all these groups, and a focal point of tension and conflict.

3 Class colour bars and class conflict: the mining companies and the white workers

Our main concern in looking at these historical developments, is with the relations and conflict between the two operator groups, the mining capitalists and the white workers. During this period, these two groups came increasingly into conflict over the system of racial discrimination, a conflict which has conventionally been seen as one between the forces of 'economic rationality' (represented by the mining companies, in their attack on the job colour bar) and of 'irrational prejudice and discrimination' (the white workers, in their defence of the job colour bar). The nature and significance of the historical behaviour of these groups, and of this conflict in particular, are here explored, and presented in a quite different light.

1. THE POST-WAR PROFITABILITY CRISIS

1 The crisis

During and immediately following the First World War, the gold mining industry entered a serious profitability crisis which, in its causes and effects, was of great significance in the historical relations between the mining companies and the white workers, and for our understanding of the nature of the system of racial discrimination.

The specific cost structure of the gold mining industry, we observed earlier on, was such as to render the profitability of the mining companies highly vulnerable in certain ways. The specific features of this structure, we noted, were the internationally fixed price of the product (precluding the transfer of cost increases to price and consumer), the very low average grade of the ore (necessitating extreme minimisation of working costs) and the high level of overhead and development costs (rendering profitability unusually and disproportionately sensitive to changes in cost and output levels). This structure determined that the fundamental imperatives of profit realisation were cost minimisation and output maximisation, and that the profitability of the mining companies was extremely vulnerable both to cost inflation and to output reduction.

For various reasons - the historical level of costs, and effective cost minimisation and output maximisation through such means as the minimisation of the cost and maximisation of the supply of forced labour, and technological innovation (the most important pre-war technological innovation was the MacArthur-Forrest cyanide process, which raised the recovery rate to nearly 100 per cent) - the period between the end of the South African War and the outbreak of the First World War was a period of unprecedented expansion of output and profit in the gold mining industry. Between 1901 and 1912, the output of the gold mines rose by 14.2 per cent per annum. (1) And annual distributed dividends rose from £2.8 million in 1902 to £10.5 million in 1909. (2)

However the next decade was to be a different story - a period of contraction and crisis. Between 1913 and 1922, the rate of output of the gold mines fell by 1.9 per cent per annum. (3) The war and immediate post-war period saw a steady rise in the level of working costs and fall in the level of output, which were reflected in falling profit margins and falling dividends, as Tables 3 and 4 indicate.

TABLE 3 Costs, output and profits, Witwatersrand gold mines, 1915-21*

	Tons milled (millions)	Working costs per ton m/d	Working profits per ton m/d	Dividends declared (£millions)
1915	28.31	17s. 5d.	8s. 5d.	7.6
1916	28.53	18s. 1d.	8s. 2d.	7.0
1917	27.25	19s. 2d.	7s. 6d.	6.6
1918	24.92	21s. 7d.	6s. 0d.	5.1
1919	24.04	22s. 11d.	5s. 6d.	5.9
1920	24.09	25s. 8d.	9s. 7d.**	8.2**
1921	23.40	25s. 8d.	9s. 6d.**	7.1**

* Witwatersrand monthly totals and averages of gold production, 'ARTCMs, 1915-21'.
**Reflects the temporary premium gold price.

TABLE 4 Costs and output, Witwatersrand gold mines, 1914 and 1921*

	1914	1921
Tons milled (millions)	25.7	23.4
Total working costs (£ millions)	21.9	30.0
Working costs per ton milled	17s. 1d.	25s. 8d.
Working costs per fine ounce milled	54s. 10d.	76s. 5d.

*Witwatersrand monthly totals and averages of gold production, 'ARTCM 1914, 1921'.

The effect of these tendencies of rising costs, falling output and falling profits was to throw a growing number of mining companies on to or below the border of profitability. These companies became known as 'low grade mines', which were defined as those mines working at a loss or at a profit of less than 2s. per ton milled. (4) In terms of this definition, in the last quarter of 1917, 14 mines, employing about a quarter of the labour force and working at an average profit of 9d. per ton, were low grade mines. (5) By September 1919, 3 of these had closed down, and 11 more mines had fallen into this category, making a total of 21 - about half of the total number of producing mines, employing about half of the labour force and working at an average loss of 0.6d. per ton. (6) Thus by the end of the war, half of the gold mining companies were unable to mine gold profitably.

This emerging profitability crisis was temporarily offset by a premium price for gold at the end of the war. Up to 1919, the gold mining companies had sold their gold directly to the Bank of England at a fixed price of 85s. per ounce. But in 1919 the gold standard was temporarily abandoned, and in July 1919 a new selling arrangement came into operation, whereby Rand gold, while still consigned to the Bank of England, was to be sold by agents of the companies in the best available market. (7) Between July 1919 and March 1920, the premium price (the price realised in excess of the normal price) fluctuated between 16 and 44 per cent over the normal price, averaging about 26 per cent. (8) The premium continued to fluctuate over the next year, and began to fall steadily towards the end of 1921.

But the underlying crisis remained and intensified; the premium merely offset its effects on profit margins. Costs were continuing to rise, and output to fall.

Without the premium, in the last quarter of 1919, 25 mines would have fallen into the category of low grade mines, working at an average loss of 0.34d. per ton. (9) Some of these mines were forced to close down. And by 1921, the number of mines that were unprofitable in relation to the normal price of gold was 28 (out of 35 producing mines). (10) Thus by 1921, over two-thirds of the producing mines were unable to mine gold profitably but for the premium, which in 1921 was falling steadily.

We noted that the immediate causes of this profitability crisis were the rising level of costs and the falling level of output. What produced these tendencies? They stemmed from three major factors: the inflationary rise in the cost of living during the First World War (which meant a rise in the cost of stores); a shortage of African labour; and the gains secured by the white workers during the war, in the form of wage increases and improvements in employment conditions and the extension of the job colour bar.

The rise in the cost of living during the war was responsible for a substantial rise in the cost of materials. Between 1914 and 1919, the cost of such items as candles, shoes and dies, rock drill steel and zinc, more than doubled, and the cost of blasting gelatine and gelignite, and of cyanide, coal and mealie meal also rose considerably. (11) And as a Commission of Inquiry observed:

> The quantity of stores used per ton of rock crushed has not altered to any notable extent since 1914, so that the rise in the cost per ton of stores used is a direct reflex of the increased cost of stores themselves. (12)

Between 1914 and 1920, the total cost of stores consumed by the gold mines rose by about 40 per cent, from about £10 million to about £14 million. (13) In addition to bringing about a sharp rise in the cost of living, the war also subjected the industry to various other charges. The total of extra-ordinary costs incurred by the gold mines during the war amounted to about £6 million. (14)

The mining companies took what measures they could to offset the effect of the increased cost of materials. In July 1917 they formed a collective agreement for the pooling of all imported stores, and for the centralised buying of such supplies by a Central Buying Committee of the Chamber of Mines. (15) But this was unable to achieve very much in the way of cost reduction, and the rising cost of living seriously undermined the vulnerable profitability of the gold mining industry, which, as the President of the Chamber observed, 'is an industry extraordinarily unfavourably situated at a time of rising prices'. (16)

Another cause of the crisis was a shortage of ultra-cheap labour during the second half of the war. During the first part of the war, while the mines did not secure their full estimated complement of African labour, their supply was rising - from 65.6 per cent of the complement in 1913, to 72.8 per cent in 1914 and the record figure of 93.8 per cent in 1915. This large supply helped to neutralise the effect of rising costs, by permitting output maximisation. But the supply began to fall off after 1915 - to 82.9 per cent in 1916, 72.6 per cent in 1917 and 61.1 per cent in 1918, while costs were continuing to rise all the time. (17) The Chamber of Mines considered that by 1918 the industry's position in relation to its African labour supply 'is now probably worse than it has ever been in the history of the Rand, having regard to the scale of operations'. (18) By the end of the war, in relation to the estimated complement the industry was short of about 40,000 African workers. (19)

This shortage reflected the growing demand for African labour by other employers, with the growth of the manufacturing industry, the increased operation of the collieries, and the continuing demands of farmers, together with the opening of new gold mines on the Far East Rand. (20) The manufacturing industry expanded dramatically during the First World War, growing at an annual rate of 18.7 per cent between 1911 and 1920 (spurred by import substitution and rising prices during the war). (21) Between 1911 and 1921, the number of manufacturing establishments in South Africa tripled, from about 2,400 to 7,000, and the number of non-whites employed in them nearly tripled as well, from 44,000 to 116,000. (22) The most important cause of the shortage, the President of the Chamber stated, was 'the expansion in the demand for native workmen in other industries'. (23)

The shortage also partly stemmed from a ban imposed by the Union government in 1913 on the importation of African workers from north of latitude 22 degrees south. This prohibition was made essentially because of the very high mortality rate of these 'tropical' Africans on the mines. (24) Allowing their continued employment at the prevailing mortality rate, the Minister of Native Affairs had declared, 'would be little less than murder'. (25) But it was also urged by proponents of the White Labour Policy, led by Creswell in Parliament. The Chamber sponsored research to find an effective vaccine against the pneumonia which killed these Africans, and made representations to the government during the war to have the ban rescinded, but without success. (26)

The third major cause of the profitability crisis lay

98   Chapter 3

in the gains secured by the white workers during the war, which had the effects of increasing the cost of white labour, of reducing output, and of further restricting the freedom of the companies to make the most profitable possible utilisation of ultra-cheap non-white labour. These gains reflected an important shift in the balance of class power in the industry during the war, which stemmed essentially from the scarcity of skilled labour during the war. This labour shortage, which derived from general war-time conditions and from the fact that, as will be seen, a large number of white mine workers left their jobs for the war, strengthened the bargaining position of the white workers.

In response to the rising cost of living and other developments, and on the basis of this shift in the balance of class power, the white mine workers pressed for and secured various gains in their conditions of employment, which are summarised in Table 5.

TABLE 5 Principal gains secured by the white workers in the Witwatersrand gold mines during the First World War*

Year	Wages	Working hours	Miscellaneous
1915	Special War Bonus for lower paid workers Paid holidays for underground workers and for some surface workers	Mechanics get 50-hour maximum work week, and time and a quarter overtime	De facto recognition of the SAIF by the Chamber of Mines
1916	Winding engine drivers get minimum rates of pay, overtime and Sunday rates, long service bonus, paid holidays Mechanics get increase in standard rates War bonus for lower paid workers raised, and extended to more workers	Mechanics get 48-hour week (plus 2 hours compulsory overtime) Winding engine drivers get 8-hour day	Joint Board of Reference between Chamber and Engine Drivers' Union set up

Chapter 3

Year	Wages	Working hours	Miscellaneous
1917	Underground workers get minimum rates, and scale of war bonus increased. Mechanics get increase in standard rates, and a special war allowance. Stationary and locomotive engine drivers, boiler attendants and firemen get minimum rates, overtime and Sunday rates, paid holidays	Mechanics get 48-hour week without compulsory overtime. Underground workers get $48\frac{1}{2}$-hour week bank to bank and short Saturday shift (began 1 January 1918)	Deduction of trade union subscriptions, and posting of trade union notices in mines accepted by Chamber. Joint Board of Reference between Chamber and Mechanics' Unions set up
1918	War Bonus becomes an automatic cost of living sliding scale. Reduction workers get minimum rates of pay	(Introduction of $48\frac{1}{2}$-hour week bank to bank)	Status Quo Agreement (extension of the job colour bar) prohibiting further displacement of white workers by non-white workers (began 1 September 1918)
1919	Cost of living allowance (war bonus) extended from 30% to 40%. Underground and surface officials get minimum rates of pay, and benefit of War Bonus. Two new paid holidays for all workers - Dingaan's Day and May Day	Reduction workers get 6-day week	Miners Phthisis Act

*Compiled from data in the 'ARTCMs 1915-19'.

The effect of these developments was to raise the cost of white labour and to reduce the output of all labour. The variation in the cost and output of labour between 1914 and 1920 is indicated in Table 6.

TABLE 6 Cost and output of labour, Witwatersrand gold mines, 1914 and 1920*

	1914	1920	Variation
Wages and salaries of white employees (£ millions)	7.1	11.3	+58.4%
Wages of African workers (£ millions)	5.3	6.0	+12.2%
Stores (£ millions)	10.2	14.2	+39.8%
No. of tons milled (millions)	26.3	24.4	- 1.9
No. of whites employed	21,875	22,668	+ 793
Tons milled per white	1,205	1,079	- 126
No. of Africans employed	179,287	183,597	+4,310
Tons milled per African	147	133	- 14

*Compiled from Tvl Ch. of Mines, Comparison of certain costs incurred in the gold mines, 'ARTCM 1921', p.151.

The cost of white labour thus rose considerably during and after the war, both absolutely and as a proportion of total costs. This in large measure reflected the wage and salary increases which, as will be noted, by 1920 amounted to a rise of about 60 per cent over the 1914 figure. While the average earnings per shift of African workers remained virtually stationary during the war, those of white workers underground rose from 20s. 3d. to 23s. 5d. (27) And the white workers secured more wage increases in 1920 and 1921. But the various other gains which they made, such as reduced working hours, paid holidays and increased compensation rates, also all increased the cost of white labour. (28)

This increase in the cost of white labour was accompanied by a fall in total and per capita output of labour, following from the reduction of working hours secured by the white workers, especially the $48\frac{1}{2}$-hour week 'bank to bank' (from surface entry to surface entry, as opposed to the previous 'face to face', which was from work place to work place). As Table 6 shows, between 1914 and 1920, while the number of workers employed in the mines increased, total output and tonnage milled per white worker and per African worker all decreased. Between 1914 and 1919, the tonnage produced annually per white and per African underground worker fell from 2,694 to 2,307 and from 240 to 210 respectively. (29)

A most significant feature of this reduction of working hours secured by the white workers was that, as is evident from these figures, it reduced the productivity of African workers, who worked under the supervision of white workers. The shortening of the working day secured by the white workers was a shortening of the working time of all workers. The introduction of the $48\frac{1}{2}$-hour week bank to bank in January 1918 reduced the working time of the African worker by an average of between one and two hours, and reduced the tonnage handled per African worker employed in tramming and shovelling by about 15 per cent. (30) Thus while the wage increases secured by the white workers did not imply any corresponding increase in the wages of African workers, the reduction of working hours secured by the white workers did have this important effect of shortening the working time of African workers.

This contraction of total and per capita output, following from the reduction of working hours, was an important cause of the profitability crisis, given the industry's specific cost structure - with its high overhead costs, the absence of profit before a high level of output, and the disproportionately great effect of inadequate output on profitability. It is worth here repeating part of the observations made by the President of the Chamber of Mines on this question, quoted earlier on in the section on the industry's cost structure.

> The loss of profit from a reduced output far exceeds the proportion of output lost, since all the profit arises only from that part of the output exceeding the critical percentage. Thus, in the case of a mine whose critical percentage is 80 per cent, a reduction of 10 per cent in tonnage means a loss not of a tenth but of a half of its profit. (31)

The profitability of the mining companies was also jeopardised by another important measure secured by the white workers during the war - the Status Quo Agreement of 1918. This extension of the job colour bar (with which we shall be concerned in the next part of this chapter) further restricted the freedom of the employers to make the most profitable utilisation of ultra-cheap forced labour, and intensified the constraining effect of the job colour bar on profitability, raising costs and curtailing output, as will be seen.

It was the conjunction of these various historical developments - the gains secured by the white workers, the rise in the cost of materials, and the shortage of African labour - in relation to the industry's specific cost structure which had the effect of placing a growing number of mines in the category of 'low grade mines'. A typical 'low grade mine' was the Simmer Deep. By 1918, this mine was operating at a loss, because of increased costs - notably of materials and of white labour - and reduced output. The cost of white labour underground per ton had risen by 86 per cent since 1914. Of this increased labour cost per ton, 27 per cent was due to wage increases and 73 per cent to lower per capita output. Between 1914 and 1918, annual output per white worker and per black worker fell by 700 and 63 tons respectively, and by 1918 the reduction plant was working at only 57 per cent of its capacity. The fall in output was due to the reduction of working hours - especially the introduction of the $48\frac{1}{2}$-hour week bank to bank, which cut an hour from the working time of African workers - and to the fact that the mine had been 'obliged to employ inefficient miners during the war', and to the fact that the African labour force was only 60 per cent of the nominal complement, which was 'one of the chief causes of decline in profit of the low grade mines'. (32) Most of the other mines had the same story to tell - rising costs, falling output, and falling profits, due to the same basic causes. (33) The number of mines falling into the category of 'low grade mines' gradually but steadily increased, as was noted earlier, and several were forced to close down. (34)

Finally, it needs to be borne in mind that the term 'low grade mine' is rather deceptive. For it suggests that some mines were 'low grade' and others 'high grade', and that the problem was essentially a geological problem of a few mines rather than a socio-economic problem of the industry as a whole.

Geologically, all the gold mines were low grade, because of the very low average grade of the Witwatersrand reef. As the President of the Chamber of Mines pointed out:

> I think it requires to be realised that when we talk of the low grade mines that with few exceptions this is a low grade industry. If you examine the industry as a whole, you will see that it is a low grade industry. (35)

However all mines possessed blocks of higher and lower grade ore. Since all the mines shared the same general cost structure, they all felt the effects of rising costs and falling output. These effects were to render lower

grade ore unpayable, and to intensify the mining of higher grade ore. As the Low Grade Mines Commission pointed out:
> The ore available for mining at any time in the mines . . . is to be found in a number of working places, and its value differs greatly in those places. Some of it is quite unpayable, other portions barely payable and others again offer a fair margin of profit. It will be evident from this that when costs rise, ore that was barely payable before becomes unpayable, and that a smaller amount is left as payable. Further, if more than a fair proportion of the best ore is mined in the struggle to survive a crisis, the balance left is so much poorer and the struggle becomes more and more difficult. This has been substantially the case with all of these mines in the past few years. (36)

While all mines felt the effect of increased costs, the specific effect on any given mine varied according to the composition of its ore reserves and its stage of development. The mines that were the most seriously affected by the rising margin of unpayability were those that had the least blocks of higher grade ore to draw upon, and those that, while still possessing sizable reserves of higher grade ore reserves, were prevented by cost increases from securing the minimum necessary level of output to cover high development and overhead costs (which rose as mines went deeper). If this tonnage could not be secured, the mine faced crisis, 'irrespective of the quantity of what would otherwise be payable ore remaining in that mine'. (37) Most of the mines forced to suspend operations by 1921 fell into this category. (38)

The problem was thus not that by the end of the war half of the mines were geologically 'low grade mines' and the other half 'high grade mines'. The problem was that over half of the mines, including many mines with high grade reserves, were unable to continue profitable operation at new levels of working costs and output. In fact, the definition of a 'low grade mine' was not geological but economic - a mine working at a loss or at a profit of less than 2s. per ton. In other words, the problem was essentially socio-economic rather than geological, a scarcity problem rather than a rarity problem, having to do with the social relations of production and the relative cost of factors of production in the industry as a whole. As a manager of a 'low grade mine' explained:
> What do you mean by saying that it must now be looked upon as a very Low Grade Mine? - Because the value of the ore has decreased and the cost of operating has increased to such an extent that there is no difference between them. A Low Grade Mine is a mine in which the

ratio of profits to revenue is a small figure, about a quarter. It has nothing to do with the absolute value of the ore, because if this mine could work at 15/- I should call it a comparatively rich mine. (39)

And as a trade union leader observed:

The position is that the low grade mines are an interminable thing. If you reduce the costs from 22/6d. to 20/-, it brings in a certain percentage of low grade ore into the reserves at a profit, and leaves an enormous amount outside. Reduce to 18/- and the same thing happens with a little more ore, and further down you get a low grade mine again, and the result is that you never end with it. It depends how much the worker will accept as reduction. If you get natives to labour for their keep only, you could include a vast deal more low grade ore into the reserves. I have never had a definition of a low grade mine yet. It simply means that a mine is whatever the management likes to make it at the time, as far as I can see. (40)

It was thus the impact of certain historical developments - the various gains secured by the white workers, the increased cost of materials, and the shortage of African labour - in relation to the specific cost and profitability structure of the gold mining industry which, by raising costs and reducing output to such an extent as to throw over half of the mining companies below the margin of payability, had the effect of plunging the industry into a serious profitability crisis, a crisis which was to have explosive consequences and far-reaching repercussions.

2 The extension of the job colour bar: the Status Quo Agreement

The exodus of many white mine workers from their jobs during the war not only raised the bargaining power of the remaining white workers, but also produced significant changes in the composition of the white labour force and in the occupational distribution of the labour force as a whole. The jobs of these workers were partly filled by a new group of white workers; and at the same time, the mining companies sought to utilise ultra-cheap non-white labour in semi-skilled work in place of more expensive white labour.

A considerable number of white mine workers left their jobs to go to the war. By the end of 1916, over 3,500 - about 20 per cent of the white labour force of the gold mines - had left for active service, with their employers' permission. (41) During the war as a whole, over 25 per cent left their jobs. (42) Most of these workers fell into the category of 'unvital work' (less skilled work) and could be replaced fairly easily. But many of the more skilled workers, such as mechanics, engine drivers, foremen, miners and shiftbosses, also left for the war and were more difficult to replace. (43) The government came to express concern to the Chamber of Mines about this exodus.

> Attention of government has been drawn to the fact that many skilled men are being recruited from industry. While appreciating keenness, government desires to remind mining managements of importance of keeping in view necessity of maintenance of industry and of avoiding mistake made in Europe, where skilled men had to be recalled from the front to maintain industrial output. (44)

The Chamber shared these fears, admitting that there were insufficient replacements for skilled workers. (45) But the Chamber could not stop white workers from leaving their jobs. (46)

One important effect of this shortage of skilled labour during the war was to increase the bargaining power of the remaining white workers, which underlay the gains which they secured during this period. Another significant effect of this exodus of white workers was to change the composition of the white labour force. For the workers who filled many of the vacant jobs were drawn from the ranks of a new and different group of white workers - the recently proletarianised and less skilled Afrikaner workers. Recently displaced from the rural areas, these workers for the most part lacked industrial skills, and, as Afrikaners, they did not share the inclination of many of the English-speaking immigrant artisans to go to the war in Europe. By the end of the war, these Afrikaner workers formed about 75 per cent of the white labour force of the gold mines, compared with about 40 per cent at the start of the war. (47) Thus for example the Simmer Deep mine lost between 30 to 40 per cent of its white labour force to the war - 'And their places were mostly filled in by raw chaps? - Yes, to a large extent that is so.' (48) And many of these new mine workers looked upon mining with some distaste, and saw mine work as a means of earning enough money to enable them to return to the land.

> You have a large number of men who, during the war, came from the country districts or from their farms. They had not come up to follow the profession of mining; they have come up merely to earn money either to buy cattle or to buy land. . . . They are here

merely to muddle through, to get through the work, to
earn the money, and to get back. (49)

These workers formed a group of semi-skilled and supervisory workers occupying an intermediate position between the mass of unskilled African workers and the skilled white workers. According to one observer:

The white conditions below ground have completely changed since the war. The bywoner Dutch from all over South Africa are the underground workers. 70%, and in some cases 80%. They never rise to better positions.
. . . They are bossed by mine captains and stopers, and they again boss the natives. (50)

And it was these new and least skilled white workers who were to be the most affected by the third important consequence of the exodus of white mine workers from their jobs to the war: the employment of ultra-cheap non-white labour in semi-skilled work.

As a result of long experience of work in the mines, and of the practice of white workers of leaving most of the manual work to Africans, a number of African workers - usually put at between 5 to 10 per cent of the African labour force - had come to acquire certain mining skills. (51) Moreover, it was frequently alleged that these African workers actually taught skills to the new white mine workers.

You say that in many cases the native teaches the white man his work underground? - Yes, in very many cases I might say.

But how does that come about? - Well, a man comes from the back veldt and goes down the mine for six months. Sometimes he learns and he finally gets a couple of machines to work himself. He is not able to do it but his natives do it, and if he were not there the natives could do it. They are skilled machine men some of these natives.

Do you mean to say that a man comes from the back veldt and will be allowed to go on machines after six months underground experience? - I am afraid it is only too true. There has been a scarcity of labour. . . .

And you maintain that the men from the back veldt know so little that the boys are teaching them? - It is quite clear that it is so. I can take you down and show you, any mine any time. (52)

Not surprisingly, therefore, during the war the mining companies began to employ such workers in semi-skilled work. While skilled jobs were reserved to white workers by the Regulations, there was no such reservation of work in the sphere of semi-skilled work, and as a Commission of Inquiry reported:

Certain work, usually described as semi-skilled, such
as drill sharpening, waste packing, pipe and track
laying, rough timbering, whitewashing and a number of
other odd jobs, had for some time past been carried out
in some mines by white men and in others by natives.
(53)
The effect of the war-time exodus of white workers was to
hasten the movement of non-white workers into semi-skilled
work. This became a cause of increasing anxiety among the
new, less skilled white workers, and as time went by these
workers began to demand the exclusion of ultra-cheap non-
white labour from semi-skilled work and to engage in militant strike action.

The first overt sign of tension came in January 1917,
when the underground white workers in the Van Ryn Deep
mine came out in a spontaneous, unofficial strike in protest against the employment of non-white labour in semi-
skilled work in various mines, and specifically against
the employment of non-whites in the Van Ryn Deep as waste-
packers (makers of supporting pillars, or 'pigstyes', in
the stopes) at 5s. per day, as opposed to the 15s. per day
received by white waste-packers. (54) The strike did not
last long, as the government intervened immediately, ad-
vising the company to withdraw the non-white workers, and
promising an inquiry. (55) The Government Mining Engineer
recommended an inquiry because 'the principle to which the
men appear to object still exists at the other mines and
is now still more likely to be a cause of disaffection
there'. (56)

The government-appointed inquiry found 'that the complaints which had resulted in open objection at Van Ryn
Deep existed elsewhere', and that the Van Ryn Deep strike
was not only due to the fear of displacement there, but
was also in protest against the fact 'that such displacement had already occurred in other mines'. (57) The white
workers feared that such displacement was the thin end of
the wedge. While the skilled workers were mostly concerned that if non-whites were employed in semi-skilled work,
it should be at the rates paid to white workers, the new
and less skilled white workers opposed the movement of
non-white workers into such work in principle. For, the
report pointed out, 'the bywoner class, a large number of
whom have migrated to the Reef in recent years, find ready
employment in the mines as waste-packers', and their opposition to the employment of non-white workers in this work
'is to be expected'. (58) The report supported this opposition, and concluded that 'it is essential that some
agreement should exist as to the classes of work limited
to Europeans only'. (59)

The Van Ryn Deep strike was a small but significant symptom of the changes and tensions developing in the gold mines during the war, as the government, employers and the Commission of Inquiry all realised. Its significance was perceptively summarised by a mining official at the time, in a letter to his uncle, Merriman, the Cape politician. The employment of non-whites in semi-skilled work had been on the increase in the past few years, he observed, and 'a good opening was afforded by their use to gradually try the removal of the colour bar question'. But the employers and the government were in a weak position because of the war, and 'great was the speed with which Barnatos [the controlling Group] and the Chamber climbed down'. A conflict over the job colour bar seemed inevitable. But 'this is not the right moment for a fight, and Wallers [the President of the Chamber] is doing his best to defer the evil day'. (60)

In February 1917, the Mine Workers' Union included in its set of demands to the Chamber of Mines a demand for the exclusion of non-white workers from semi-skilled work. The Chamber refused to agree to this demand, out of an alleged concern for the rights of non-white workers. It portrayed itself as confronted with something of a moral dilemma:

> The question of the 'colour bar', and the general economic and industrial relationship between the European and the coloured population, is one of the most difficult of South African problems. The European population is naturally desirous of maintaining its position and retaining for itself the fields of employment which it has held in the past. The coloured population, on the other hand, claims the right to work and to progress. (61)

The Chamber claimed that it would be unjust to exclude non-white workers employed in semi-skilled work from their jobs. But at the same time it wanted it to be clear that it was not against the job colour bar in skilled work. The gold mines had been 'singled out, through the mining regulations, for legal restrictions to safeguard the position of the skilled European employee', and the Chamber 'has not attacked and has no intention of attacking these regulations'. The Chamber therefore took up the position that it 'is prepared to recommend to its members that the status quo as at present existing on each mine shall be maintained'. (62)

The terms offered by the Chamber in February 1917 were rejected by the white workers, who made new demands in July. These included demands 'that no drills or tools be sharpened or repaired by cheap or coloured labour', and 'that waste-packing be done by white men'. (63) In its reply, the Chamber again professed that 'it has a responsibility not only to its white employees but also to its coloured employees, and that it is its duty to endeavour to hold the balance as evenly as possible between them'. (64) But the Chamber repeated its offer to maintain the status quo:

> As regards the relative scope of employment of European and Coloured employees, the status quo as existing at each mine to be maintained, no billets which are now held by European workmen to be given to Coloured workmen, and vice versa. (65)

The workers accepted the rest of the Chamber's offers - a $48\frac{1}{2}$-hour week, an extension of the war bonus, and minimum rates for underground workers - but not this offer. (66)

In 1918, the various mining unions, in a new set of demands to the Chamber, repeated the demand for the exclusion of non-white workers from drill-sharpening, in a more militant vein: 'Coloured drill-sharpeners on the Witwatersrand mines to be dismissed, failing which, after 30 days from receipt by the Chamber of Mines of this demand, federated unions will refuse to cooperate with coloured drill-sharpeners.' (67) The Chamber again replied that in its view 'it would not be a just action to deprive arbitrarily natives and coloured men of a means of livelihood which they have enjoyed for years', while again repeating its offer to maintain the status quo. (68) The unions continued to press for complete exclusion. (69) And the Chamber reiterated that it 'is prepared to maintain for the European mine employees the work which is at present being carried out by them, and its offer, if accepted, would effectively prevent any encroachment by the coloured population on that position'. (70) This offer was finally accepted by the white workers, and the Status Quo Agreement,

> that the status quo as existing on each mine with regard to the relative scope of employment of European and coloured employees should be maintained, that is to say, that no billets which are held by European workmen should be given to coloured workmen, and vice versa, (71)

came into effect on 1 September 1918.

Why did the white workers and the mining companies come to make this Agreement? What did it signify? The involvement of the white workers in the Agreement is not difficult to explain. For them, it represented a protectionist response to the new war-time developments in the industry, extending job protection to the new, less skilled white workers, who were not protected by the job colour bar in the Regulations. As far as the white workers were concerned, the Agreement was 'an attempt to defend the already badly undermined position of the white workers on the mines' against the attempts of the mining companies to extend the scope of employment of ultra-cheap labour at the expense of white workers. (72) Such a protectionist measure was seen to be necessary, as was the job colour bar in the Regulations, by the various measures utilised by the employers to secure such labour, 'to keep the natives' wages and conditions down to the level that a ring of employers can force them', which 'led to a steady and progressive encroachment by the natives on the position of the white workers'. (73) Like the job colour bar in skilled work, the Agreement reflected 'the insecurity of the white man's position and the force which is keeping the native down'. (74) But more specifically, the Agreement was seen as a necessary response to the policy of the mining companies during the war of 'continuously substituting natives and coloured people for white workers in a number of occupations that had been previously exclusively filled by white men'. (75)

    It was felt at the time [of the Agreement] that the Chamber was taking a mean advantage of the absence on Active Service of a considerable number of mine employees and utilising an occasion of national extremity for the purpose of advancing their well known policy of eliminating white men from the mining industry. (76)

The reason why the Mine Workers' Union accepted the Status Quo Agreement instead of continuing to press for the complete exclusion of non-white labour from semi-skilled work was because the Chamber made its offers to the mining unions as a package deal, which had to be accepted or rejected as a whole, and 'pressure was brought to bear by other unions upon the Mine Workers' Union to accept the conditions because they had to be accepted as a whole'. (77) A sign of the militant mood within the Union was that its General Council's consent to the Agreement was only carried by the chairman's casting vote. (78) Opposition to the Agreement continued within the Union. (79) The white workers saw it as something of an interim measure, as 'merely a temporary barricade . . . until the nation as a whole can decide definitely and irrevocably . . . upon the policy to be adopted'. (80) They wanted the Agreement

    to prevent the complete flooding of the white workers' position until the nation can be aroused to the dangers of the present labour policy of the mines, just as the child who plugged the hole in the dyke with his finger

until assistance to repair the dyke could be obtained, saved his country from disaster. (81)
But what of the involvement of the Chamber of Mines in the Status Quo Agreement? Here we see the Chamber actually initiating an extension of the job colour bar. The Chamber's role in the Agreement is to be explained as part of its general strategy towards the white workers during the war. This was a strategy of extreme accommodation, designed to minimise class conflict and to stem a rising tide of workers' militancy. And this strategy is to be explained by the basic shift in the balance of class power in the industry during the war, consequent upon the shortage of skilled labour. This shift placed the white mine workers in a strong market position, and the new white workers displayed a growing grass-roots militancy. For the Chamber of Mines, the Status Quo Agreement was a kind of time-buying ceasefire agreement, a tactical compromise during a period of class weakness to delay class confrontation until the balance of class power had swung more in its favour. The Chamber's role in the Agreement thus needs to be seen as part of a general strategy, and in the context of the class situation which generated this strategy.

This strategy was most clearly articulated by the Chamber's war-time President, Evelyn Wallers, who was President of the Chamber for an unprecedented period of five years (as opposed to the usual one) including the four years from 1915 to 1919, and under whose leadership this strategy was developed and implemented. Its starting point was a recognition by the companies of the war-time change in the balance of class power - of the fact that, as Wallers put it, 'the "swing of the pendulum" under the law of supply and demand is at present in favour of the men'. (82) This condition made it necessary and expedient to pursue a strategy of minimising class conflict and of containing working class militancy, through such means as the propagation of the idea of a consensus of interests between capital and white labour, the institutionalisation of a framework of 'industrial relations' to stabilise relations between them, and the granting of various concessions to the white workers.

The companies had not forgotten the turbulent class conflict on the Rand in 1913 and early 1914, and the militancy of the white workers at that time. As Wallers observed to the Chamber: 'Before the war both employers and employed were clearly preparing themselves in every possible way for a struggle of very great magnitude.' (83) But the war had seemingly dissolved this antagonism, for 'when war intervened, all became aware of the real

struggle that was ahead; conditions of industrial relationship presented themselves in a more correct light and at their true value'. (84) With the war, the mining companies thus found themselves in a certain sense 'saved by the bell'; class relations were now seen 'in a more correct light and at their true value'. And the new conditions created by the war presented the companies with an opportunity of securing a more stable relationship with the white workers. As Wallers declared:
> There are few questions which have been more vitally affected by the war than that of the relation between employer and employed, and few lessons of greater importance taught to us by the war than the definite necessity of the proper adjustment of that relationship. (85)

In what direction did this relationship need to be adjusted? It was first of all necessary to stress that, as far as the mining companies and the white workers were concerned, 'neither side - neither Capital nor Labour - can carry on without the other, that there is definite identity of interest, and that justice and common sense will prevail in the joint working of that interest'. (86) It was then necessary to institutionalise this alleged consensus of interests in a formal and stable framework of industrial relations. Employers had to rid themselves of nineteenth-century attitudes to labour and to accept the right of the white workers to organise and act collectively in pursuit of their 'legitimate' aspirations. (87)
> The aspirations on the part of workmen the world over towards reasonable working hours, the maintenance of good wages and a definite and improved status in industry are perfectly legitimate and right, and every thinking man in the employing and managing sections of the community recognises that fact. (88)

The correct course for the companies was a system of industrial relations which helped the white workers to secure these 'legitimate' aspirations peacefully, through industrial councils, industrial agreements, 'cooling off periods' and so on. (89) The growth of the industrial council movement in Great Britain was seen as 'confirmation . . . in a very satisfactory form, of the wisdom of the lines upon which we have been thinking and working'. (90)

Such a policy of conciliation and concessions was conducive, Wallers explained, to the stabilisation of relations between the employers and the white workers and to the containment of radical and 'extremist' tendencies among the latter. It was through such a strategy 'that the extremists . . . who are seeking trouble rather than

peace . . . must be effectively and faithfully dealt with'. (91) And it was these elements who 'constitute the real danger'. (92)
They are the definite obstruction to well-ordered, well-considered progress; they seek to obscure the identity of interest that in fact exists, and the co-operation between employer and employed that must be realised if really good industrial and social conditions are to be secured. (93)
Such a strategy was seen to be all the more important in view of the Russian revolution and the growth of industrial unionism and the workers' control movement, all of which expressed tendencies 'usually accompanied by the opinion that the employing and managing sections of the community should be eliminated'. (94) To avoid such a fate, the employers in the gold mines would be wise to accept and co-operate with the moderate aspirations of the white workers. (95)
The behaviour of the Chamber of Mines, under the leadership of Wallers, towards the white workers during the war was an implementation of this accommodationist strategy. And the Status Quo Agreement may be seen as one of many specific developments that followed logically and deliberately from this strategy. Others comprised the recognition of and co-operation with the white trade unions and their co-ordinating body (the South African Industrial Federation), the establishment of joint boards of reference between the Chamber and various unions, and the various gains secured by the white workers in wages, working conditions and working hours.
The 'Wallers policy' had the general and long-term aim of stabilising relations between the mining companies and the white workers, and the short-term aim of averting confrontation between them over the emerging profitability crisis until the balance of class power was more in favour of the employers. In relation to these aims, it was fairly successful. There was no costly, large-scale conflict between the companies and the white workers during the war. Given the fact that the 'swing of the pendulum' was 'in favour of the men', and that 'if the men had decided to exploit the principle of supply and demand to its full extent . . . many mines would have had to close down', the President of the Chamber expressed appreciation for the fact that 'they have not endeavoured to exact the full toll under that law', which was seen to confirm the wisdom of the Chamber's policy. (96) And the 'pendulum' seemed likely to swing in a different direction soon. A mining official expressed the prevailing view of employers that the end of the war would bring an end to the labour

shortage and strengthen the hand of the employers:
The return of the men from active service will of
course give you a larger number of men to choose from?
- Yes.
And therefore the Management itself will be able
presumably to bring about a better state of discipline?
- Undoubtedly. (97)
However the short-term success of the Chamber's accommodationist strategy was both costly and limited. All the
concessions to the white workers during the war undermined
the profitability of the mining companies. While the
Chamber accepted that its goals could only be secured at a
price, the price which it had to pay was very high, as was
noted earlier. Moreover, the Chamber's policy, including
the Status Quo Agreement, did not succeed in eliminating
conflict between the companies and the white workers and
radical tendencies among the latter during the war. For
the last part of the war and the end of the war saw a
rising tide of militancy among the white workers, especially the new Afrikaner mine workers, which increasingly
perturbed the employers and the government.
This increasing activism at grass-roots level was most
generally evident in the growth of a militant shop
stewards movement. Works Committees of shaft and shop
stewards were formed in the mines, and came to wield considerable local and immediate power over the employers,
through such sanctions as 'go slows' and 'lightning
strikes'. Commenting on the reduction of managerial power
during the war, a Commission of Inquiry reported that:
'The chief interference with the managers has been on the
part of the trade union officials, more particularly of
shaft and shop stewards'. (98) The power and influence of
these Committees had reached, in its view, a 'deplorable
extent'. (99) And as time went by, the new Afrikaner mine
workers became increasingly militant, supporting their demands for such things as the exclusion of non-white
workers from semi-skilled work with various unofficial
strikes, that arose at the grass-roots level, sometimes in
defiance of union leaders. Such strikes began to break
out in various mines in 1917 (notably in the Van Ryn Deep
mine in January, the Meyer and Charlton mine in February
and the Randfontein mine in April and May). Unrest in the
mines towards the end of the war, a Commission noted, took
the form of lightning strikes, which 'waste large sums of
money, give undesirable opportunities to extremists, and
have a disturbing effect upon the natives'. (100) Between
1914 and 1919, the number of illegitimate absentee shifts
taken by white workers per year rose by 82,128. (101)
Such unofficial strikes and grass-roots militancy among

the white workers expressed an instability which disturbed
the Chamber of Mines, challenging its policy of containment and stabilisation. The President of the Chamber reported that:
> The great difficulty so far in dealing with the Union
> embracing the greatest body of workers on the mines,
> namely, the South African Mine Workers' Union, has been
> the meeting of the situations continually arising
> through action by local branches or by employees on in-
> dividual mines. (102)

These local strikes and disputes broke agreements between
the Chamber and the unions, negating a general principle
of the Chamber's policy, a principle 'of the greatest importance', which lay 'within the arrangement made that no
sectional or drastic action shall be taken in a dispute by
either side before the question has been referred to a
Board of Reference'. (103) The Chamber had taken steps to
institutionalise the board of reference system, with its
'cooling off periods' etc., and the unions co-operated in
this. But the Industrial Federation and the union leadership did not wield complete control over the white
workers. Not all of the latter were union members, and
among union members themselves the question of local
branch autonomy was very much at issue. After an unofficial strike in 1917, the Inspector of White Labour reported that 'there is a restless feeling abroad amongst
numbers who are not in membership of the union which is
liable to burst out at any time', that a movement was
afoot 'to force the pace, which may end in serious
trouble', and that 'the Conference idea is looked at as a
pretext for delay'. (104) Reporting on the militant mood
of the white mine workers, another government official
stated, more bluntly, that: 'You will see that one does
not know what the men will do next; they are like
children.' (105)

A situation of 'not knowing what the men will do next'
was not one to reassure the Chamber of Mines. While intensifying its conciliatory policy during the last part of
the war, it was at the same time sufficiently perturbed by
the growing signs of instability that, as the Government
Mining Engineer cabled to the Minister of Mines: 'Mining
houses generally anxious to know feeling of government regarding strikes, since demands of men are growing and impossible position may arise at any moment.' (106)

The 'feelings of the government' about developments in
the gold mines were far from happy. While it also sought
to accommodate the white mine workers during the war, the
government became increasingly concerned about the rising
tide of militancy among them, especially among the new

Afrikaner mine workers, during the latter part of the war, so much so that, at the urging of the Secretary of Mines, it made contingency plans for the suppression of a general strike on the Rand.

After the Van Ryn Deep strike of January 1917, the Secretary of Mines reported confidentially to the Minister that the recent unrest 'tends to show that a new factor has arisen which must be taken into consideration in regard to industrial and labour questions on the mines'. (107) This new factor, he continued, was the new group of white workers in the gold mines.

> The new element to which I refer is the large percentage of the younger Dutch-speaking Afrikanders who have been gradually coming into the mining industry. These do not, as a rule, join the Miners' Union very readily, but there is reason to think that some organisation, more or less of a political character, is being carried on amongst them. It would appear that the greater part of the talking and agitating during the past few days has been due to these younger Afrikanders. . . . This is entirely a new danger. (108)

The Secretary thought 'that the Government should be made aware of the new circumstances arising in the mines in order to enable some kind of preparation to be made, and have a plan of defence ready'. (109) For what was likely, he prophesied, was 'a third rebellion, started on industrial lines instead of having its origin in the country districts'. (110) It would not be long before these fears came true.

Concerned about the contents of this report, the Secretary of Justice asked the Commissioner of Police to have it verified. (111) The police confirmed the fact that 'a large number of Dutch-speaking Afrikaners, approximately 2,500, mostly from the Orange Free State, have obtained employment on the mines of the East Rand in the place of old employees who left on active service'. (112) These new workers were playing the leading role in the agitation against the employment of non-white workers in semi-skilled work, and they were also anxious about being replaced by workers returning from the war. Were a major strike to break out, it would 'have the support of an element with less respect for law and order than was the case in the strikes of July 1913 and January 1914'. (113)

After another strike in 1917, and ensuing negotiations between the Chamber and the white workers, the Secretary of Mines confided to the Governor-General that the situation in the mines was 'not without danger of disturbing influences'. Relations between the Chamber and the white workers were so important that 'we cannot regard the

Chapter 3

relations between the two parties from merely an academic viewpoint'. There was a need for a 'reliable striking force'.

It is of serious importance to us to have some reliable striking force which can be depended upon in the country, instead of remaining in the condition in which we were last month, when we were frankly told that if trouble occurred the Defence Force could not be called out, the Burgher Commandos could not be relied upon, the Special Constable Force was not existent owing to removals, men going to the front, etc., and the police were unreliable. (114)

After another strike, the Secretary again warned of the growing militancy of the rank and file workers, some of whom, organised in the local branches of the Mine Workers' Union, resisted attempts by the Union's moderate leaders to restrain strike initiatives by the local branches. It was, he again emphasised, 'our duty to be prepared'. (115) The Commissioner of Police then warned 'that should a Strike take place, and consequent trouble demand Police attention, I have not sufficient men to cope with any large or serious disturbance', and suggested that a scheme should be worked out with the Defence Department 'for protection of life and property in case of a general Strike on the Witwatersrand Mines'. (116) The Minister of Justice then requested the police to implement this suggestion. (117)

As a result, the police and the Defence Department organised a contingency plan for mobilising police from all over South Africa for emergency duty on the Rand in the event of a strike.

It is proposed to just send them a one word telegram 'MOBILISE', and the different Divisions will at once notify their members, who will concentrate at different points on the Railway and entrain for the Rand, where they will be assigned their areas of duty.

This would include 'a small striking force of horsemen . . . made up from the Transvaal Division'. (118) The Minister of Justice gave his approval to the plan, and by October 1917 the Commissioner of Police was able to report that all arrangements had been completed, and that full mobilisation could be achieved within four days. (119) This advance planning by the government for class conflict on the Rand reflected its concern about war-time developments, and a determination not to be taken by surprise by such conflict. In the event, however, when such conflict did break out in 1922, the government had plenty of time to amass its forces.

Thus while the Chamber's accommodationist policy towards the white workers during the war - of which the Status Quo Agreement formed a part - succeeded in averting serious class conflict and major 'official' strikes in this period, the mood of the white mine workers was becoming increasingly militant as time went by, to the concern of the employers and the government. This militancy was most pronounced amongst the new, less skilled white workers, as the Secretary of Mines and the police noted. Concerning unrest among white workers during the war, mining officials were of the view that:

> Any trouble as far as white labour is concerned does not refer to the higher class of working men - the better class - composed of two thirds to three quarters of the men. . . . We are not dealing with the top men here - the top two thirds who have been giving no trouble. . . . It is simply the things that took place with the lower one third that gave the trouble. (120)

These workers were the least secure of the white workers, the most exposed to the danger of displacement by ultra-cheap labour, a danger which was becoming increasingly real during the war. And while the rest of the white mine workers may have 'given less trouble' during the war, this was at the cost to the companies of the substantial gains - including the Status Quo Agreement - which they secured for all of the white workers.

What did the Status Quo Agreement signify? The Agreement was an extension of the job colour bar, which both stemmed from, and was to be a cause of, significant developments in the gold mines. On the one hand, it was a response to war-time changes in the labour force and labour market and to the tendency of the mining companies during the war of employing ultra-exploitable workers in more skilled work. The job colour bar in the Mining Regulations protected the more skilled white workers. The Agreement extended protection to the less skilled white workers, prescribing that no jobs held by white workers in 1918 could be given to non-white workers. On the other hand, coinciding as it did with the emerging profitability crisis, it was to have the effect of intensifying this crisis. For as an extension of the job colour bar, it was an extension of the job colour bar's contradiction of profit maximisation, which further restricted the freedom of the employers to make the most profitable possible utilisation of labour. Soon, the Chamber of Mines was to be demanding the dissolution of the Agreement, and was finally to withdraw unilaterally from it, with explosive consequences.

2. THE OFFENSIVE OF THE MINING COMPANIES AGAINST THE WHITE WORKERS

1 The mining companies and the job colour bar

By the end of the First World War, the gold mining companies were thus faced with a serious profitability crisis. The premium gold price alleviated the crisis, but only temporarily, and only by offsetting its effects, not by affecting its causes, which intensified. The Chamber of Mines realised this all too well. While it appreciated the premium, since it had 'for the time being, saved the situation', it was, the President of the Chamber declared, 'of no use to delude ourselves or others with the idea that this premium on gold is going to be permanent'. (1) The premium merely reflected temporary currency instability. 'What has really happened', the President observed, 'is not that gold has appreciated but that the currency for which we sell it has depreciated.' (2) And this currency depreciation had the effect of increasing the price not only of gold but also of everything else as well, 'so that what we receive at one end, we pay out at the other in increased and increasing cost of stores and of living'. (3) The premium price did not eliminate the causes of the profitability crisis; it did not mean an end to cost inflation, or to output reduction. 'The problem of the low grade mines', the President declared, 'is thus not solved, but merely postponed.' (4) The price of gold would eventually fall and return to its fixed level, and then, the President declared, clearly and ominously: 'When that time comes, we shall be faced with the necessity of adopting one of two alternative policies. Either half the industry must be closed down . . . or the costs of production, including the cost of labour, must be reduced.' (5)

The fundamental problem for the mining companies was how to realise the second of these policies. How were 'the costs of production, including the cost of labour' to be reduced? The diagnosis was correct. The premium merely lessened the effects of the crisis; if half of the mining companies were to be prevented from 'going under' and if the profitability of the gold mines was to be ensured, the crisis would have to be overcome through action upon its causes.

The specific historical response of the mining companies to the profitability crisis was determined by their varying degree of ability to influence the various causes of the crisis. As we have seen, the rising level of costs and the falling level of output, which constituted the crisis, stemmed from the impact of certain historical developments - the rise in the cost of materials, a shortage of ultra-cheap labour, and the various gains secured by the white workers - within the specific cost structure of the gold mining industry.

The mining companies had little ability to resolve the crisis through action upon the first two of these causal factors. They could do little about the rising cost of stores: they had already during the war obtained what small relief was possible through such practices as centralised buying, and no further margin for cost reduction existed in this area. (6) Nor, with the increased demand for African labour among various employers, and with the continuing ban on the importation of tropical African labour, were the mining companies able to raise output and reduce unit costs through increasing the supply of ultra-cheap labour; and raising this supply through wage increases would have had a disastrous effect on costs. The only course open to the mining companies was that of extracting more profit from the existing labour force. This could be done in two basic ways - paying workers less and securing more work from them. This meant acting upon the third cause of the crisis - the gains secured by the white workers: higher wages, reduced working hours, and the extension of the job colour bar. For the labour costs of African workers were already ultra-low, and there was no possibility of any radical cost reduction in that area. That left two other courses: a reduction of white labour costs, and an increase in the work and responsibility of both white and African workers. White labour costs could be reduced through the replacement of expensive white labour by ultra-cheap black labour, and labour productivity could be increased through a reorganisation of labour. Both of these imperatives were obstructed by the job colour bar, and their realisation necessitated an attack on the job colour bar, and thus on the position of the white workers.

Until the end of the First World War, as was observed earlier, the policy of the Chamber of Mines towards the job colour bar had been a mixture of peaceful co-existence and active co-operation, as part of its long-term and short-term accommodation of the white labour aristocracy. But with the new and critical configuration of conditions which had emerged by the end of the war, producing the profitability crisis, the job colour bar now assumed a dual significance for the mining companies. The crisis intensified the relative importance of its contradiction of profitability, in its effects on both costs and output; and, unlike the other causal factors behind the crisis, the job colour bar was amenable to effective counteraction by the employers - the only such factor that was.

The mining companies were therefore to seek to overcome the profitability crisis through a structural reorganisation of labour in the mines, aimed at minimising costs and maximising output through a more profitable allocation and utilisation of labour, involving both a reduction of white labour costs and a maximisation of the work and responsibility of all workers.

On the one hand, therefore, the companies were concerned to reduce the cost of white labour. In addition to wage reductions, and retrenchments without replacements, an important means for achieving this was the substitution of ultra-cheap forced labour for expensive white labour in certain occupations. Such substitution was doubly advantageous to employers - ultra-cheap labour was employed both more productively and in place of much more expensive labour (it will be remembered that white wages were on average about ten times higher than African wages).

The area in which this substitution was to take place was that of semi-skilled work, in such occupations as drill-sharpening, winch and locomotive driving, timbering and waste-packing. Some African workers had already moved into such employment - a tendency which called forth the Status Quo Agreement, which was designed to prevent the displacement of white workers in these jobs. But the worsening profitability crisis made such displacement of increasing importance for the mining companies. 'There are employed on the mines', the Chamber of Mines stated, 'a certain proportion of natives who, by reason of their long mining experience, character and ability, could be much more usefully employed than they are at present.' (7) What stood in the way of this, it went on to complain, was the job colour bar. (8)

The other major imperative was to maximise the work and responsibility of all workers. On the one hand, one of the major aims of the companies was to increase the amount of work performed by African workers while underground. The job colour bar considerably restricted the amount of this work. Because of the job colour bar, mine managers declared, 'it is impossible to obtain eight hours work per day from underground natives'. (9) This was because various Mining Regulations prohibited various activities by African workers without the presence and personal supervision of a white miner. (10) African workers would go down the mines at about 4.30 a.m., but usually not start work until about 7.30 a.m., because they had to wait until the working place had been made safe under the personal supervision of the white miner, which took considerable time. On most mines, the average work time spent at the face by white workers was about seven hours, and between two to four of these hours were spent in such preparatory activities as dressing down, lashing, starting holes and charging up, 'with the result that in certain classes of underground work such as hand and machine drilling, the natives seldom have more than five hours and often as little as three in which to finish their task'. (11) This problem became more acute as mines deepened and expanded and as the white workers secured reductions in working hours.

> When the mines were shallower and the working day of miners was longer, the effect of these Regulations was not so serious, but today when mines are deep and cover large areas these Regulations cause a great waste of working hours. (12)

The working hours of the African workers were limited by those of the white workers, and, as was noted earlier, the reduction in the latter during the war produced a corresponding reduction in the former.

The mining companies were therefore concerned to eliminate this particular effect of the job colour bar, so as to 'save the wastage of native labour that exists today through their hanging about doing nothing for a very long time'. (13) They wanted the Regulations amended 'so as to allow of a competent native with the necessary native assistants to enter the working place, make safe and prepare it for drilling over without waiting for the ganger'. (14) They wanted African workers to be able to do the safety and preparatory work - to make the necessary watering, dressing down, clearing of benches, blowing over, plugging of holes, rigging up, fixing of hoses, preparation of jumpers, marking of drill hole positions, and general preparation of the working place - without the personal presence of the white miner. (15) This would permit an estimated one to three extra hours of work per shift by African workers. (16) And as a mine manager explained:

> The law permits us to work natives eight hours, and we can only work them on an average about five or six hours, and it is our business to try to get eight hours or as near as eight as possible. (17)

As the Chamber of Mines saw it, 'The whole idea is to get more work out of the natives while they are below instead of having them doing nothing.' (18)

By the same token, the mining companies also wanted to extend the work and responsibility of white workers. Their aim was to have fewer white workers, with greater work and responsibility. They were opposed to the restriction of particular jobs to particular workers, and the 'one man, one job' principle, whereby, for instance, a miner in charge of drilling could not do his own timbering, and so on. (19) Their policy, as will be seen, was to be to retrench many white workers in supporting work and to extend the responsibility of remaining whites, especially the miners, to include this work, which in practice meant that the white workers were to have to extend more responsibility to African workers.

The mining companies were thus concerned to reduce costs and to raise output through a reorganisation of labour. A manager of a 'low grade mine' gave an example of how this would work. His mine employed about sixty white timbermen. If African workers were substituted for some of them, and if the area of work which remaining white workers had to be responsible for was tripled, the number of white timbermen could be reduced by about two-thirds, saving the mine over £1,000 per month. (20)

What stood in the way of this more profitable utilisation of labour by the companies was the job colour bar of the white workers, both in the Mining Regulations, which restricted skilled jobs and various duties (such as responsibility for making safe) to white workers and curtailed the working time of African workers, and in the Status Quo Agreement, which extended job protection to white workers in semi-skilled work, and which came to be regarded by the white workers as a general anti-displacement agreement and not just an anti-substitution agreement. The Agreement was invoked by the white workers, the Chamber complained, to prevent the displacement of what the Chamber alleged to be 'redundant' workers - for instance to prevent the companies 'from combining two gangs under one ganger'. (21) As a Commission of Inquiry reported:

Attempts . . . on the part of the manager of a mine to get rid of redundant or inefficient men were often met by the Unions by an appeal to the Status Quo Agreement. If, for instance, it was proposed for reasons of efficiency or economy, to combine two gangs of natives under one of two European overseers and so to dispense with the services of the less efficient, the Unions would intervene on the ground that the Status Quo Agreement would be contravened thereby. . . . It was mainly on this account that it was deemed desirable to put an end to it once and for all. (22)

The job colour bar protected the position of expensive white labour, and restricted the working time and responsibility of all workers and the occupational mobility of the more skilled African workers.

In order to resolve the profitability crisis, the

mining companies were thus to seek to reduce the scope of
operation of the job colour bar, so as to secure the more
profitable employment of ultra-cheap African labour. To
this end, they were to seek both the abolition of the
Status Quo Agreement, so as to make substitutions in semi-
skilled work, and the amendment of the Mining Regulations,
so as 'to permit natives to be used as working leading
hands to assist the European supervisor in performing and
directing the work'. (23)

> To give effect to the Chamber's suggestion, it would be
> necessary to set up machinery whereby the more expert
> natives . . . can obtain a certificate identifying them
> as such, and arranging that these natives could be
> given authority and responsibility which is not now
> possible. (24)

Precisely how these African workers would be utilised, and
the degree of labour reorganisation, would vary from mine
to mine, but 'Broadly speaking, it is suggested that they
be used as authorised assistants to the European supervisor and entitled, when so instructed, to act as his
deputy on their own initiative and responsibility.' (25)

The purpose of these changes would be both to reduce
labour costs and to maximise work.

> I take it from your evidence that the benefit you
> expect to derive from relaxation of the colour bar is
> an increased amount of work from the native rather than
> a saving in wages? - It would happen both ways. You
> would certainly save a good deal in white wages and get
> better work out of the boys you have. If we can re-
> organise the work on the mines, we can do with less
> white men, and get greater tonnage out of the same
> number of boys who remain. (26)

Various kinds of economies could be secured, this mining
official explained. Some white workers would be dismissed
without being replaced, others would be replaced by African workers, while those whites retained would be made responsible for a much larger work area and number of Africans, and African workers would be employed more productively. (27) The premium gold price was useful, but a
substantial reorganisation of labour was far more important, the Chamber insisted, since only this would act upon
the causes of the crisis and restore profitability.

> You consider that the question of allowing more scope
> to the native and the removal of the colour bar is of
> greater importance than getting an immediate increase
> in the price of your gold? - I think it is of very much
> more importance giving the natives more scope and re-
> ducing the working costs. You may get a temporary in-
> crease in the price of your gold, but if you can bring

your unpayable ore into the payable category it will be most important for the industry. (28)
The only effective course open to the mining companies to overcome the profitability crisis was thus to secure more profit from the labour force, through reducing white labour costs and extending the work and responsibility of all workers. However this course involved an attack on the white workers, and particularly on the job colour bar of the white workers. The job colour bar was the chief obstruction in its way, and its successful realisation necessitated a reduction of the scope of operation of the job colour bar. The significance of the job colour bar to the mining companies in this crisis was aptly summarised by a mining official:

Is the colour bar the greatest stumbling block to the mines being worked profitably? - No, it is not the greatest stumbling block, but it is the only thing over which we have any control which will enable the mines to continue working. The greatest stumbling block is the poverty of the ore. (29)

But in pursuing this course, and in seeking to take action over 'the only thing over which we have any control', the mining companies were headed for confrontation with the white workers.

2 The strike and uprising of 1922

It was during 1921 that this confrontation began to take shape. After reaching a record level in February 1920, the premium price fluctuated for a period and then began to fall steadily during 1921, while costs remained at a record high level and output and profits continued to fall. The white workers continued to secure gains, with more wage increases in 1920 and 1921, so that by 1921 white labour costs were 60 per cent higher than in 1914. (30)

The profitability crisis thus remained and intensified in the immediate post-war period, despite the premium price. But at the same time, the balance of class power swung more in favour of the employers. The labour shortage during the war, we noted earlier, had 'swung the pendulum in favour of the men', as the President of the Chamber of Mines had put it. But this shortage came to an end with the end of the war, and in its place came rising unemployment among white workers. This unemployment stemmed from such factors as the continuing proletarianisation and urbanisation of unskilled rural whites, the return of soldiers from the war, the post-war depression in Europe and a depression in South Africa beginning at the end of 1920. Many returning workers were unable to find employment. By the end of 1919, there were about 4,000 unemployed returned soldiers in the Union. (31) White unemployment on the Rand, as in South Africa as a whole, intensified during 1920 and 1921. By May 1921, about 5,000 white workers on the Rand were unemployed. (32) Some idea of the state of the labour market for white mine workers is provided by the statistics of the government-administered employment exchange. In 1920, about 1,400 unemployed white mine workers applied for mining jobs to the exchange, while the employers made requests for only about 290 such workers, about 280 of whom obtained employment; in 1921, about 1,700 applied, with the employers requesting only about 180, and only about 175 obtaining employment. (33) This large pool of unemployed white mine workers shifted the balance of class power in favour of the mining companies.

While this unemployment strengthened the hand of the employers, it did not dampen the militant mood of the white workers on the Rand - a militancy which had risen during the war, was buoyed on by the gains secured during this period, was intensified by unemployment and fears of displacement, and was not unaffected by such events as the Russian revolution. The immediate post-war period saw the largest number of workers on strike in South Africa's entire history: in the three years 1919-21 a total of 1.5 million white workers were involved in industrial strikes (compared with a total of 0.13 million for the 13 years between 1923 and 1934). (34) A sign of the times was the establishment of a workers' 'Soviet' in Johannesburg in 1919, when, following from a strike of various groups of white workers in April, the white workers took over the government of Johannesburg, ousting the town council and setting up a Provisional Board of Control (which was disbanded when government officials, who hastened to Johannesburg, promised various concessions on wages and other issues). (35) In May 1920, the South African Industrial Federation (the generally conservative trade union co-ordinating body) decided in favour of a policy of nationalisation of all gold and coal mines, and of the establishment of a legal minimum ratio between white and non-white workers. (36) During 1920 and 1921 the white workers on the Rand held many meetings to protest against unemployment. A mass meeting in October 1920, chaired by the Mine Workers' Union, passed a resolution: 'That we, the workers of the Witwatersrand, in mass meeting assembled, do hereby most emphatically protest against the continuation of the system of capitalism at present in force, which can, at a moment's notice, throw our comrades out of work.' It called for a take-over of control of the economy by the workers, 'which will result in the destruction of the system that produces only for profit and the substitution of a system of production for use, which will give equal opportunities in all things to all those who are prepared to work'. (37) 'It was rather interesting to note', a newspaper observed, 'that every reference to the Russian Bolsheviks and their accomplishment was cheered loudly.' (38)

It was against this background of continuing profitability crisis, unemployment and militancy among the white workers, that, during 1921, the Chamber of Mines and the mining unions engaged in a long drawn-out series of negotiations over wages and the job colour bar, in an attempt to find a mutually acceptable solution to the profitability crisis. But, despite concessions by the white workers, these negotiations did not meet the requirements of the mining companies, and at the end of 1921 the Chamber of Mines declared its intention to implement the changes which it sought, which provoked a strike and uprising by white workers on the Rand.

The first line of attack taken by the Chamber in the negotiations concerned wages. In February 1920 the white workers had secured a wage increase of £2.4 per week. In May 1921, the Chamber informed them that because of the falling price of gold, a wage reduction was necessary. (39) After a conference with the white workers, the Chamber proposed a reduction of 3s. per shift in the wages of most white workers, to take effect in 1922. The premium price was falling, wages were being reduced in other parts of the world, and, the Chamber stated,
> unless a substantial reduction can be made in the cost of production, an increasing number of mines will become unable to carry on. . . . The mines cannot reduce the cost of stores by any means other than those which are habitually used, so that it is necessary to secure a reduction of wages. (40)

The Chamber calculated that this proposal would affect 15,260 workers, and save the companies about £58,000 per month as of January 1922. (41)

In reply, the white workers stated that overseas wage reductions were irrelevant, that wage rates had to be based on more than just cost of living fluctuations, that white wages had not been adjusted to cover even half the increase in the cost of living, and that as far as the 'low grade mines' were concerned, 'the trade unions do not admit the right of employers to adjust wages on a basis of the poorest paying part of their industry'. (42) They rejected the Chamber's proposed wage cut as unjustified. The Chamber reiterated its concern about falling price and profits and rising costs. The industry's capital requirements, for both mining and development work, were very high, it stated, 'but there is little or no prospect of capital being forthcoming . . . unless it can be clearly demonstrated that there is a determination abroad that the cost of production shall and must be substantially reduced at the earliest opportunity'. (43) The President of the Chamber declared that: 'We cannot wait until the price drops out of sight and deal with it at a moment's notice then. We must make preparations for the fall that is bound to come, and we think it is necessary to take immediate steps.' (44) The negotiations continued until finally in August 1921 the Chamber and the white workers reached agreement over a new cost of living based sliding scale of wage rates. Future wage adjustments were to be based on quarterly fluctuations in the cost of living, with minimum and maximum levels of adjustment, and wage reductions of 1s. 6d. per shift would come into force on this basis as of August 1921. (45)

The other problem to which the mining companies came to turn their attention, both to reduce white labour costs and to maximise labour productivity, was the job colour bar. At this stage, in 1920 and 1921, they were specifically concerned with one aspect of the job colour bar - its effect of limiting the amount of work performed by African workers underground, a problem which, as was noted earlier, had intensified with the reduction in working hours secured by the white workers, and which expressed itself in falling output and productivity. This problem derived essentially from certain job colour bar Regulations prescribing that the examination and making safe of working places had to take place under the direct personal supervision of white workers. The effect of this, as General Smuts summarised it, was 'that we do not get the full and proper use out of the vast labour force we have collected from all parts of Southern Africa on these fields'. (46) Because of time spent in waiting until the large number of working places had been examined and made safe by the smaller number of white miners (as well as in getting to and from working places), African workers performed on average only between 5 and 6 hours of work per shift.

In 1920, following from certain recommendations of the Low Grade Mines Commission, the Chamber of Mines and the Mine Workers' Union entered into negotiations about these Regulations. (47) These did not produce any immediate results. But in June 1921, the Chamber of Mines urged the Prime Minister for action towards the amendment of the Regulations. (48) And at the end of the month, certain of the Regulations dealing with making safe were amended, after the Government Mining Engineer had secured agreement between the Chamber and the Union. (49) However as time went by, this change did not have the intended effect of increasing the work performed by Africans. (50) This provoked renewed efforts by the mining companies and the government to amend one Regulation still further. The Secretary of Mines informed the Mine Workers' Union that, because of the falling premium price, it was now proposed to amend Regulation 106(7)(a) in such a way as to diminish the extent of participation by white workers in making safe, by replacing provisions prescribing the 'personal and direct supervision' of the white miner with a looser formulation, such as 'control'. (51) The Mine Workers' Union expressed strong opposition to this proposal, fearing retrenchment and work extension. (52) Then the Prime Minister, General Smuts, convened a special conference on this issue. The gist of the discussions was that the white workers wanted to make safe with experienced African workers under their personal supervision; the Chamber wanted African workers to be able to do this alone; the white workers feared that such a system would mean displacement and work extension. The conference produced an agreement to replace the old Regulation 106(7)(a) with a new one, which provided for a system of night examinations. This the white workers agreed to because it left responsibility for deciding whether to be personally present in any place up to the white worker. (53)

But by now, the end of 1921, the amendment of a few Regulations held out no solution to the intensifying profitability crisis of the mining companies. The proposed amendment, the President of the Chamber stated, 'does not go nearly far enough, and it does not carry with it the germ of the solution for the present grave situation', and he wanted it to be clearly understood that 'we feel that other issues will be involved and are involved in the present situation, apart from the Regulations altogether'. (54) These other issues, the Chamber now stated for the first time, were the Status Quo Agreement, and the wages of the highest paid workers, and the mining companies were going to find it necessary to 'be at liberty to allocate and distribute and use their labour in whatever direction it is thought fit, without the operation of any trade union restrictions'. (55) After the agreement to amend the Regulation, the President repeated his warning that: 'While this Regulation will be helpful, and we shall do our best with it, there are other things we have to face. It is no use running away from them. We have to face them.' (56)

The time had come 'to face them', the Chamber decided, by the end of 1921. In the last three months of the year, while working costs remained at a record high level, the premium price fell by 7s. 5d. per ounce. In November, 7 mines were operating at a loss or a profit of less than 1s. per ton; by December, the number of mines in this position had doubled, to 15. The Chamber calculated that when the price of gold reached its normal level, about two-thirds of the producing mines would be unpayable at the prevailing levels of costs and output. (57)

The negotiations of 1921 had failed to bring about or to augur any significant and rapid improvement in profitability. With the premium falling steadily and costs higher than ever before, the Chamber of Mines decided that the time had arrived to implement the radical changes which it considered necessary to overcome the crisis. On 8 December, the Chamber moved into a new stage of confrontation with the white workers. The negotiations over the Regulations, it now told the white workers, had come nowhere near solving the crisis. The Chamber now proposed a three-fold solution, comprising a reduction of the wages of the highest paid miners, the abolition of the Status Quo Agreement, and a reorganisation of underground work. The job colour bar should be restricted to skilled work, it stated, and it was necessary 'that the mines should make greater use of native labour in semi-skilled occupations'. The Chamber disclaimed any intention of wanting to employ African workers in skilled work; it only wanted to employ them in semi-skilled work. These proposals, the Chamber concluded, would mean the retrenchment of about 2,000 of the less skilled white workers. This was the only way to reduce costs to a level 'which will show a reasonable return on capital even when gold has dropped to its normal price'. (58)

This was followed by a conference between the Chamber and the unions. The Chamber pointed to the worsening condition of the mining companies and to the necessity of being able to operate profitably at the normal price of gold, and they repeated their three demands - to reduce some wages, to reorganise labour in such a way as to eliminate the system of 'one man, one job', and to eliminate the job colour bar in semi-skilled work provided by the Status Quo Agreement. (59) The white workers refused to open negotiations until the Chamber gave full details of its reorganisation plans - they were unwilling to give the Chamber a 'blank cheque' for labour reorganisation, and while they were concerned about the position of the 'low grade mines', they were not about to accept the Chamber's 'taking advantage of temporary circumstances to bring about some permanent revolutionary changes in the industry' (to which the President of the Chamber replied that: 'I think it requires to be realised that when we talk of the low grade mines that with few exceptions this is a low grade industry'). (60) The Chamber then listed various semi-skilled jobs in which it wished to substitute African for white workers (such as drill-sharpening, waste-packing, winch and haulage driving, and timbering). The Chamber repeated that it had no desire to displace skilled whites, but merely wanted to get rid of less skilled white workers, who, it alleged, 'having failed in other occupations, now seek to shelter behind the Status Quo Agreement and certain of the Mining Regulations, to the detriment of the mines and all concerned therewith'. (61) Then a few days later, on 28 December, the Chamber gave formal notice to the Industrial Federation of its intention to implement its proposals as of 1 February 1922, because of the urgency of the profitability crisis. (62)

In response to this notice, the Industrial Federation decided to hold a strike ballot, to be taken on 8 January 1922. (63) This ballot resulted overwhelmingly in favour of strike action, and the Federation informed the Chamber that a strike would be declared unless the Chamber withdrew its notice. (64) At a conference on 9 January, the white workers again rejected the general scope of the Chamber's proposals and its ultimatum approach, while the Chamber refused to withdraw its notice. (65) On 10 January, the white workers in the gold mines, the power stations and the engineering shops came out on strike (joining white coal miners, who had already struck some days before, in opposition to proposed wage cuts). The companies notified them that they would be dismissed if not back at work by 16 January.

The striking workers were led by the Augmented Executive. At the end of December, the Federation (which had been negotiating for the workers) decided to augment its executive by including representatives of all the unions involved in the dispute, and this enlarged executive became known as the Augmented Executive. (66) At the grass-roots level, leadership was provided by the shop and shaft stewards committees, which had been formed during the war. At the same time, a new type of organisation arose alongside that of the unions - that of the commandos. These commandos were semi-military formations of between 50 and 500 men, which came into being towards the end of January in all sectors of the Rand. These were innovations of the Afrikaner workers, who transposed the traditional fighting formation of the Afrikaner farmers to a new setting, that of urban, industrial class conflict. The commandos were led by 'generals', who were for the most part elected from the ranks of the mine workers. At first the commandos were used to discourage 'scab' labour and for routine duties; later they provided the armed force of the workers when warfare broke out on the Rand.

Once the strike had begun, the government arranged a conference between the companies and the workers under Justice Curlewis. This conference, which continued for two weeks, proved inconclusive. The same arguments came forth from both sides, and neither side was prepared to make concessions acceptable to the other. While both were prepared to discuss certain questions, the mining companies refused to retract their demands and the white workers refused to discuss the question of the abolition of the Status Quo Agreement. (67) A union leader expressed the sentiments of both sides at the end of the conference when he declared: 'What is the use, we have met here for 12 days, and on any dispute we have dealt with, we are in exactly the same position as when we started - not the slightest improvement in the position of any dispute under consideration.' (68)

After the failure of the Curlewis conference to reach agreement, the Chamber of Mines, stating that 'a patched-up compromise of the present dispute offers no solution of the problem', extended its terms of settlement. Concerning the job colour bar, the Chamber's position now was that it was to be free to make any rearrangements of labour that it thought necessary (subject to a ratio of 1 to 10.5 whites to Africans for the first two years), as a result of which a number of white workers would be retrenched and not re-employed, and 'Underground men re-engaged (other than mechanics and engine drivers) will be taken on for general mining work and will be required to do whatever mining work is required of them by the management.' And the Chamber extended its wage demands: the cost of living allowances on white wages were to be completely withdrawn by the end of June, and all standard wage rates were to return to their pre-war level. And two paid holidays - May Day and Dingaan's Day - were to be abolished. (69)

Early in February, the Prime Minister, General Smuts, made an attempt to reach a settlement. He suggested that the white workers return to work immediately on the best terms they could get, pending an impartial inquiry into the dispute, the recommendations of which could form the basis of a more permanent settlement. As a result of this initiative, the Chamber met with the Prime Minister, and agreed to make a concession - that the Status Quo Agreement would only be abolished in the least profitable mines, whilst its termination in other mines would be suspended until the issue had been considered by Parliament and the proposed Commission of Inquiry. The Prime Minister then met with the Federation, which, after some negotiations, finally agreed to recommend a return to work on pre-strike conditions, pending the report of the Commission, and on the condition of the continuation of the Status Quo Agreement or of some equally effective alternative form of protection. But this did not meet with the Chamber's agreement. (70)

These new negotiations thus failed to secure agreement, and on 11 February Smuts publicly urged the workers to return to work, as 'the continuance of this unhappy state of affairs cannot be tolerated any longer'. He urged the workers to accept the Chamber's latest terms, and he announced that the government 'will use all its powers to protect those who listen to this appeal, and the police have instructions . . . to give protection to all miners who return to their former employment'. And he called on the companies to resume operations as soon as possible. (71) Thenceforward, the policy of General Smuts was to 'let things develop'. 'We shall draw a ring', he told Parliament, 'We shall preserve law and order and shall allow the disputants to fight it out within the ring.' (72) He did not think the government should appoint a Commission of Inquiry: 'we should let things develop.' (73)

The mining companies then attempted to restart operations where possible. In the next two weeks, a small number of white workers - about 5 per cent of the white labour force - trickled back to work. (74) During this time, the Augmented Executive came to consider renewing negotiations, and on 4 March it made a conciliatory move to the Chamber, offering to hold new talks with it at the earliest possible time, 'for the purpose of discussing possible terms upon which the strike might be declared off'. (75)

It was the Chamber's reply to this offer which was to end any further possibility of a negotiated settlement and to usher in a new stage of conflict. The Chamber replied that 'such a conference would obviously be futile, nor in the opinion of the Chamber is there anything to be gained by further discussions with the Federation'. The representatives of the workers, it claimed, 'were either incompetent or unwilling to grasp even the elementary fact that the industry was in a very critical position', and the

Chamber 'will not waste further time in attempting to convince persons of that mental calibre'. The Chamber did not want 'to hold debating society meetings'. It was restarting operations, and the Federation merely wanted to obstruct this by getting 'their orators to expend a few million more words'. The Chamber restated its conditions of settlement, which, it warned, would not stand open interminably, and, for good measure, it concluded by attacking the Federation on the grounds that 'The members of the Chamber are occupied with the winning of coal or gold, and they see no reason why they should discuss that business with representatives of slaughtermen and tramwaymen.' (76) The gist of the letter, apart from its insulting tone, was that the Chamber was no longer willing to deal with the Federation.

The arrogant and uncompromising tone of this letter provoked widespread anger and indignation among the workers. Some even considered that it was a deliberate attempt to provoke violent confrontation and the repression of the strike by the forces of the State. (77) Whatever may have been the intentions behind it, it was certainly to contribute to such an effect. Its immediate effect was to pass the leadership of the strike into more militant hands.

The bad reception of the Chamber's letter led the Chamber to make a public statement attempting to justify its contents and to offset the adverse publicity. The restarting of the mines, it claimed, meant, in effect, the repudiation of the Federation as the representative of the mine workers. 'What more in effect did the Chamber's letter say than this?' it asked.

> The Chamber . . . in its letter, leaving on one side the question of particular phrases, on the advisability of which a difference of opinion may exist, said nothing but what was in its view - and presumably in that of the government - the right policy.

The Chamber was prepared to listen to what trade union leaders had to say, 'but unfortunately, the terms on which the mines can be placed in a position to continue to give employment are governed by economic and not by debateable considerations'. (78)

The Chamber's reply forced the Augmented Executive to make a new move, and the decision which it took was to call a ballot of the striking workers on whether to continue the strike, a decision which was seen by many to mean that the Executive 'had decided to throw in its hand'. (79) This led the more militant leaders, formed around a Council of Action, to form a Committee of Action to assume responsibility for the strike and to press for the continuation and escalation of strike action. At a mass meeting on 5 March, the workers overwhelmingly rejected the Federation's proposal. Faced with this repudiation of its policy, and subject to considerable pressure from the rank and file, the commandos and the Committee of Action (who all surrounded the building in which the Executive was meeting, and held an all day meeting), the Federation reluctantly decided to call a general strike, and ceded leadership of the strike to the Committee and the commandos.

The call for a general strike met with little response outside the Rand and even on the Rand - with important groups of workers like the railway and printing workers not joining the strike. This attitude of other workers had been in evidence for some time, and it is right to observe that 'the call for a general strike was more of a gesture than a serious attempt to retrieve a desperate situation'. (80) The leadership of the strike was now split, with the commandos resisting attempts by the Committee to centralise leadership. And at this time - on 7 March - occurred a series of assaults on Africans. This had the important political effect of arousing fears among the white public at large of an African uprising (though, because of their timing - all within 24 hours - and their apparent co-ordination, they were considered by many to be the work of agents provocateurs). This, together with intensifying rumours about a 'bolshevik plot' which accompanied the assumption of power by the militants, had the effect of dampening support for the strikers in the surrounding countryside - which had been sustaining the strikers with food and which the strikers hoped would send in commandos in the event of armed conflict.

After the declaration of a general strike, the government and the striking workers intensified their preparations for armed conflict, which erupted on 10 March, when the workers went on the offensive and the government proclaimed martial law. The government surrounded the Rand with about 7,000 armed forces, supported by bomber planes, artillery, machine guns, armoured trains and cars, and tanks. The warfare passed through two stages. Between 10 and 12 March, the workers' commandos attacked surrounding police and military forces on the Rand, securing control over much of the Rand. During the next few days, the forces of the government attacked and overwhelmed the workers. Fighting raged along the Rand, with the government bombing the positions of the workers by plane and making effective use of artillery. By the end of 14 March, the government had put down the uprising and secured control of the Rand. Accurate figures of casualties were difficult to arrive at, because some workers were buried or treated secretly. But probably between about 150 and 220 were killed, and between about 500 and 600 wounded. (81) About 5,000 people were arrested, about 1,000 of whom appeared in court. Eighteen were sentenced to death and 4 were hanged.

The strike was officially terminated on 16 March, and the white workers returned to work unconditionally, on the Chamber's extended terms of settlement - freedom for the mining companies to reorganise labour as they saw fit, and a comprehensive reduction of wages and benefits. 'Agreements made with the workmen's unions prior to the strike', the Chamber stated, referring to the Status Quo Agreement, 'were declared to have lapsed.' (82)

It is not one of the purposes of this study to give a detailed account of the strike and uprising of 1922. (83) Its concern with these events is essentially with their causes, effects and general significance - with elucidating the way in which they were generated and determined by a specific structure and historical situation of class relations, expressed specific contradictions within this structure and situation and determined further developments within them, and illustrated the class nature and dynamics of the system of racial discrimination. In pursuit of these concerns, we have observed the specific configuration of structural and historical conditions which may be said to have produced and to explain these events; and we shall go on to examine the changes and conditions which followed from them. The events themselves must be seen as the most dramatic (though merely one of many) manifestations of a struggle between the mining companies and the white workers over the determination of the precise mode of operation of the system of racial discrimination according to their specific, different and in certain ways contradictory class interests and class problems - a struggle, that is, over the relative scope of operation of their respective class colour bars. The continuing course and outcome of this struggle is what we have now to go on to observe.

3 The reorganisation of labour and the displacement of white workers

It was noted earlier that the only course open to the mining companies to overcome the profitability crisis was that of making more profitable use of labour, which meant reducing the cost of white labour and increasing the productivity of all labour. This course was obstructed by the job colour bar of the white workers, and its realisation thus necessitated an attack upon the position of the white workers. This attack provoked the strike and violent confrontation of 1922, a confrontation from which the mining companies emerged victorious. This victory enabled the companies to set about implementing the two imperatives of minimising white labour costs and maximising labour productivity. These were partly secured through a cut in the wages of white workers; but they were mainly realised through a comprehensive reorganisation of labour and reduction of the scope of the job colour bar.

After the strike, the companies reduced the wages of all white workers. They had originally been concerned only to reduce the wages of the highest paid miners; but with the continuation of the strike, they raised their demands to include a cut in the wages of all white workers and the abolition of some paid holidays. The wages of the white workers were reduced by varying degrees, ranging between about 25 per cent and 50 per cent, as Table 7 indicates.

TABLE 7 Wages (per shift) of white workers, Witwatersrand gold mines, June 1921 and May 1922*

	1921 s. d.	1922 s. d.
Amalgamators	27 9	21 6
Banksmen	24 8	17 5
Engine drivers, winding (electric)	31 5	24 3
Engine drivers, winding (other)	31 11	24 2
Engine drivers, winches (electric)	24 4	17 3
Fitters	29 0	22 11
Miners: machine stoping		
Contract	49 10	28 8
Day's pay	33 5	23 6
Miners: hand stoping		
Contract	41 8	28 8
Day's pay	28 9	22 3
Miners: machine developing		
Contract	61 7	36 10
Day's pay	31 5	22 3
Miners: hand developing		
Contract	41 11	26 11
Day's pay	38 10	22 0
Miners: shaft sinking		
Contract	68 1	52 10
Day's pay	46 0	26 5
Pipemen	28 8	26 1

138 Chapter 3

	1921 s. d.	1922 s. d.
Platelayers	28 8	26 1
Pumpmen	29 0	22 10
Skipmen and onsetters	25 9	18 4
Timbermen (shaft)	32 2	23 11
Trammers	25 10	18 8

*'South African Mining and Engineering Journal', 7 October 1922, p.73.

And the two additional paid holidays secured by the white workers during the war - May Day and Dingaan's Day - were abolished.

But the most important change implemented by the mining companies after the 1922 strike was a radical reorganisation of labour in the mines, designed to reduce white labour costs and to raise labour productivity. This involved the substitution of ultra-cheap African workers for white workers in certain jobs and the retrenchment of other white workers without replacement, the extension of the work and responsibility of the remaining workers, and technological innovation.

The goals of the employers were thus secured in various ways. They were partly achieved through the direct substitution of African workers for white workers in semi-skilled work - a process which had already been developing during the war, but which was greatly accelerated after the 1922 strike. This may be seen in Table 8, a comparison of the racial distribution of labour in the main semi-skilled occupations in 1921 and 1924. It was in this sphere of semi-skilled work that most of the labour substitution occurred. (84)

After 1922 the various mining unions all complained about this same problem - the displacement of white workers from semi-skilled work. The Engine Drivers' Association expressed concern about the fact that, between 1921 and 1924, the number of white hauling drivers underground fell from 781 to 703, while the number of African hauling drivers underground rose from 170 to 461. (85) The Reduction Workers' Association complained that between 1921 and 1924 the number of white workers employed in reduction works had been cut from 1,825 to 1,454, while the number of Africans employed in them had risen from 7,971 to 9,722, with most of the displacement taking place in various semi-skilled jobs. (86) The Boilermakers' Society complained that African workers were being put on to work

TABLE 8 Labour substitution and the displacement of white workers in semi-skilled work after 1922*

	1921 (Dec.) White	1921 (Dec.) African	1924 (Sept.) White	1924 (Sept.) African
Drill-sharpening	397	1,583	297	2,526
Winch driving	99	382	32	547
Locomotive driving	90	361	67	523
Timbering	1,253	12,346	864	14,439
Waste-packing	312	3,276	67	4,791
Pipe-fitting and plate-laying	695	5,210	461	6,346

*Tvl Ch. of Mines, Statement showing numbers of workers employed in connection with certain occupations in the mines, 1921 and 1924 (Annexure A of Statement of the Tvl Ch. of Mines to the Mining Regulations Commission); SAEDFA Archs.

hitherto done by white workers, such as truck repair work, at the expense of white workers. (87) The Society of Woodworkers expressed the same grievance: African workers were now being employed in such work as repair and maintenance work in the compounds, previously done by white workers at much higher rates. (88) And so it went on. In virtually all areas of semi-skilled work, white workers were being replaced by workers from the forced labour sector.

The minimisation of white labour costs and the maximisation of labour productivity were also partly secured through the extension of the work and responsibility of the remaining white workers, which accelerated the displacement of certain white workers and the occupational mobility of African workers.

Underground, this involved the extension of the responsibility both of the white miner and of the remaining white workers engaged in such supporting work as wastepacking, timbering, pipe-fitting, track-laying and stonewalling. Up until 1922, the white miner was responsible only for rock breaking, and for one gang of African workers. After 1922, he was made responsible for the supporting work in his stope as well, and for a larger gang of African workers. As the Mining Regulations Commission reported: 'Here the process has consisted in combining under a single European supervisor two or three gangs of natives, up to such time under separate control. The single European supervisor has had his sphere of responsibility doubled or trebled.' (89) According to one miner, as a result of the post-strike labour reorganisation, 'one man is doing the work that three men did before the strike', and 'everything today is sacrificed for the sake of lower costs'. (90) Another miner reported that after the reorganisation, he had been made responsible for tramming, timbering, developing, machine stoping, hand stoping, pipe-fitting and track-laying, that he had been the only miner on one level of the mine, and had been placed in charge of between 80 to 90 African workers. This work extension made it impossible to adhere to the Mining Regulations. 'What I should like to point out to the Commission', he declared, 'is that I personally have broken the Mining Regulations every hour in the day.' (91) Another miner expressed the same view - which was expressed by all miners giving evidence to this Commission:

You state that the Regulations are contravened daily by the men having too many places or too many natives to supervise. Now does the management know that these Regulations are being contravened in the way you say? - Certainly they do. They can see for themselves, and the miners also mention it very often to them, pointing out, as I have done, that they have too many places to look after. . . .
Is it your suggestion that the policy prevailing today is this - they tell you that you must not break the Regulations, but at the same time they know you can only get through your work by breaking them? - Yes.
And if you say it is impossible for you to do this work, they get rid of you? - That is so. (92)

The effect of this extension of the miner's responsibility was to accelerate the already noted displacement of white workers in supporting work, and to displace a number of white miners - which was reflected in the fact that between 1921 and 1924 the total number of white miners fell from 3,355 to 3,165. (93) Its other main effect was that of extending the responsibility of the more skilled African workers, on whom the miner had increasingly to rely for the supervision and performance of much of the supporting work peripheral to rock breaking. As an official of the Mine Workers' Union explained:

We have constant complaints from the men themselves that they have far too much work to do to allow them to comply with the Regulations. Take for instance a man who is running eight or nine developing ends. I have asked these members to tell me how it is they get through, and they say they cannot. What do they do?

There is only one thing for them to do, and that is to
leave it to the boss-boy. That is how the gradual
elimination of the white man is going on along this
Reef in favour of the coloured worker. (94)
The responsibility of the other white workers underground
was also increased. As was noted, it was in the sphere of
semi-skilled supporting work that most of the substitution
of African workers for white workers took place. At the
same time, the responsibility of the remaining white workers
was considerably extended. Thus the tendency was to
reduce the number of white timbermen from several per
level of a mine to one per two or three levels, to reduce
the number of white pipe-fitters from about one per level
to about one per four levels, to reduce the number of
white trammers from two per level to one per several
levels, and so on. (95) As a miner observed:

There were underground timbermen in 1914; a stope
timberman was employed, building pigstyes, he was a
white employee. A man would go around the stopes and
packs. It is not so now. One white man will probably
run two or three levels building pigstyes with natives.
. . .
The coloured man is gradually encroaching on that
particular sphere of work? - Yes, he is taking it all,
slowly, it is true, but still he is taking it. (96)

These changes underground were also reflected in the growing
importance of the occupational category of 'general
miner'. By 1924, about 75 per cent of the white workers
underground were signed on as 'general miners'. (97) This
was symptomatic of the curtailment of the system of 'one
man, one job' secured by the companies through the labour
reorganisation.

A similar process of work extension was implemented on
the surface, in the reduction works. The Reduction
Workers' Association reported 'that work has increased and
responsibility has increased out of all proportion to the
number of men engaged'. (98) Between 1921 and 1924, while
the tonnage of ore milled by the reduction works rose by
14.5 per cent, the number of whites employed in them was
reduced by about 15 per cent, and the responsibility of
the remaining white workers was extended, to include more
work processes and a larger number of African workers.
(99)

The profit maximisation sought by the mining companies
was thus partly realised through work extension. The
'South African Mining and Engineering Journal', which reflected
the views of the employers, noted that the drop in
the number of white workers after 1922 was due not only to
substitution, but also to 'the elimination of redundant

men and the placing legitimately of more work on the remaining men'. (100) The Mining Regulations Commission reported a marked increase after 1922 in the practice 'of extending the sphere of the European miner's responsibility beyond what we conceive to be its justifiable limits'. (101) It observed that:

> This tendency to enlarge the European miner's sphere of responsibility is the result of a variety of forces, of which the obligation constantly cast upon managers to secure a maximum of output at a minimum of working costs is the most compelling. Combining with another, viz: the marked advance during recent years in the efficiency of the native boss-boy, it has been instrumental in so far extending the European miner's responsibility as virtually to reduce his control over the work of his natives in many cases to a mere shadow, they looking upon the boss-boy rather than upon him as their real supervisor. (102)

The extension of the white worker's responsibility was thus leading to 'an increasing employment of native labour in spheres formerly occupied exclusively by European workers'. (103)

The minimisation of white labour costs and the maximisation of labour productivity were also both secured through technological innovation. Given the industry's particular cost structure, the mining companies had always placed great importance on the development and application of labour-saving technology. It is true that:

> The problem of costs would, naturally, have been even more intractable, and the future of gold mining in South Africa even more speculative, if it had not been for the continuous improvement in mining technique, improvements which were of course in part the direct result of the pressure of rising costs on profitability. (104)

One of the most important technological innovations had been the new MacArthur-Forrest cyanide process of ore reduction, first introduced in the 1890s. After 1922, the mining companies were able to take full advantage of three other technological developments - the jack-hammer drill, the drill-sharpening machine, and the corduroy process of gold extraction.

The most important technological development of this period was the jack-hammer drill, which revolutionised rock breaking in stoping work. The jack-hammer could drill between 20 and 40 holes per shift, compared with the 4 to 6 holes per shift of the old Holman drill. (105) The jack-hammer was a special type of machine drill, first introduced experimentally in 1916, because of a shortage of

African labour. But, as the Chamber of Mines observed: 'Small improvements were obtained from time to time, but the restrictions of the Status Quo understanding and the rooted prejudice of the miners to any alteration in methods of operating machines effectively blocked progress until after the 1922 upheaval.' (106) The victory of the mining companies in this upheaval enabled them to introduce the jack-hammer on a large scale. By 1923, the improved version of the jack-hammer (wet, hollow steel, improved bits), together with the labour reorganisation, had achieved 'amazing results', according to the President of the Chamber, with the 'astonishing result of drilling 63 feet per shift' compared with the 16 feet per shift drilled by an older type of machine drill in the labour conditions of 1920. (107) By 1925, rock drilling efficiency was 120 per cent greater than in 1921. (108) This widespread introduction of the jack-hammer enabled the companies to dispense with a number of white miners: between 1921 and 1924, the number of white miners employed in hand stoping fell from 930 to 547. (109)

The introduction of a drill-sharpening machine, and of the corduroy process, displaced white workers through the dilution and elimination of their jobs. Drill-sharpening had been a fairly skilled job, done by hand by white workers, assisted by African workers. A new machine, the dolly hammer machine, was developed to sharpen drills. It greatly simplified the work of drill-sharpening, turning it into a semi-skilled machine job that could easily be performed by the more experienced African workers after a very short period of training. (110) The machine was first introduced on one mine just before the war, and was brought into operation on a large scale after 1922. Between 1921 and 1924, the number of whites employed in drill-sharpening was reduced by 25 per cent, while the number of Africans employed in this work rose by 50 per cent. (111) Likewise in the reduction works, after 1922 the mining companies began to replace the old system of stamp milling and plate amalgamation with a new system of reduction and gold extraction - the corduroy blanket process. The Reduction Workers' Association claimed that: 'The introduction of corduroy blankets in place of plate amalgamation has offered the controllers of the gold mining industry another opportunity to eliminate white men and to substitute a far greater amount of natives for the eliminated whites.' (112) The introduction of the corduroy process led to the retrenchment of about 10 per cent of the white workers employed in reduction works before the 1922 strike, and 'generally speaking, whenever these white men are eliminated, natives are introduced', and the responsibilities of the remaining white workers were extended. (113)

The changes implemented by the mining companies resulted in the displacement of a large number of white workers. By August 1922, the number of whites employed in the gold mines had been reduced by about 4,400 - 20 per cent of the pre-strike figure. (114) How much more permanent displacement took place, however, it is impossible to state precisely, since some of these retrenched workers were later re-employed by the mines and others found employment elsewhere, and since the displacement involved not only the retrenchment of workers but also the destruction, through the labour reorganisation, of many jobs previously held by whites. The number of white workers (excluding salaried staff) employed in the gold mines in 1924, according to the Chamber's calculations, was about 1,700 fewer than in 1921. (115) The government estimated that in 1924 there were about 1,500 white mine workers unemployed on the Rand who had been employed before the strike. (116) A fair estimate of the total displacement might be that the reorganisation of labour after the strike resulted in the permanent displacement of about 2,000 white workers from the mines, together with the elimination of a large number - probably between 1,000 and 2,000 - of jobs previously held by whites. And the ratio of white to non-white workers in the gold mines increased after 1922 from the average of about 1 to 8 of the previous decade to about 1 to 10. (117)

It was by means of this comprehensive reorganisation of labour in the mines that the mining companies achieved their goal - the more profitable utilisation of labour through the reduction of white labour costs and the maximisation of labour productivity - and successfully overcame the profitability crisis. Table 9 compares the operating figures of the gold mines for 1921 and 1924. The changes implemented by the mining companies after the defeat of the white workers in 1922 thus achieved the desired effect of substantially reducing working costs and raising output and profits. The positive effect of these changes on the position of the mining companies was 'enormous', the Chamber of Mines stated, increasing the payable tonnage of those mines producing at the end of 1921 by 60 per cent. (118) The changes saved 24 companies from the insolvency which pre-strike conditions were pushing them into, which showed, the President of the Chamber declared, 'how absolutely essential it was to reduce working costs from the high figure which they had attained in 1921'. (119)

TABLE 9 Operating figures, Witwatersrand gold mines, before and after 1922*

	1921	1923	1924
Tons milled (millions)	23.4	26.5	28.2
Working costs per ton milled	25s. 8d.	20s. 0d.	19s. 7d.
Number of whites employed	18,949	17,761	16,429
Total salaries and wages (£ millions)	16.6	13.2	13.7
Salaries and wages to whites (£ millions)	10.6	6.8	7.3
Dividends declared (£ millions)	7.2	8.4	9.5

*Compiled from the annual operating figures for the Witwatersrand gold mines, 'ARTCMs 1921, 1923, 1924'.

The mining companies thus successfully overcame the profitability crisis through this labour reorganisation, which they were able to implement after their victory in the confrontation with the white workers. But the matter was not to rest there. The economic benefits which the companies secured through the way in which they resolved the crisis were to be politically costly. The white workers had lost a battle in 1922, but they had not lost the war.

4 The legal invalidation of the job colour bar: the Hildick-Smith judgment

The reorganisation of labour in the mines after the 1922 strike, which included the abolition of the Status Quo Agreement, was accompanied, in 1923, by a test case in the courts concerning the legality of the job colour bar in the Mining Regulations, which resulted in a Supreme Court judgment that the job colour bar in the Regulations was illegal.

In August 1923, a Manager of the Crown Mines, Mr Hildick-Smith, was charged before a Magistrate's Court, in an action brought by the government, for contravening the job colour bar in the Mining Regulations by permitting an African worker to drive an electric locomotive underground - work which was restricted to white workers by Regulation

179. (120) The locomotive driven by this African worker had recently run over and killed another African worker. (121) The Magistrate, who remarked at the beginning of the case that: 'I quite understand that this case will not be settled here', acquitted Hildick-Smith on the grounds that the Regulation in question was ultra vires the enabling Act, because the Regulation was racially discriminatory and Section 4 of the Mines and Works Act (the section which empowered the government to make Regulations) did not sanction racially discriminatory Regulations. (122) 'The right to discriminate between whites and coloured persons', it was stated in a supporting opinion, 'is nowhere explicitly conferred, and is not to be necessarily inferred from any of the Subsections of Section 4.' (123) The implication of the Magistrate's judgment was that all of the discriminatory Regulations forming the job colour bar in the Regulations were illegal.

The Attorney-General appealed for the government to the Supreme Court for a ruling on the Magistrate's judgment. The Supreme Court ruled in favour of the Magistrate's verdict. The Supreme Court judges agreed that the enabling Act - the Mines and Works Act of 1911 - did not authorise racial discrimination. It permitted discrimination on such grounds as age and skill, Judge Krause observed,

> But, here, Regulation 179 does not discriminate between persons so employed and entitled to be so employed because of their skill or want of skill or other personal disqualifications; it absolutely prohibits a large section of the population from being so employed at all, because the colour of their skin does not happen to be white. (124)

When the legislature had intended such discrimination, it had conferred the right to make it in the enabling Act. (125) But this had not been the case with the Mines and Works Act, and the racial discrimination in the Regulations was thus 'prima facie repugnant to the general law of the land . . . because it says that something is unlawful which the law does not say is unlawful'. (126) It was an established principle of South African law, Judge Tindall agreed, that a Regulation discriminating on a racial basis was unreasonable and ultra vires if it was not authorised by the enabling Act, and

> I have come to the conclusion that Regulation 179 discriminates between white and coloured . . . that Act No. 12 of 1911 confers no power on the Governor-General to make this discrimination and therefore that the Regulation is ultra vires. I think the matter is not open to doubt. (127)

Again, the implication was that the job colour bar in all of the discriminatory Regulations was illegal, for being ultra vires the Mines and Works Act.

The questions arise as to why this case took place and why at the time which it did, as to who was behind it, and as to what it signified. Although the employers would seem logically to have been the likely initiators of such a move against the job colour bar, in fact this was not the case. The action was initiated by the government through the Department of Mines, because, it appears, of the growing contravention of the Mining Regulations after the labour reorganisation of 1922 and because of the dubious legal status of the discriminatory Regulations, which the Department was responsible for enforcing.

The administration and enforcement of the Mining Regulations was one of the responsibilities of the Department of Mines and Industries. The labour reorganisation of 1922 involved, we noted, a reduction of the job colour bar and an extension of the work and responsibility of workers, which led to an increasing contravention of the Regulations. The Department became increasingly concerned about this, and about the legal status of the discriminatory Regulations, which was very much in question. The Department doubted their legality, the Government Mining Engineer declared, and it was generally accepted that they were ultra vires. (128) Officials affirmed that 'it has been common knowledge for years past that they were ultra vires'. (129) But the Department had to operate on the principle that they were intra vires - that they were legal. (130)

It was the increasing contravention of these Regulations following the 1922 labour reorganisation which drove the Department to take action. The Department knew that colour bar Regulations were being contravened, an Inspector of Mines explained, 'and there was some doubt in regard to this colour bar question, so we decided to go to court'. (131) The Government Mining Engineer decided to bring a test case to clarify the legal status of these Regulations, when a suitable occasion presented itself. As an Inspector of Mines explained to the Mining Regulations Commission:

The Crown Mines prosecution, how did it originate? - It was pushed by our Department. We knew it was being done on the Crown Mines, and in my district they were using native drivers on the Van Ryn Deep, and we had doubts as to whether they were right or wrong. We discussed it at several Inspectors' meetings, and Sir Robert [the Government Mining Engineer] said: 'We will bring a test case: the first district that has a

really clear case will take action'. . . . The Crown
Mines was the first clear case. (132)

After the 1922 strike, the Crown Mines substituted African
drivers for white drivers on the main locomotive haulage
engines underground.

That was a palpable and obvious thing, and after a
short time there was an accident in these haulages and
the question came up. We did not prosecute at first in
regard to that owing to the doubt as to whether the
Regulation was ultra vires or not, and it went on for
about eighteen months. (133)

Eventually the Inspector for this District suggested that
the Department should press for a legal ruling, and it was
decided to take action.

It seems to be rather a mystery as to who took the initiative in bringing this case forward? - . . . I discussed it with the Government Mining Engineer and he
suggested that we prosecute the Manager . . . my own
feeling was that it was a very unsatisfactory position
for this work to be going on in that rather indefinite
way. (134)

This move was made on their own initiative, the Inspector
stated; they had not been approached about this matter by
the employers or by the white workers. (135)

What had actually been the case, however, was one
thing; what appeared to be the case, and what the judgment appeared to symbolise and foreshadow, were another.
The white workers felt that the Chamber of Mines was the
moving force behind this test case and that the employers
would take advantage of the judgment. The white workers
had enjoyed legal protection, one miner stated, 'until it
was decided otherwise in the courts of law by the Chamber
of Mines'. (136) A union leader echoed the views of many
white workers when he alleged that the Chamber was behind
the whole affair:

That is one of the methods of the Chamber of Mines.
They do not do anything. They allow other people to do
it for them. Anyone who took notice of the Crown Mines
case knows how it was managed and conducted. They did
not take any interest in it outwardly, but at the root
of the whole thing the Chamber of Mines was the moving
spirit. . . . They said: 'We are not taking any notice
of this', and the government had to get somebody to put
up a sham fight. (137)

And the white workers feared that the companies were
taking and would take advantage of the new situation to
increase the substitution of African workers for white
workers. 'It certainly had that effect in our opinion', a
union leader stated. (138) Since the judgment, the white

workers alleged, other mines had followed the example of the Crown Mines in replacing white locomotive drivers with African workers. (139)

There is no evidence that the Chamber of Mines actually initiated the case (though it was obviously 'behind the case' in the sense that it was its labour reorganisation which provoked the Department of Mines to take action). And in fact the mining companies did not set about taking advantage of the judgment. This might seem paradoxical. Here were the white workers in a weak position after their defeat in 1922. Here was the job colour bar in the Regulations declared to be illegal. Why did the mining companies not follow through their victory and seek to get rid of the job colour bar altogether?

The answer to this is that the companies were concerned not with abolishing the job colour bar but merely with reducing its scope. Ideally they might have preferred to have a labour force made up entirely of forced labour, and they did sometimes object, on an ideological level, to the job colour bar per se. But in reality they accepted the job colour bar, and had rational reasons for doing so, and their opposition to it during this period was merely concerned with curtailing its scope of operation. Given the economic and political power of the white workers as a whole, in the mines, on the Rand and in South Africa generally, it was clear that any attempt by the employers to abolish the job colour bar altogether would have provoked a far greater conflagration than that of 1922, and the potential costs and dangers of such a policy far outweighed its potential benefits; and the job colour bar did have the positive effect for the companies of reinforcing the division of the working class. The Chamber of Mines thus accepted that politically free and economically expensive labour - white labour - had something of a permanent place in the mines, and it was prepared to and did accommodate the job colour bar. What it was seriously concerned with was the precise size of the free labour sector and the precise scope of operation of the job colour bar. It wanted to reduce and eliminate the operation of the job colour bar in the sphere of semi-skilled work (to which it had been formally extended by the Status Quo Agreement), and to restrict its operation to the sphere of skilled work. It wanted to restrict the position of white workers in the industry to that of a small 'labour aristocracy' of skilled and supervisory workers, and to substitute African workers for white workers in semi-skilled work. And it was to this effect that the labour reorganisation following the 1922 strike reduced the job colour bar. This did involve, in addition to the abolition of the Status Quo Agreement, the contravention of certain Mining Regulations (as in the case of locomotive driving); but on the whole the discriminatory Regulations concerned skilled work, and while certain skilled white workers were displaced in 1922, on the grounds of redundancy and through work extension and technological innovation, substitution and most of the displacement took place in semi-skilled work.

While all this may have been the case, however, to the white workers the Hildick-Smith judgment seemed to symbolise and foreshadow an increasing threat to their security. The political significance of the case lay not in what the employers sought or planned to gain from it but in what it was seen to represent by the white workers. They had lost the protection of the Status Quo Agreement, abolished in 1922. Then they had undergone the labour reorganisation implemented after their defeat in 1922. Now the job colour bar in the Mining Regulations was ruled to be illegal. Their security thus appeared to be threatened on all sides, and the legal judgment seemed to be an ominous portent for the future. But this accumulation of attacks upon and threats to the white workers was to provoke the latter into a determined counter-attack against the employers.

3. THE COUNTER-ATTACK OF THE WHITE WORKERS

Defeat in the 1922 conflict, the ensuing labour reorganisation, the abolition of the Status Quo Agreement and the legal invalidation of the job colour bar in the Mining Regulations, thus all left the white mine workers more insecure than ever before, and fearful for their future security. They had been subdued by the armed forces of the State. They were now to seek to use the power of the State, to an unprecedented degree, to protect and strengthen their position, to reinforce the job colour bar and to check the power and policies of the employers. After the upheaval of 1922, the two opposition parties - the Labour Party and the Nationalist Party - formed a political alliance, which, with the support of the white workers, won the general election of 1924. The new government supported and implemented a protectionist policy for the white workers. In response to the situation in the gold mines and pressures from the white workers, it appointed a Commission of Inquiry into the contravention of the job colour bar and the position of the white workers in the industry, and it acted to legalise the job colour bar, with the 'Colour Bar Act' of 1926.

1 The Pact government

After their defeat on the industrial front in 1922, the white workers turned to more conventional forms of political action. Such an approach had already been countenanced during the strike, when, for instance, the Industrial Federation had issued a statement declaring that:
> The attitude of the Prime Minister indicates that the government is backing the present attack by the employers on the white workers. . . . We therefore request the workers and also all sympathisers to take the necessary steps in conjunction with ourselves to defeat the present government and substitute one calculated to protect the interests of the white race in South Africa. (1)

And in the new and embittered political climate which followed the conflagration of 1922, it was to be such a 'substitution' of government which was to snatch some degree of victory for the white workers from the jaws of defeat.

The white mine workers took certain initiatives of their own to secure protection and allies. Thus in 1923, the mining unions met together and 'It was decided to circulate all public bodies with a view to obtaining their sympathy in supporting our claims as white workers against the Chamber of Mines policy of placing natives in jobs that should be reserved for whites.' (2) They issued and circulated a manifesto on 'the trend of South Africa towards a black industrial basis'. The attack on the white workers, the manifesto stated, was increasing unemployment among whites, which 'is the price the white race pays for the "promise" of capitalism in South Africa', a promise which was not redeemable 'unless we pledge our future progress deeper to overseas pawnbrokers'. The white workers wanted to enlarge their sphere of employment, it declared, and to ally with other groups against the power and policies of the mining capitalists.
> We do not say that any honest work is degrading of the white race. We cannot see any future for a race of white supervisors; we want to make this land produce a civilised livelihood for every willing worker. We claim that the interests of farmers, commercial men and trade unions are identical in this matter. We want the cooperation of these sectors to carve a future for our race. (3)

These sectors did not benefit from the reduced purchasing power of the white workers. (4) The great obstacle to the better economic development of South Africa, the unions stated in a circular letter accompanying the manifesto, was the concentration of ownership of the bulk of land and mineral resources in a few hands, and what was needed was an alliance of the less well-off against these large property owners. 'The trade unions feel that the time has arrived', they stated, 'for some measure of cooperation between workers, farmers and the commercial community with a view to discovering some method of alleviating or remedying the position.' (5)

This particular initiative did not lead anywhere. (6) But more significant and successful moves in the same direction were taking place at other levels, as the two opposition parties, the Labour and the Nationalist Parties, made their way into a political alliance that was to have important consequences.

While the immediate spur to this alliance was the political climate following the events of 1922, the alliance reflected, and may fruitfully be explained by, the common socio-economic base of the two parties and the specific configuration of structural and historical conditions in South Africa at this time. While a close examination of this would take us beyond the scope of this study, a few general observations may be made in passing.

The dominant white group in South Africa did not form a single and undifferentiated class, but comprised different and internally differentiated classes. The principal class differentiation was between a class of owners of property in the means of production and a class of white workers separated from such ownership and having to sell their labour power to the former. And these classes were also internally differentiated - the principal differentiations being between large property owners and small property owners, and between skilled workers and unskilled 'poor whites'. What would appear to have been happening at this time was that certain long-term structural developments and conditions (the concentration of ownership of finance capital and of land in the hands of small groups of property owners, and the continuing commercialisation of farming) were combining with certain post-war economic developments (depression and tight-money policies, high unemployment among white workers, and the labour reorganisation in the mines) in such a way as to have the effect of intensifying the insecurity both of small property owners and of the white workers, and of producing a convergence of interests between them in opposition to large property owners. Both could benefit in various ways from control of the government and the State, and each needed the other to achieve such control.

These two groups came increasingly to be represented politically by two parties - the Labour Party and the

Nationalist Party. The political articulation of these groups was in part determined by the ethnic differentiation within the white group between English-speaking and Afrikaner-speaking whites. The Labour Party represented English-speaking white workers, and came increasingly to appeal to the less well-off generally within the English-speaking community. The Nationalist Party represented Afrikaner small property owners and Afrikaner workers. These ethnic differentiations corresponded, to some extent, with socio-economic differentiations, with the latter party being more of a rural party, essentially concerned with land ownership - actual and aspired to - whereas the Labour Party was rooted in the urban sector. The convergence of the problems and interests of small property owners and white workers, stemming from prevailing economic conditions and developments, was to generate a political coming-together of these two parties.

The explanation of the alliance which arose between the Nationalist and Labour Parties at this time (and of South Africa's political history generally) in terms of such a class analysis requires further systematic exploration and development, which cannot be gone into more fully here. However, it may be pointed out that this analysis finds confirmation in the correspondence between the two party leaders, Creswell and Hertzog, which initiated the formation of this alliance.

It is noteworthy that Creswell made his first approach to Hertzog before the 1922 strike - in October 1921, and that this was in a letter devoted essentially to a discussion of the socio-economic situation in South Africa and expressing opposition to the concentration of property ownership. There were only two large banks in South Africa (in addition to the Central Reserve Bank), Creswell complained, and what he found disturbing was

> the enormous real power that this union in a practically closed ring of the Financial Credit power and the Industrial power gives to those who enjoy it and who continually plan behind the scenes over the whole economic policy and development of the people.

The large capitalists were also the main employers of African labour, and would tend to use their power to inhibit the growth of new enterprises which might threaten their labour supply. The structure of economic and financial power in South Africa required examination, Creswell declared, and he wondered whether 'in contemplating the world position your own thoughts have led you to suspect that it is this concentration of Credit Power and Industrial Power which is the great danger to the development of society'. (7)

Hertzog replied in a positive vein, remarking that:
'The fear expressed by you that the big birds of prey may at any time swoop down and carry away the fruits of our labours, is a real one, and has engaged much of my attention.' The war had made the rich richer and the poor poorer,

> and the over-accumulation of money in the hands of a few has put them in such a favourable position of joint scheming and joint oppression, that I fear with you that lesser individual enterprises are more than ever at the mercy of the few.

The fiscal policies of the Smuts government, such as credit restriction and high interest rates, had increased the dependence of the 'lower industrial class' and the farmers on the 'moneyed corporations', at the expense of the general welfare of the people. Hertzog concluded:

> I cannot but feel that the policy of the government has led to a wholesale surrender to Capitalistic influences, or at any rate is leading thereto. The more the people is thrown into helplessness and the government into debt, the more will the moneyed few extend their influence and their enterprises, and the more will they become the real governing factor.

It was not that Hertzog was opposed to capitalism. 'I have no feeling of antagonism against Capital,' he declared. 'I heartily wish every citizen of the Union was a capitalist.' What he was opposed to was the inequitable distribution of capital and the excessive power of 'the moneyed few'. (8) More letters between the two leaders gave expression to the same sentiments.

The aftermath of the events of 1922 presented the two parties with a golden opportunity to reach for political power, with the Smuts government very unpopular and discredited and with the white workers aroused to an unprecedented sense of grievance. But since neither of the two parties, nor any one of the classes which they represented, possessed the electoral strength to gain control of the government and the State on its own, an alliance between them became mutually expedient. And after the 1922 upheaval the two parties moved towards such an alliance.

Members of the two parties had in fact held informal meetings during the strike, in February. (9) But the first official move came in July 1922, when Creswell met Hertzog 'to see whether any basis of cooperation was possible'. (10) The parties negotiated over the following months, and in April 1923 they formed a pact to fight the next general election in alliance together. Summarising the gist of the talks between the party leaders, Creswell wrote that:

Chapter 3

> We found ourselves broadly in agreement in our view that the present government acts as though dominated by the conviction that the interests of this country are best served by its taking what may be termed the 'BIG FINANCE' view of our various internal and economic problems ... and that the necessity to combat this trend of policy ... is largely the cause of the common opposition of our two Parties to the present government and the Party supporting it. (11)

An electoral alliance between the two parties was necessary, Creswell stated, to avoid splitting the opposition vote. But for such an alliance to be successful, it was necessary to dispel certain fears among voters - that the Nationalists were determined to secede from the Empire, and that the Labour Party 'is a Bolshevik group'. (12) The Labour Party thus watered down the 'socialist objective' in its programme in its annual conference in 1923, and the Nationalists promised not to change South Africa's constitutional status.

Opposition to the Smuts government had been growing before the 1922 strike. But the effect of the events of 1922 was greatly to intensify this opposition, the strength of which was revealed in a by-election in Wakkerstrom in April 1924, in which the South African Party lost a traditionally strong seat. As a result of this defeat, Smuts called a general election for June 1924. The Nationalist-Labour Pact won this election, the Nationalists gaining 63 seats and Labour 18, making a total of 81 against the 53 won by the South African Party. (13) After being in the hands of the South African Party for 14 years - since the formation of the Union of South Africa in 1910 - the power of the government and the State were now assumed by a Nationalist-Labour coalition. The two parties decided to extend their electoral pact into a governing alliance. A government was formed with General Hertzog as Prime Minister, and including two Labour Party leaders - Creswell and Boydell - as Ministers. Creswell became a newly created Minister of Labour. The government's general aim was to be one of economic and social reform, including attempts to solve the problem of white unemployment, the establishment of a Ministry of Labour, co-operation with the labour movement, the implementation of a segregationist 'native policy', the establishment of a State Bank, and various other measures. The government was 'to keep the workers' interests in all phases before the government'. The two parties were to sit and remain as separate parties, and care was to be taken to avoid tensions between the two ethnic groups - English and Afrikaner - particularly over the issues of socialism and republicanism. (14)

156 Chapter 3

The long-time and leading advocate of the white labour policy, the political scourge of the mining companies, the leader of the Labour Party - Frederick Creswell - was now the Minister of Labour. He immediately called a conference of trade unionists to discuss the unemployment problem. This conference adopted a wide range of demands and proposals concerning white unemployment. This unemployment, it declared, was largely the result of undercutting from ultra-cheap non-white labour in the urban areas. The government was asked to implement a minimum 'civilised' wage through Wage Boards, to set apart more land for Africans, to repeal all tax and recruitment measures which forced Africans off the land into wage labour in the urban areas, to encourage Africans to stay on the land through technical rather than scholastic education, and to move towards the 'repatriation' of Africans who had migrated to urban areas since May 1921 and engaged in work other than unskilled labour in the mines. (15) The conference adopted many other, more specific, resolutions on race relations and unemployment. It favoured the elimination of non-white labour from certain occupations and industries, such as bakeries, breweries, the food and liquor industry, and hospital services. For the mines, it proposed a reduction of the ratio of white to non-white workers, and a limitation on the number of African workers over whom a white mine worker could be made responsible. The conference advocated a 'civilised labour policy', through which white labour would be given preference over non-white labour in unskilled work. The government was requested to implement this policy directly in all government employment and public works, and indirectly through making the availability of protectionist tariffs to employers contingent upon a satisfactory ratio of white to non-white labour. (16)

The new Pact government acted to protect the white workers, implementing many of the resolutions of this conference. The White Labour Policy of providing employment opportunities for unskilled whites in unskilled labour at 'civilised' wages became official government policy, as the Civilised Labour Policy, and was implemented in such areas as the railways and harbours and the postal service. (17) The government amended the customs tariff system in 1925 to make tariff protection dependent upon the observance by employers of 'satisfactory labour conditions'. (18) The government passed a Wage Act in 1925 to provide, through a Wage Board, for the establishment of 'civilised' minimum wage levels for unorganised and unskilled workers (which, by excluding such areas as agriculture and domestic service, effectively applied only to unskilled white

2 The 'Colour Bar Act'

After the change of government, the new Ministry of Labour conducted a review, with other government departments, of the situation in the gold mines. Because of unemployment, and bitterness over 1922, the review observed, discontent among the white mine workers remained very high. The workers feared that the mining companies would continue to displace white labour, and they might take more militant action, but they appeared to have widespread confidence that the new government would act to protect them. 'The mines must eventually conform to the national interest', the review concluded, and the government should take steps to protect the white mine workers, which might include 'legislative steps . . . to restore the old position of the colour bar recently overset by judgement of court'. (20) And the white mine workers themselves lost no time in pressing their claims on the new government. After the trade union conference convened by Creswell, representatives of the white mine workers met with government Ministers to press their case. They informed the Ministers about the discontent in their ranks over the displacement, work extension and wage cuts which followed the 1922 strike - a discontent which might explode into another strike, they warned, unless the government took some action. What they particularly wanted was a Commission of Inquiry into their grievances, and the legalisation of the job colour bar. (21) In response to its policy review and to these representations from the workers, the government appointed such a Commission, and soon introduced a Bill to legalise the job colour bar.

This Commission was appointed in November 1924, to examine the contravention of Mining Regulations in the mines, and 'the present position in these mines in regard to the respective spheres of work of white and coloured persons'. (22) The white workers presented it with much evidence - which was considered earlier - about the displacement and work extension produced by the labour reorganisation of 1922. These changes were blamed for the increasing contravention of the Mining Regulations, and for generally jeopardising the security of the white workers. If these policies were allowed to continue unchecked, the Mine Workers' Union declared, virtually all of the white mine workers would eventually be eliminated from their jobs. (23) The white mine workers demanded stronger protection against the policies of the companies. Because of the Hildick-Smith judgment, they wanted the Mines and Works Act amended so that, as the Mine Workers' Union put it, 'it shall be lawful to frame Regulations discriminating between white and coloured workers'. (24) They also wanted certain Regulations amended, to check work extension and displacement. But the first necessity was to legalise the job colour bar by amending the Act. The white workers also favoured the idea of a minimum wage per job - a rate-for-the-job system; but in the absence of such a system, they considered that discrimination on a racial basis was necessary. In the view of the Mine Workers' Union:

> The real point on that is that whites have been ousted by coloured labour. It is not because a man is white or coloured, but owing to the fact that the latter is cheap. It is now a question of cheap labour versus what is called 'dear labour', and we consider we will have to ask the commission to use the word 'colour' in the absence of a minimum wage, but when that is introduced we believe that most of the difficulties in regard to the coloured question will automatically drop out. (25)

The Commission reported in 1925. Concerning the first term of reference - the Mining Regulations - it found that certain important Regulations concerning labour underground were being habitually and increasingly contravened. (26) The Commission concluded that the condition 'that cries out most insistently for rectification is the practice of assigning to the European miner an area of supervision and responsibility too wide for him effectively to control'. (27) To deal with this, it recommended that:

> the average limits of the European miner's area of responsibility should be considerably curtailed, and that, in the interests of health and safety, the employment of natives be restricted to the lower grades of mining occupations, all posts involving any exercise of supervision over others being confined to European workers, since mine natives in the present state of their development and the terms of their relationship with Europeans are unfitted to occupy them. (28)

Looking at the broader issues of group relations in the mines and the position of the white workers, the Commission confirmed that the process of displacement of white workers was already far advanced in semi-skilled work, and believed that it could extend considerably into skilled work. It disagreed with the view of the Chamber of Mines

> that a process which has flourished for years back in the sphere of semi-skilled occupations is going

suddenly and immediately to stop at the highly artificial line which is drawn to separate these from what we have called the skilled. (29)

The Government Mining Engineer himself had recently declared that:

I have no reason to doubt that, as natives become more skilled in various occupations, economic law will in years to come operate as it always has, and that the more expensive white man will be replaced to an increasing extent by native labour. (30)

The causes which had produced displacement of whites in semi-skilled work (the ultra-cheapness of African labour, the forced labour system, the acquisition of skills by African workers) were still in operation and would undermine the position of the skilled whites. (31) This was in fact already evident in two areas. With the extension of the miner's work and responsibility, African 'boss-boys' were being given increasingly responsible work. And openings for the white worker to many skilled occupations through apprenticeships in ancillary jobs 'have by reason of native competition, been shut in his face'. Many skilled workers received their training in semi-skilled work, 'and the policy which excludes the European from the latter, must inevitably cut him off from the former calling'. (32)

The Commission rejected the two main grounds on which the mining companies sought to justify the displacement of white workers - those of redundancy and inefficiency, and of technological innovation. Concerning the latter, it declared that:

Such consideration as we have given to the question in the light of the evidence prevents our coming to the conclusion that any recent improvement in the efficiency of machinery is in the fullest sense a justification of the elimination of European in favour of native labour, however cheap. (33)

But it was the issue of redundancy that proved to be the basic bone of contention. The Chamber admitted that the majority of displaced whites fell into the category of 'redundant' rather than that of 'inefficient' or of 'displaced by machinery'. This raised the whole question, the Commission stated, of the meaning of the term 'redundancy'.

Whether the continuation of two gangs of natives, under one or two European overseers, does really render the other, whose services are eventually dispensed with, redundant, is a question the answer to which of course depends upon the limits we assign to this somewhat elastic term. (34)

The Commission adopted the following criterion and came to the following conclusion:
> If the process results in the European, who is retained, being saddled with a responsibility greater than he can carry, his dismissed co-worker cannot truly be said to have become redundant, and as we have no doubt that in connection with the vast majority of the dismissals of European underground workers that took place in 1922 this condition was actually fulfilled, we are unable to conclude either that the Europeans in question had become redundant or that their dismissal was justified. (35)

The Commission therefore concluded that the displacement of white workers after 1922 could not be attributed to redundancy, and that what it actually stemmed from was the policy of the mining companies of maximising profitability through making the most profitable possible utilisation of ultra-cheap forced labour at the expense of white labour.
> The decrease in the number of European employees, which has gone hand in hand with an increase in the quantity of ore handled, while the number of native employees has remained practically constant, we are unable to attribute to any other cause than a deliberate policy, consistently pursued throughout the period under review, of displacing European in favour of cheap coloured labour. (36)

The Commission concluded that:
> Infinitely the most serious result . . . of the policy pursued during recent years, and far transcending all others in importance, is the elimination it seems bound, if unchecked, to bring about of the European worker from the entire range of mining occupations. (37)

This was especially the case, it considered, since 'the "colour bar" has no present existence in law', because of the Hildick-Smith judgment. (38) The companies had disclaimed any intention of taking advantage of this ruling, but
> on the evidence of the past few years we have very little doubt that the vast majority of such employers will, in the absence of legislative prohibition, continue their policy of replacing European by native workers, whenever economic considerations appear to call for such substitution and those of health and safety are not glaringly opposed to it. (39)

The Commission's concluding recommendations - 'The best means of safeguarding the interests of the European mine worker' - reflected these general concerns and fears. It was necessary 'to rescue the European miner from the economic fetters which at present render him the easy victim of advancing native competition'. (40) To this end, the Commission recommended that the practice of reserving certain jobs to white workers should be continued, that the job colour bar in the Mining Regulations should be legalised, and that the Mines and Works Act should be amended to that effect. (41) The white workers needed such protection for the purpose 'of counteracting the force of the economic advantages at present enjoyed by the native'. (42)

The report of the Mining Regulations Commission thus harmonised with the general labour policy of the new Pact government, giving unequivocal support to the protectionist demands of the white workers. It was the first government Commission up to this time (of many Commissions, and with the exception of the Transvaal Mining Industry Commission report of 1908) to have analysed class and race relations in the gold mining industry from the perspective of the white workers rather than that of the mining capitalists. As such, it not surprisingly provoked a hostile response from the Chamber of Mines and its allies. The 'Mining Journal' (which shared and propagated the Chamber's views) constantly attacked the Commission, disliking its broad terms of reference, alleging that it was partisan and incompetent, complaining that workers giving evidence 'have hardly distinguished themselves ... except as ardent protestants of doctrines which are untenable from the point of view of the ABC of logic, and as disciples of faiths which have no substratum of fact or reason', (43) and declaring that:

> There really ought to be some sort of law passed which would make it a punishable offence for people to detain busy men before a Court of Industrial Inquisition and to waste their time by compelling them to listen to and refute all sorts of absurd statements. (44)

On the publication of the Commission's report, the President of the Chamber of Mines declared that:

> The Commissioners appear to have ignored the economic aspect of mining, the primary purpose of which is to win minerals at a profit and not the mere carrying out of regulations which are in no way connected with safety and health, but which are designed to create employment for redundant persons. (45)

The 'Mining Journal' weighed in with the opinion that it was an 'innocuous document', and that 'having regard to the personnel of the Commission, it is a matter for congratulation that it goes no further than it does', and it wondered how much the Commission had cost 'and whether the people of the country have received value for their money'. (46)

The Chamber of Mines may not have received value for its money, but the white workers were not to be disappointed. Their primary concern was to have the job colour bar legalised. 'Unless the Act is amended', a union leader had told government Ministers, echoing the feelings of the white mine workers, 'there is no future for the white men in the industry.' (47) And the new government, in its review of the situation on the Rand had concluded that such a move was an important priority, a move that was also to be recommended by the Mining Regulations Commission. And in 1925, the government introduced a Bill to amend the Mines and Works Act.

It was a simple little Bill, proposing to amend Section 4 of the Mines and Works Act of 1911 so as to make it legal for the government to make Regulations under the Act discriminating on a racial basis, and thus to legalise the job colour bar in the Mining Regulations. This little Bill was, however, to make a very stormy passage through Parliament, provoking prolonged and controversial debate in both Houses, being thrown out by the Senate in 1925, reintroduced and again rejected by the Senate in 1926, and finally passed by a majority of both Houses in the first joint sitting of both Houses, in 1926.

The immediate reason for the Bill, the government stated, was the Hildick-Smith judgment. 'The consequence of that judgement', the Minister of Mines declared, 'was that the whole position in the Transvaal was thrown into the melting pot.' (48) And 'it would be criminal on the part of this government to allow the position created by the judgement in the Transvaal to drift'. (49) 'We are not going to allow matters to rest on the favours and good graces of the Chamber of Mines', he told the House. 'It must be properly defined what is white man's work and what is Kaffir's.' (50) The Bill was being introduced because 'the whole matter must be put on a proper and a lawful basis'. (51)

But the general and long-term concern of the Bill, according to its proponents, was to protect the white workers against 'the adventitious and artificial advantages in favour of the native . . . which make him more attractive to the employer as a source of labour'. (52) 'The whole system there', the Minister of Mines declared, about the position of African workers in the mines, 'is all through a striking example of the colour bar. The native is kept under control, but not the white man.' (53) The job colour bar was necessary as a defence against the colour bars utilised by the mining companies. The white workers required such protection because of their particular position in the class structure, in contrast with

that of the employers. 'There is no director of a company
... whose living is menaced. Therefore they can afford
to look at this matter in an abstract way, and stand for
"justice" and "right" and so on.' (54) The white workers
had to be protected against the capitalists, 'whose whole
and sole object is to get their commodities produced and
their business run on the cheapest possible scale with the
cheapest possible labour in order to make the greatest
possible profit'. (55) They had to be defended from the
employer who would always seek the 'cheapest possible
labour, whether it comes from China or tropical Africa, or
who would even give the employment to baboons if they
could do the work'. (56) The Bill was 'something which
will restore that which was taken away from the white men
on the Witwatersrand by force of arms', and which would
compensate for 'the low wage competition of the natives'.
(57) The white workers had to be protected against the
'class of employer who, if he could get green men or blue
men cheaper than black men, would do so', and against the
flooding of industry by ultra-cheap African workers 'under
such conditions that justify us in describing them as
serfs', workers who were 'merely used as competitive factors against our own local people'. (58) If the employers
were allowed to continue with their policies unchecked, a
Senator warned,

> the position in South Africa would simply be this:
> black labour and white capital. That would be the
> whole position and so far as the white worker is con-
> cerned he would be eliminated. It is now the duty of
> the present government to see that that policy of drift
> is stopped and that the white man is put into a proper
> safe position. (59)

'This is an economic question', another declared. 'It is
a question as to whether or not there is to be competition
for certain jobs, mostly on the Witwatersrand gold mines.'
(60) And 'our Christian spirit', another stated, 'carries
us in the direction of wanting to keep these avenues of
labour open to our white children'. (61) It was necessary, the Prime Minister declared, 'to find a way by which
the colour line will serve as a deciding factor to settle
what work shall be exclusively done by whites'. (62)

While opposition to the Bill was expressed from various
quarters on various grounds, it was of an essentially
pragmatic nature. What concerned the opposition party -
the South African Party - was not a problem of ends and
principles, but one of means. The basic point at issue,
in the view of General Smuts, was not the issue of white
supremacy but was the question of how best to preserve and
stabilise white supremacy.

Make no mistake, my whole political effort and public life in this country has been to establish and render firm and secure white civilisation in this country. But there are ways of doing it and the question is whether this Bill and the statutory enactment of this colour bar . . . is the way to establish the white position in South Africa. I am very doubtful about it. (63)

The South African Party thus opposed statutory discrimination, on the grounds that it would 'embarrass us in every way possible', and that 'getting round us a ring fence of hate from all the other communities in South Africa' was not, according to Smuts, 'the way to establish a white South Africa'. (64) Racial domination was already well established in practice; there was no need to go on reinforcing it officially. 'No doubt we have a colour bar in the South Africa Act', Smuts declared. 'Let us leave it there; it is fundamental. Do not pile on the agony and do not make the position of the white man in South Africa impossible.' (65)

These pragmatic considerations were echoed by other opponents of the Bill. The Bill was said to be objectionable because its effect would be 'that feeling among the natives is going to be enormously accentuated'. The Bill was an unnecessary 'outward and visible sign of the intention of the government and the people who put them into power to keep the native down', the effect of which would be that 'agitation is bound to arise to a greater degree than would otherwise have been the case'. (66) The Bill was to be opposed because it would tend to provoke 'a most serious disturbance in the native mind'. (67) And it was also objectionable because to protect white workers 'by these artificial methods would absolutely lead to disaster and failure'; they could only be saved by 'efficiency and hard work'. (68) And while the job colour bar in the mines was in itself acceptable, its incorporation into statute law was unnecessary, because 'custom will protect the European better than any law'. (69)

The Bill was passed by the House of Assembly with a clear majority, but was rejected by the Senate, in which the South African Party still held a majority (because of the appointment of SAP Senators before the change of government). The Bill was therefore reintroduced to and again passed by the House of Assembly in 1926, and again rejected by the Senate, after more lengthy debates covering the same ground as those of 1925. (70) After the Bill's second rejection by the Senate, the government convened a joint sitting of both Houses (under Section 63 of the South Africa Act) - the first time this procedure had been implemented in the Union's history. It was time, the Minister of Mines told the joint sitting, that the Bill, which was 'closely connected with . . . the great problem of the solution of the native question', was incorporated into law. (71) 'We would be unworthy of the trust reposed in us by the white civilisation of the whole country', he asserted, 'if we drew back from the attempt to solve this great and weighty problem.' (72)

Leading the opposition, General Smuts reitereated the view of the South African Party that when you had effective de facto racial discrimination, there was no need to 'raise all this feeling all over the country' and thus to threaten the status quo by making it more overt. The position of his Party was: 'Let us stick to the old colour bar Regulations as they have been working in the mines', a course which 'would lead to no outcry in this country'. (73) The Bill would simply aggravate race relations and 'is going to make impossible any policy of appeasement and settlement between white and black in this country'. (74) It was not the right means to go about securing the future of white supremacy. As another leading member of the South African Party told the Minister of Mines:

The members who sit on this side of the House are quite as anxious to protect white civilisation as he is, and, if necessary, to extend the colour bar, but we object to the method in which he intends to do it. (75)

Moreover, while white supremacy had to be maintained, it was important for employers to be able to make the most of the 'asset' of African labour. It was necessary 'to make the right use of the great asset which Providence has given us in the natives of this country'. But how could 'we make a right use of this great gift or asset if we circumscribe the natives by legislation so that they cannot give the best they are capable of, and are not allowed to use their powers for the development of the country'. (76)

The Prime Minister, General Hertzog, confessed to have found it 'painful' to listen to the speech of General Smuts, who, he alleged, 'has never yet in this assembly delivered a speech which is unfortunately so contemptible'. (77) For General Smuts to say that the government was only concerned 'to stir up the feelings of all sections of the population, while we are trying to straighten out his mess, and to reproach us with it, is contemptible'. (78) The native policy of the South African Party was merely opportunistic, and 'the time has come for South Africa to no longer follow the policy of laisser aller. . . . What South Africa must do is to keep its eye on the future and to fix the point we are aiming at.' (79) Moralistic objections to the Bill were an insult to the white workers, implying that 'more than half of our people ... are animated by nothing but prejudice against colour, and that they are supporting this measure for that reason'. (80) The crux of the matter was 'the inequality in competition for a living between the two races', and the fact that 'the white man in South Africa has to fight an unequal battle against the natives of South Africa', all of which necessitated protectionist measures like the Bill, without which there would be a repetition of the bloodshed of 1922. (81)

The same outlook was expressed by Frederick Creswell, the leader of the Labour Party. High sounding moral condemnations of racial discrimination, by churchmen and others, were irrelevant if they ignored the particular economic structures and conditions of particular societies, he declared. 'It is easy for these reverend gentlemen, who have little contact with the realities of life, to say "Ah, this is wrong. This is violating moral justice."' (82) Such objections ignored the class problems of the white workers, and the fact that the more productive employment of African workers could merely mean the greater exploitation of these workers. (83) As for politicians, such as those in the South African Party, who said 'Let us have discrimination, but not on the law books; let us make discrimination, but not be seen to be doing so', for such a position 'no decent man can have anything but scorn and contempt'. (84) A legal job colour bar was in fact only 'a flimsy protection in face of economic and industrial currents which you set going by other institutions which we have', and after a while the new Wage Act might make racial discrimination unnecessary; but for the moment, there was no point in 'throwing away even that flimsy protection while those institutions and those economic and industrial currents consequent on them are in full swing'. (85) In conclusion, the Minister of Mines reiterated that the driving concern behind the Bill was not colour prejudice but was the need to protect white workers against the 'semi-servile condition' of the African workers, and against the colour bars of the employers - against the fact that 'the native is preferred by the mining companies owing to the compound system, pass laws, right of prosecution for desertion, and so on'. (86)

After being debated for about thirty-five days over two years in both Houses of Parliament, the Bill was finally enacted into law by the joint sitting of both Houses. The new Mines and Works Act Amendment Act of 1926 - or 'Colour Bar Act', as it became known - amended the Mines and Works Act of 1911 so as to legalise racial discrimination in the Regulations promulgated under the Act. (87) And over the next few years, the Regulations were amended, incorporating many demands of the white workers. (88)

The pendulum had thus come full circle. The State, which in 1922 had served as the instrument for the repression of the white workers, was now in the hands of their representatives, and implementing a protectionist policy for them, reinforcing and extending the employment colour bars, to protect skilled and unskilled white workers from the negative effects of the exploitation colour bars of the employers on their conditions and prospects of employment.

4 Class colour bars and class conflict: the African workers

From an examination of the historical behaviour of, and relations between, the groups operating the system of racial discrimination in the gold mines - the mining companies and the white workers - we turn now to an examination of the historical behaviour, and treatment, of the group over which it operated - the African workers. The period during and following the First World War was highly significant not only in the former but also in the latter. It was during this period that African workers on the Rand first came, on any significant scale, collectively to express grievances about and to take action against their oppression. The structure of this oppression, and the place of the system of racial discrimination in it, were considered in Part 1. We have now to observe the historical response of the African workers to this structure and this system - their growing unrest, their attempts to improve their situation, and the grievances which lay behind this unrest - and the repression of these attempts through the effective historical operation of the system of racial discrimination.

1. UNREST, CONFLICT AND REPRESSION

There was little significant unrest among African mine workers before the strike of white workers on the Rand in 1913. This strike had important politicising effects on the African workers, who, impressed by the militancy of the white workers, came to express their own grievances and to engage in strike action. When the strike first broke out, in June 1913, numbers of African workers refused to go to work, which appears at this stage to have been due largely to pressure from the white workers, who asked African workers to join the strike and also intimidated

them with various threats. (1) A mining official recounted that:
> The reason the natives gave me for refusing to go underground was that the Europeans who were on strike had threatened to do them harm and blow them up underground if they should proceed to work. . . . What the natives told me was that the strikers stated it was perfectly easy for them to take off a red ribbon and go into the mine, offering themselves for service as strike breakers, to do harm to the natives while they were at work. (2)

In some cases, the white workers had threatened to cut the shaft ropes as the Africans were being hoisted in and out of the mines, and in others, to blow them up underground. (3)

But as the strike progressed, African workers began to hold meetings, to discuss grievances and to refuse to work on account of their grievances. The response of the mining companies to this outbreak of African unrest was in all cases swiftly repressive. It was to call in the police and the army, to arrest the leaders and to force the Africans back to work. On 6 July, African workers in one mine prepared to hold a large meeting to discuss grievances, but were prevented from doing so by the police, and on another mine a demonstration by African workers was put down by mounted police, and the leaders arrested and sentenced to six months hard labour. (4) By 8 July, 9,000 African workers in four mines were refusing to work. In response to this, the army was called in, and it surrounded and entered the compounds, and the Director of Native Labour (the State official responsible for administering the labour controls applicable to African workers) gave the striking workers the choice of returning to work or being arrested. 'The display of force', he later recounted, 'supplied the necessary influence and the natives agreed to return to their duties.' (5) Forty leaders were arrested and sentenced to three months hard labour. Other striking Africans were encouraged to 'return to their duties' in the same way. On 9 July, 2,000 African workers in one mine refused to work, put out pickets, and threatened to kill 'scab' workers. As they 'refused to listen to reason', the Director of Native Labour repeated his formula of sending in troops and threatening mass arrests; the workers returned to work and the leaders were arrested. (6) Altogether, about 13,000 African workers engaged in strike action during the 1913 disturbances.

The 1913 strike undoubtedly politicised many African mine workers. They were impressed by the militancy of the

white workers, and by the readiness of the employers and
the government to make concessions to them in contrast to
their harshly repressive treatment of striking African
workers. During the strike, the labour officials of the
Chamber of Mines found that African workers 'could not be
persuaded that those who were on strike were not in the
right', and were often confronted with the arguments that
'if the strikers are in the wrong, how is it that the
government is not dealing with it', and that 'if we
natives were on strike, we should be put in gaol for doing
these things'. (7) Towards the end of the strike, the
African workers on one mine nailed a manifesto of protest
and demands on the compound office door, declaring that:
> We want some legal understanding in regard to our pay
> and position. We do not see the miners who kick us
> underground, they are absent and we are working. Why
> should we be sent underground without anything being
> said in regard to the black man's position? Is it
> thought that the black men have sold themselves? (8)

Taken by surprise by the militancy of white workers and
the unrest among African workers in the 1913 strike, and
aware of the role played by intimidation and government
inaction in the development of the latter unrest, the
government and employers made careful preparations for
dealing with any future outbreak of class conflict on the
Rand and for checking African participation in it. These
preparations were personally taken in hand by General
Smuts (then Minister of Finance). (9) In accordance with
the instructions of General Smuts, the Chamber of Mines
made arrangements to move African workers away from the
Rand at very short notice should the need arise, and recommended that mounted police should be stationed at
various compounds around the Rand. (10) When, early in
1914, the white railway workers on the Rand came out on
strike, with calls for a general strike, a special message
from the Prime Minister, General Botha, was read out to
all African workers in the mine compounds. Botha informed
them that the railway workers had struck work, and that
the strike might spread to the mines. He wanted to empha-
sise to the African workers that: 'The dispute has nothing whatever to do with the natives. Your duty is to obey
the instructions of your compound manager. When you are
required to work you shall do so.' He went on to promise
that the troops which had been sent into Johannesburg
would protect all African workers who wanted to continue
working. But he warned 'that the hand of the government
will be heavy on any who may disobey these orders'. (11)
Apart from a few sporadic outbreaks of unrest, the African
workers did not participate in the 1914 strike, which was

short-lived and met with far less success among the white
workers than that of 1913, due in large measure to the
speedy and repressive response of the government, which
kidnapped the strike leaders and deported them to England.
The Director of Native Labour cabled the government that:
> During recent crisis natives were much impressed by
> strong measures taken for maintenance of law and order,
> and freely expressed their thanks for the decided and
> decisive action of the government which not only gave
> them protection but enabled almost all being continu-
> ally employed. (12)

Botha's message had been well received by the African
workers, and they had been struck by the sight of whites
being obliged to carry passes (under the martial law which
had been declared in the Transvaal). (13)

However the response of the African workers to the 1913
strike had shown them becoming aroused over their grievances and beginning to assert themselves in a militant
manner.

> The natives had not only been interested spectators of
> the methods employed by the European strikers, but some
> had actually followed their lead in fomenting dissatis-
> faction, urging natives to strike and picketing and
> threatening those who did not comply with their
> demands. (14)

The immediate response of employers and government was, as
we observed, to put such unrest down by force and to
arrest the workers' leaders. But they also became concerned to contain and discourage the development of this
unrest. As the Director of Native Labour explained:
> Having reason to believe that this lead would be fol-
> lowed by certain native agitators, and realising how
> lamentable it would be were the government to be placed
> in the position of having to make concessions to na-
> tives as a result of demands being formulated in re-
> spect of known grievances, the Director recommended
> that such a move be anticipated and that a Commission
> be appointed. (15)

On the basis of these pragmatic calculations, such a Commission, known as the Native Grievances Inquiry, was duly
appointed, to inquire into African grievances and into the
effectiveness of the compound system as a form of control
over Africans. (16) Concerning the former, it made about
80 recommendations for the improvement of African labour
conditions on the mines. These concerned improvements in
such areas as the provision of food (e.g. unlimited porridge rations, better and cleaner food distribution,
catering for special tribal tastes, hot rations before
work), the provision of medical services (e.g. fully

qualified medical personnel, periodical medical inspections, consultation of relatives before amputations, the screening-off of beds of dying workers), technical improvements (e.g. larger cages, shelters near shafts, double gates at hauling stations, better drill distribution), the reckoning of shifts against contracts, transport facilities, deferred pay and other matters. Although known as the Native Grievances Inquiry, the Commission had as its second term of reference to inquire into the control that could be exercised over African workers in compounds, especially during unrest and conflict. And it recommended that control over Africans in the compounds be tightened up, and that compounds should be constructed in such a way as to be easily and quickly closable in the event of such unrest.

The great majority of the Inquiry's recommendations concerned improvements of a quantitative kind in the immediate labour and living conditions of African workers, in such areas as food, accommodation and working conditions. The Chamber of Mines agreed in principle to nearly all of them, and most of them were implemented. (17) But these were not structural changes. The ultra-subordinate class position of African workers, which, as we shall see, is what their fundamental grievances stemmed from and concerned, did not receive much of the Commission's attention, and was not changed as a result of it. African workers remained rightless, powerless and ultra-cheap. The system of ultra-exploitation of African labour persisted undiminished. Consequently, the Commission was not to have the desired effect of neutralising discontent among African workers.

Unrest among African workers on the Rand greatly intensified during and following the First World War. The most important immediate cause of this was the effective stabilisation by employers of the very low level of African wages during a period of rapidly rising prices and of rising wants, needs, expectations and political consciousness among Africans. It also reflected the exposure of African workers to the presence and activities of the white workers and the gains secured by the latter during this period, to the influence of white socialists, who helped to organise African workers, and to the growth of political organisation and leadership among urban Africans. This unrest of African workers during this period expressed the beginnings of systematic and widespread awareness of and opposition to the ultra-exploitation of their labour.

During the first years of the war, there were sporadic outbreaks of unrest among African workers in various

mines. (18) A police official reported in 1916 that:
> The natives have started holding meetings, resorting to picketting and are in fact organising in the same manner as the miners did in the 1913 and 1914 strikes. ... I am convinced that, in the event of any further industrial disturbance, the government will not be able to count on the loyalty of the natives as they have done in the past. (19)

The response of the companies was, again, to call in the police, who arrested the leaders, who were imprisoned or deported from the Rand - the policy of arresting leaders being favoured, the Director of Native Labour affirmed, because of its apparent effectiveness in checking unrest and bringing about a return to work by the rest of the workers. (20)

African unrest on the mines reached a new peak early in 1918, when the African mine workers implemented a boycott of the trading stores on the Rand in protest against rising prices and low wages. In February, African workers on one mine decided to boycott the stores near their compound, 'owing to the heavy increase in the prices of all commodities required by them'. (21) They organised pickets, and the boycott quickly spread to other compounds. In fact, it nearly became a strike. In one mine,
> the labourers told the mine manager that unless he could get the cost of goods at the stores reduced to pre-war prices they would not go down into the mine the following day, and it was with some difficulty that this attitude was overcome. (22)

A Commission of Inquiry into the boycott was appointed, and it found that while 'the methods of trade at the Reef stores are pernicious' (because of the prevalence of bargaining and the absence of standard prices), the high prices being charged were not a form of profiteering but merely a reflection of the increased cost of living. (23) This was confirmed by another Commission, which made a detailed investigation of the accounts of the store-keepers, and found that selling prices had risen less than the cost of goods, that expenses had risen, that the amount of net profits had not appreciably changed since before the war, and that the percentage of net profits on sales had fallen, from 15 per cent in 1914 to 10.6 per cent in 1917. (24)

These were most significant findings. For they implied that the source of the discontent of the African mine workers lay not in exorbitant prices but in the falling purchasing power of their wages, as of money generally, which could only be redressed by a corresponding increase in wages. The Commissioner inquiring into the boycott thus concluded his report by stating that in the prevailing conditions, and especially if they worsened,

> I fear that a determined effort will be made by the mine boys to obtain increased pay. Such a thing is only mentioned in Johannesburg with bated breath, and even then in a whisper, as the consequences of such a demand might have serious results. . . . A careful perusal of the native evidence shows a steady trend of thought in this direction. (25)

It was not to be long before this prediction was to come true.

Following this boycott, and following a successful strike for wage increases by white municipal workers in Johannesburg in May 1918, African municipal workers came out on strike for higher wages. They were given the usual choice of returning to work or being arrested. Over a hundred African workers were then arrested, and sentenced under the Master and Servant Laws to two months imprisonment with hard labour, and

> In passing sentence, the magistrate told the accused that they would be set to do the work they had refused to do, and would be guarded by armed men, and would be liable to be shot if they attempted to escape. (26)

The arrest of the leaders and participants in this strike provoked widespread discontent and protest among Africans on the Rand, and triggered off a campaign of opposition to ultra-low wages and to the forced labour system that was to be unprecedented in its dimensions and significance.

On 19 June, the Transvaal Native Congress convened a mass meeting of about 1,000 Africans drawn from various parts of the Rand. A resolution was put to the meeting that every African worker on the Rand was to receive a wage increase of 1s. per day as of 1 July, failing which Africans would declare a general strike on the Rand. Did they all agree? 'The whole hall said yes, and also those outside the hall.' (27) A Congress leader declared that: 'The white workers do not write to the Governor-General when they want more pay. They strike and get what they should. Why should we not do the same?' (28)

This demand was transmitted to employers in a circular from the Congress, which stated that while the African workers were an 'indispensable class of the community', the value of their wages was constantly declining due to rises in the cost of living, and nothing was being done about it, whereas 'Other sections of the working class community, being articulate and more influential, have in many cases secured increase of pay to meet the increased cost of living.' Now 'it was felt that the time had arrived for the native workers to press for consideration of their case'. This wage grievance was shared by all African workers on the Rand. 'The fact is', the circular declared, 'that today the native worker is giving his labour for the barest subsistence and is undergoing something like sweating.' It concluded by demanding an increase of 1s. per day in the wages of all African workers on the Rand as of 1 July 1918. (29)

More mass meetings were held by Africans on the Rand in support of this wage demand. These meetings, convened by the Transvaal Native Congress, were characterised by growing militancy, both in the content of speeches and in the mood and behaviour of the assembled Africans. The general tenor of the speeches is well captured in the words of one Congress leader to a meeting of about 1,000 Africans on 29 June:

God gave you Africa to live in. He gave you anything he knew was necessary for you. He gave you a land and gold, which you gave away to other people. After you gave them the country, they treated you worse than dogs. Today you are carrying passes. Today you have got no place. Today they are telling you that you will get a place in heaven. There is one thing sure my friends, it is this, if you have no place on earth you have no place in heaven. (30)

At a meeting of about 10,000 Africans the next day, Africans in the crowd tore up a Union Jack, and 'this appeared to be the signal for general lawlessness, and gangs of natives endeavoured to stop trams, motor cars and vehicles of every description, stones being thrown at trams as they passed'. (31)

However, on the offer of a meeting with the Prime Minister, General Botha, who wrote to the Congress expressing a willingness to discuss African grievances with a deputation from the Congress, the latter decided to call off the threatened strike. A deputation met Botha in July, and the government appointed a Commission of Inquiry into unrest among Africans on the Witwatersrand. Africans were told to express their grievances to the Commissioner, the Chief Magistrate of the Transkei (Mr J.B. Moffat). (32)

Groups of African workers in the mines and municipalities nevertheless did come out on strike on 1 July and during July. On one mine, all the African workers refused to work, and many were arrested after refusing 'to co-operate in maintaining law and order'. (33) On another mine, 1,500 African workers struck work and marched out of their compound in a protest demonstration. Their main grievance was that 'they were not receiving sufficient money for the various works which they did and wanted

more'. (34) A newspaper reported that:
> It appeared that the natives . . . were actuated by the belief that in order to get an extra shilling a day, they had merely to demand it and enforce that demand by refusing to work and by making a public demonstration. Mr. Taberer [of the Native Recruiting Corporation] explained to them the fatuity and hopelessness of their conduct. (35)

The Moffat Commission reported in September 1918. It focused much of its attention on the job colour bar, which had been very far from being the main grievance of the African workers, and it did not recommend any increase in wages. It alleged that the rise in the cost of living was not causing serious hardship to mine workers and was only marginally affecting municipal workers. It concluded in favour of the pass system, but recommended certain reforms and improvements in its administration. (36)

With the appointment of the Moffat Commission, the news of peace in Europe, and the decision of the Native Congress to elect and send a delegation of Africans to the Peace Conference in Europe, the issue of wages temporarily receded into the background. As a Congress leader explained to a meeting of Africans on the Rand:
> Some of you wondered what became of the 1/- we have been asking for. We have not given up the 1/- increase of pay business yet. While we were still engaged in asking for this 1/-, the news of the Peace came. Then President Wilson of America announced that now was the chance for every person to get his rights. We are now going overseas to get your rights at the Peace Conference. (37)

The deputation to the Peace Conference was seen as another means of securing redress of grievances, in this case by appealing to world opinion and concern for human rights. As a Congress leader declared to a meeting:
> We dig the gold out of the mines but when it comes to be divided we are not wanted. Look at these buildings built by the white people, and yet we have not got them. When the money of Parliament is being divided we are not wanted at all. We want to go overseas to let them know that there are two nations here, white and black. (38)

But early in 1919, the agitation among Africans on the Rand over wages resurfaced in a more militant form. The 1918 campaign had failed to secure wage increases; and nothing struck the African workers more forcefully than the crucial role played by the coercive labour controls of the forced labour system in bringing about this failure. The latter were now to become the focus of opposition as well. An important component of this system, as we noted in Part 1, was the pass system. It reinforced the coercive contract provision of the Master and Servant Laws by restricting the freedom of Africans in urban areas to organise and act effectively together. To Africans, the pass system was the most immediately evident manifestation of the forced labour system, and it came to symbolise and to be identified with the whole system. Early in 1919, the Congress decided to mobilise the widespread and deeply felt opposition of the Africans on the Rand against the pass system. The campaign for wage increases was now to become as well a campaign against the forced labour system, which was now to be seen as the main obstacle preventing African workers from improving their position; and new and more militant tactics were to make their appearance in this campaign.

At meetings of Africans on the Rand early in 1919, African leaders began to advocate a new tactic for the wage campaign - passive resistance against the pass system. On a particular day, passes would be destroyed or handed in, and 'after that', according to a Congress official, 'we can easily see to the 1/- increase and I think we can be able to get it'. (39) This campaign against the Pass Laws gathered pace during March, and then exploded in fierce and widespread unrest.

On 31 March 1919, a mass meeting of Africans decided to take action against passes, and a crowd of about 1,000 of them then converged on the Johannesburg Pass Office and handed in their passes. The police were unable to do anything because of their small numbers and the large size of the crowd, and the Africans left to spread their anti-pass action around the Rand. (40) But the police were reinforced, and on 2 April they arrested the leaders of an anti-pass demonstration. The crowd of Africans followed the police to the charge office, and began to demonstrate and to throw missiles at the police, who then arrested a large number of them. The next day, a large crowd of Africans arrived at the Pass Office and handed in a sack containing their passes. (41) The Africans held many more meetings. The arrest of leaders meant, according to one speaker, that 'we must all be leaders', and the militant action had to be pressed further, according to another, 'because the government has failed to give us the shilling increase we want, and we must demand our freedom and be under their control no more, because they deceive us'. (42) Groups of Africans were organised to go around all parts of the Rand to spread the anti-pass campaign. (43)

The important new development was thus that the wage campaign was now part and parcel of a campaign against the forced labour system and its coercive labour controls, which were identified as the obstacle to wage increases. 'This Pass Law is the thing that makes us do not get the 1/- increase we want', a Congress leader declared. (44) And as the Congress declared in a circular to Africans on the Rand: 'We came to the conclusion that passes prevent money. It was agreed to throw away the passes which bind us on to many things. Passes were therefore thrown away by men.' (45)

As a result of this militant agitation, another deputation of Africans from the Rand met with the government. At the conference, the Africans attacked the system of coercive labour controls, which they blamed for their failure to secure wage increases and for keeping Africans 'in a state of economic bondage', and for preventing the African worker 'from selling his labour to the best advantage'. (46) The government released eight African leaders from prison, appointed a Commission to investigate allegations of police brutality, and promised to look into the question of the Pass Laws. The Commission exculpated the police, but emphasised 'the urgent necessity of not losing any time in tackling the question of the existing Pass Laws and the administration of these Laws here'. (47) Privately, the Commissioner warned the government that 'a large section of the natives were very upset in connection with the Pass Laws and their administration'. (48)

Agitation and demonstration continued sporadically despite the appointment of the Commission and the government's promises to look into the pass system. One meeting of Africans turned into a battle between Africans and police, as the latter attempted to stop the meeting from taking place. Africans threw their passes into sacks, and many were arrested. (49) An African woman just released from prison told another meeting that 'if any man comes to me and says he loves me and I find that he has a pass I will kill him stone dead as I don't want this pass'. (50) In one suburb, a crowd of Africans took a sack full of their passes to the Pass Office, and 'when the white man opened the door we gave them to him, he asked us why do we give them away, we told him that we don't want them and we are fed up with them'. (51) There was a great deal of resentment among Africans over the fact that while they had remained loyal during the war, and had actually helped to fight it, unlike the Afrikaners - some of whom had rebelled against it, their position in South Africa remained unchanged. The Africans had not rebelled, a Congress leader complained, 'and some of our friends have died in the sea while keeping the King, and still our grievances are not heard by the government'. (52)

Chapter 4

The wage campaign of the African workers on the Rand finally reached a phase of resolution early in 1920. Towards the end of 1919, the agitation over low wages and the increased cost of living was renewed. The Congress had investigated the cost of living, and found that an unmarried man could not live adequately on less than £2 per week, and a family on less than £4 per week, whereas African wages on the Rand averaged at about £3 per month. As a result, Africans were being forced into theft, liquor selling and prostitution. (53) It was decided that all African workers should press employers for a wage increase, and that in the event of refusals, strike action would be considered. (54) Demands for wage increases were duly made. Then it was decided to send a deputation to employers to press for higher wages. (55) And on 9 January, a deputation of Africans met in conference with representatives of the employers and the government over the wages issue.

Nothing had come, the Africans complained, of their recent demands for an all-round 1s. increase, and, 'Things have gone from bad to worse and our people - our women - are becoming liquor sellers and thieves, and we must again apply for assistance and consideration owing to this high cost of living.' (56) Another member of the deputation 'thanked the gentlemen for meeting them and said they were there owing to the feeling of hunger. He thought they were approaching a time when they would have to steal and eat cats, for which they will be prosecuted.' (57) Because of such things as landlessness and high grazing rents, Africans 'have to come to town and die before you. That is why we have to put before you that we shall rob you and steal your property and goods. We have no adequate lands to plough in the country.' (58) No specific demands were made or conclusions reached: the employers agreed to consider the general demand for wage increases, and to hold another conference in two weeks. At this following conference, the employers' representatives agreed to recommend that African workers who had to provide for their own food and lodging (which excluded African workers in the gold mines) should receive wage increases. (59)

The Congress reported back to a meeting of about 3,000 Africans, a great many of whom were mine workers, that the employers had agreed on a wage increase for all African workers except mine workers. This provoked much opposition. It was wrong, said one speaker, reflecting the general sentiment of the meeting, to exclude the mine workers, 'who were kept closed up in compounds and treated almost as though they were in gaol'; the mine workers were dissatisfied and would have to fight for their rights. (60)

Discontent had been as widespread among the African mine workers as among the other African workers on the Rand, and with their boycott of 1918 they had been the first to take protest action against the falling value of their wages. Mine workers played a leading part in the wage campaign, attending the meetings convened by the Congress in considerable numbers; and there was also a keen interest in the compounds in the anti-pass campaign. (61) The news of the wage and anti-pass agitation circulated around the compounds, from mine workers who participated in it and from African political activists who visited the compounds. According to one report on the situation in the mines, 'at present there are 24 educated natives visiting the Reef compounds who deliver leaflets and preach the socialist propaganda to the mine natives'. It concluded:

> That the behaviour of the natives on the Reef today is not what it was some seven years ago is without doubt, and in the event of a strike being declared, it will in my opinion be impossible to keep them in order. (62)

The exclusion of the African mine workers from the wage increases was followed very shortly by the largest strike of African workers in the gold mines - and in South Africa as a whole - up to that time. Between 17 and 27 February 1920, about 71,000 African mine workers in 21 mines came out on strike and, as the President of the Chamber of Mines put it, 'practically paralysed the industry'. (63) Hitherto, the President declared, African workers had expressed their grievances in 'something in the nature of a riot', but now 'there was for the first time, a native strike in the true sense of the word . . . an absolutely peaceful cessation of work'. (64)

This strike was essentially concerned with wages. The distinctive features of the wages of African mine workers during this period - as for the rest of the twentieth century - were threefold: their ultra-low level, the stabilisation of this ultra-low level over time, and their falling real value. The first of these we have already noted in the first part of the study - the average wage of African workers was negligible, about 2s. per day compared with about 20s. per day for white workers. The second of these may be seen in Table 10. Thus between 1911 and 1919, when the wages of the white mine workers rose by 40 per cent, the average earnings of the African mine workers remained virtually stationary.

TABLE 10 Average earnings per shift, African workers, Witwatersrand gold mines, 1911-19*

Year	s.	d.
1911	1	11.3
1912	1	11.6
1913	1	11.0
1914	1	11.7
1915	1	11.4
1916	1	11.1
1917	1	11.1
1918	1	11.5
1919	2	0.3

*'Report of the Low Grade Mines Commission' (1920), p.31.

This stabilisation of African money wages over time, during a period of rising cost of living, constituted a progressive reduction of their real value. Some idea of this decline may be gauged from the fact that between 1910 and 1920 the **wholesale** price index in South Africa rose from 1,000 to 2,512 - representing a very substantial increase in the cost of living, and from the fact that, despite the considerable wage gains secured by the white mine workers during this period, the index of the real value of their wages showed a progressive decline during this period (from 1,000 in 1910 to 933 in 1914 to 758 in 1919). (65) These figures suggest a massive drop in the real value of the wages of African mine workers during this period.

The fundamental cause of the strike was the deep discontent among the African mine workers over these various aspects of their wages, a discontent which had been steadily intensifying during the war, as the cost of living rose, as the white workers secured wage increases and as the agitation of African workers on the Rand gathered pace, while all the time their wages remained fixed at their ultra-low level, and a discontent which was quickly translated into strike action by the refusal of the employers to concede any wage increase to African mine workers. Grievances were also expressed about the high prices charged by stores and about the job colour bar. But the crucial issue, both to the African workers and to the mining companies, was that of wages (and the latter grievances were closely involved with wages). The Chamber of Mines itself recognised that: 'There is no doubt that the natives have viewed with considerable impatience the increase of pay to the European workers, and that they are

feeling very strongly that they also should obtain an increase.' (66) And as a government official reported:
It is difficult for natives to understand the reason for the rise in prices. They maintain that the war is over and still the prices charged for clothing, and in fact for every article of food and every necessity of life, have gone up considerably since peace was declared; that they have had no reply to their frequent representations and now renew their attempt to get relief by asking for the alternative remedy of higher wages as a set-off against increased prices. (67)

The growing discontent among the African workers over their economic position had already found expression in the store boycott of 1918. It now assumed far greater dimensions as 70,000 African mine workers came out on strike.

During the strike, the African workers made various wage demands, the smallest of which was for an increase of 3s. per shift in their wage rates. (68) The Chamber of Mines calculated that if this, the minimum wage demand, was granted, it would cost the industry £8 million per annum, and would, at 1920 cost and price levels, put twenty-three mining companies out of business; with gold at its normal price, it would leave all of the companies profitless except eight, but in fact, since these would be unable to meet the industry's standing charges alone, 'the whole mining industry would be rendered unpayable'. (69) There could hardly be a clearer indication of the extreme dependence of the gold mining industry on ultra-cheap labour than is provided by these calculations.

It was in view of these facts that the Chamber of Mines 'refused to make any further advance in native rates of pay', and was 'unable to make even the minimum advance asked for without closing down the industry'. (70) The African mine workers were 'informed that the highest rate possible was being paid to them compatible with continuance of work by the industry'. (71) And the strike was quickly put down with the usual formula - a demonstration and application of force with the introduction of troops into the compounds, the choice of arrest or return to work, and the arrest of leaders. Compounds were isolated from each other and dealt with one at a time, the striking workers being told that the rest of the workers had returned to work. In some compounds, such as that of the Village Deep mine, the African workers put up resistance, and some were shot dead and many wounded as the troops subdued them and forced them back to work. (72)

The African mine workers were thus forced to return to work unconditionally, without any wage increase whatsoever. The only change which emerged from the strike concerned the prices charged by the Rand stores. The Chamber sought to introduce a new system of stores supplying African workers with goods at close to cost price. This aroused strong opposition from the traders, who succeeded in obstructing the plan. Eventually an arrangement was arrived at whereby the store prices were somewhat reduced. (73) As far as the job colour bar was concerned, the Chamber declared that it was unable to make changes, and that:

> There seems to be an impression in some quarters that the removal of the colour bar would meet the native's grievance, but it should be clearly understood that the removal of the colour bar, even if it were possible, in opposition to the wishes of the great bulk of the European population of the Witwatersrand, would advantage only the comparatively small number of skilled or semi-skilled natives; to the great mass it would make no difference whatever. (74)

This is a statement of considerable significance - one of the few occasions when the Chamber openly recognised that as far as the mass of African mine workers was concerned, the job colour bar was of very marginal importance (the real beneficiaries from any reduction of the scope of the job colour bar being not the African workers but the mining companies). This contrasted with the usual tendency of the Chamber and of other employers and of Commissions of Inquiry of defining the job colour bar as the most serious injustice and most important form of racial discrimination suffered by the African workers.

The only other response of the Chamber of Mines was to recommend a reinforcement of the armed control of African mine workers. The strike indicated, the Chamber warned the government, 'that the native is advancing more rapidly than we had anticipated, and that we should take measures accordingly'. Fearing 'that at no distant date further attempts will be made to organise strikes among the natives', the Chamber recommended that the force of mounted police stationed on the Rand be strengthened, to guard against the 'considerable loss of life and damage to property among the Europeans' that would be likely 'in the event of the natives taking the law into their own hands'. (75)

The strike thus failed to secure any redress of the main grievance of the African mine workers, and the response which their strike action elicited was one of repression. The mining companies thus successfully stabilised the ultra-low level of African wages over time. The ultra-cheapness of African labour - the keystone of the profitability of the gold mining industry - was effectively maintained. The African mine workers did not participate in the 1922 strike. It was to be another two decades before they were to make another attempt to secure wage increases through strike action, an attempt that was to meet with the same response and the same failure.

2. THE AFRICAN WORKERS AND THE CLASS COLOUR BARS: STRUCTURAL GRIEVANCES

We have observed how the African workers were structurally affected by the system of racial discrimination, and we have observed their historical response to their situation. This historical behaviour expressed a growing sense of structural grievance - a growing consciousness of and opposition to their class oppression and the role played by the system of racial discrimination in this oppression. What was this consciousness? How did the African workers come to see their situation and the system of racial discrimination? What were their fundamental grievances?

In this regard, it is as well to bear in mind that the prevailing view of employers and Commissions of Inquiry, and of most of the historiography of industrialisation and race relations in South Africa, has been that the most serious racial discrimination suffered by the African mine workers - and African workers generally - was the job colour bar (a view which continues to predominate among employers, economists and others in South Africa today, and which we shall have occasion to discuss in the Conclusions). The structural analysis of the system of racial discrimination made in the first part of the study gives good grounds for rejecting this view, and for concluding that, on the contrary, the system of ultra-exploitation of labour constituted by the exploitation colour bars of the employers was far more oppressive of the African workers than the job colour bar. And what an examination of the grievances of African workers indicates is that this was in fact the way they felt about the system of racial discrimination. What emerges - not surprisingly, but not conforming to the prevailing view - is that their most fundamental grievances concerned wages and the exploitation colour bars, that the job colour bar was of much less concern, and that where it was it was very much of a wages issue.

Chapter 4

1 The African workers and the exploitation colour bars

At the end of the First World War, the Director of Native Labour stated to a Commission of Inquiry that:

> For some years past, a considerable element of discontent has prevailed among the natives in the Witwatersrand area. So far as those employed on gold mines are concerned, it may be said that the cry for 'more money' is the main thing that exercises the minds of the majority.

A small minority of African mine workers, he continued, were concerned about the job colour bar, but this concern was also largely a concern for higher wages: these workers

> are no longer contented with their lot as unskilled labourers paid at current contract rates, but aspire to work of a semi-skilled and, in some cases, even skilled nature, with consequent increased opportunity of earning higher wages. (1)

The evidence - most clearly the evidence of African mine workers and their representatives to the major Commissions of Inquiry during this period - everywhere confirms this view. (2) For the great majority of African mine workers, the crucial issue was that of ultra-low wages and wage minimisation; and the interest of the minority in more skilled work was largely based on the expectation of higher wages in such work.

The main wage grievance of the African mine workers concerned the ultra-low level of their standard wage rates, and the system of wage minimisation. But as the cost of living rose, and as the white workers secured wage increases, their wage grievances became focused as well on the stationary level of their wages and on the system of discriminatory and coercive labour controls responsible for this.

No grievance was more universally in evidence than that 'the men are not paid according to the amount of work they do'. (3) The standard rate of wages of African mine workers was, the Native Congress stated, 'not in any sense commensurate with the nature and the hours of work'. (4) 'In the mining industry particularly, where there are many risks and other difficulties of work and distance from home, the nature of the work has to be taken into consideration when assessing a standard rate of pay.' (5) African mine workers 'appreciate that their labour is serviceable and valuable and that at the present average rate of pay they do not get full compensation for what their labour gives or produces'. (6)

Thus the evidence of African mine workers to the Native

Grievances Inquiry of 1913-14 consisted for the most part
of an unending stream of complaints about low wages and
about the wage minimisation system, especially the loafer
ticket system and the maximum average system, which were
described earlier on. As one African mine worker stated:
> All the natives here are complaining of the same thing,
> that they do not get money. When we left our homes, we
> were told that there was a lot of money . . . but since
> we have been here we do not get money. We work for
> nothing, merely for porridge. (7)

And in the words of another:
> We all have the same complaint about our money. . . .
> We do not get sufficient money. . . . We are in need of
> money and we came here to earn money but we do not get
> enough money to support our families. We receive many
> letters from our people at home asking us to send
> money, and we have no money to send them. (8)

And of another: 'On account of the small pay given to us,
we are not even able to support our mothers and fathers at
home.' (9) And of another: 'These complaints are most
painful to our hearts, because it seems to us now that we
came here to work for porridge and not for the money which
was promised to us.' (10)

The African mine workers objected very strongly to the
loafer ticket system of unpaid and extra-contractual
labour, whereby Africans engaged in, and paid for, drilling work were made to do a certain amount of lashing and
tramming work before drilling. This often resulted in
their not drilling the minimum number of inches for which
the piece-work rates of payment began, in which case they
were given no pay (later, a token payment) for the shift,
and the shift was not recognised as a contract shift,
which meant that the African worker had to do an extra
shift to complete his contract. In such cases the shift
ticket of the African worker was marked in a particular
way, to cancel pay for the shift and to withhold recognition of the shift as a contract shift. Such tickets were
known as 'loafer tickets' (and also as 'porridge tickets'), and such workers were thus penalised in two ways.
As an African mine worker pointed out: 'They get a double
punishment, because they do not get their tickets marked
and they are not paid for that day and the contract is not
going on.' (11)

This practice was a source of acute grievance to the
African mine workers. In the words of one:
> We all complain about money because we do not get
> money. We bore the holes but we do not get the pay.
> We do lashing work but we are not paid for lashing.
> Our tickets are not marked for lashing. A hammer boy

who has done lashing work but does not finish his hole gets a loafer's ticket. (12)

And of another:
We drill four holes with the machine but the boss does not give us tickets and we get no money. For the five holes we drill we do not get any money. We have a great complaint about this because we came here to earn good wages and we do not get them. (13)

And of another:
We have all a complaint that we do not get money. I work very hard. First of all I have to do lashing and push rock into the box hole. When I have finished lashing, then I have to do my drill work. A white man who has been sitting in his box will come back and say that I have not done my work that day and he gives me no ticket. That is my chief complaint. (14)

And of another:
When I came here, I came here for money but I do not get money. This is the complaint we have to lay before you and we have no other complaint. We have come to these fields for money, but I get my ticket marked 'porridge' for the day. Money is not marked on my ticket while I am still alive, and I want my tickets marked with money so that when I die here on the gold fields my mother will be able to get what I earned when still alive. (15)

This grievance against the loafer ticket system was a universal complaint among Africans employed in drilling work, the majority of the African mine workers.

The system of wage minimisation through the fixation of ultra-low wage rates both in standard time rates and, through the maximum average system, in piece-work rates, also figured prominently among the wage grievances of the African mine workers. An intensification of the latter grievances before the war originated, a Committee of Inquiry reported, 'in the schedule of wages promulgated by the Native Recruiting Corporation and in its application'. (16) The introduction of the maximum average system was one of the causes of participation by African workers in the 1913 strike of the white workers, for it had the effect of limiting and reducing the earnings of many African workers, and, as this Inquiry reported, 'this cutting is not and cannot be understood by the average native, more especially by old hands, who have been accustomed to the higher rates'. (17) Certain work stoppages by African workers were due specifically to the news that they could not earn more than 2s. 3d. per shift. (18) The Economic Commission reported in 1914 that:

The native desires to be paid according to his

strength; and he complains of the small amount he
earns. . . . The maximum average day's pay of 2/3d.
fixed by the Native Recruiting Corporation is especially felt by the natives as a grievance. (19)
The African mine workers strongly resented the standardisation of their wage rates at an ultra-low level, and the minimisation of their piece-work earnings. (20)

These fundamental wage grievances intensified during and following the First World War, when the wages of African mine workers were kept stationary, while the cost of living, the material needs, wants and expectations of the African workers and their families, and the wages of the white workers all rose considerably. This expressed itself in the growing and increasingly militant unrest among African workers on the Rand over wages during this period. Given the rising cost of living and the rising needs and wants of the African workers and their dependents, the stabilisation of the wages of the African mine workers at their ultra-low level over time - which we noted earlier - meant that African wages were falling in real value and becoming increasingly inadequate as a means of livelihood.

The mining companies sought to justify this stationary level of the already ultra-low wage rates of African mine workers with the claims that these workers were not affected by the rising cost of living (because the companies provided food and accommodation), that the rising needs and wants of African workers were irrelevant in any consideration of their cost of living, and that dependents in rural areas were less affected by the increase in the cost of living than were Africans living on the Rand. Thus, in its evidence to the Moffat Commission, which inquired into the unrest of 1918, the Chamber of Mines stated that because African mine workers received free food and accommodation, it was 'of opinion that so far as the personal cost of living of the natives employed on the mines is concerned, there has been no increase justifying an increase in wages'. (21) The fact that the African worker's needs and wants had risen was considered irrelevant - only his minimum subsistence requirements were relevant: 'Only articles the consumption of which is necessary to maintain the subsistence standard to which he is accustomed should be taken into account in estimating his increased cost of living through the war.' (22) And the very low standard of African wages was considered to be fair remuneration, on the grounds that it compared not unfavourably with the wages of other African workers, when food and accommodation were taken into account. (23) In his report, the Commissioner accepted the Chamber's position. The wage grievances of the African mine workers were not considered to be important. The reason given in support of this conclusion was the fact that many African workers returned to work on the mines, and 'it seems unlikely that these would have been content to re-enrol had they felt that their employment at the rates of pay offered would impose any really serious hardship on them'. (24) From this fact, and from the fact that many Africans came to the mines 'voluntarily' (i.e. independently of the recruiting corporations), 'it must be assumed that they are prepared to work for the wages offered in spite of the fact that the purchasing value of the money earned is reduced owing to war conditions'. (25) This dubious reasoning was thought to settle the matter. The Commissioner did not consider or explore the possibility that Africans left their homes and families to work in the gold mines for long periods for negligible wages of falling value because of economic compulsion, and that they 'accepted' these wages because of extra-economic compulsion; and he devoted most of his criticisms to the job colour bar, which was, as usual, defined as the primary problem.

The claims made by the Chamber of Mines about African wages and the cost of living were highly questionable, and were contested and rejected by the African mine workers and their representatives. In the first place, African mine workers were not provided with all necessities. They had to purchase their own clothing and boots. And the cost of an outfit of clothing rose from 18s. before the war to 38s. in 1918, and of a pair of boots from 12s. 6d. to 20s. (26)

But African workers rejected the view that their cost of living should be assessed only in subsistence terms. Their needs and wants were growing, and this also constituted an increase in their cost of living. As an African leader explained:

For example, while the native of olden times used to live largely on sour milk and mealies, that same native must have his coffee and sugar at least once a day. At his own home too, and some bread also as often as he can. So his mode of life is quite different now to what it was ten years ago, and also the natives today are ambitious to have beds, even in their kraals, whereas in the past they had mats. The storekeepers are selling these things now in large numbers, and you find these things in even the rawest native huts. Therefore it is very fair to suggest that the cost of living is very much higher than it was 20 years ago. (27)

Low African wages were often justified by employers, the Native Congress observed, 'on the idea that the native had no needs'. But, it pointed out, 'in these days it would be altogether erroneous to hold that idea', for 'the needs of the ordinary man in the kraals have increased and are increasing rapidly', and 'the cost of living has gone high, while wages of native workers have remained low and stationary'. (28) The growing needs and expectations of Africans for consumer goods, for education, and for other goods and services, combined with the rise in the cost of living during the war, meant that 'an average wage of £3 a month becomes ridiculously inadequate'. (29) African mine workers and their families now required more food and clothing, and wished to provide education for their children, and they were unable to satisfy their needs and aspirations with the wages which they earned on the mines. (30)

Moreover, the African mine workers had dependents in the rural areas, who were totally affected by the rising cost of living, contrary to the allegation of the employers that the cost of living had risen less in these areas than on the Rand. This allegation was investigated by a Commission of Inquiry into the cost of living. It found that in 1918 the cost of living in the rural areas from which African mine workers came was as high as - and in some cases higher than - the cost of living on the Rand. Prices in Basutoland were roughly the same as those on the Rand, and in the Transkei they were much higher. (31)

Grievance over the stationary level of wages was fostered not only by the rising cost of living and a changing standard of living, but also by the wage increases secured by the white workers. African mine workers resented the fact that 'the wage of the white miner has been increased on the cost of living, but nothing of the sort took place with the natives'. (32) This representative of the African mine workers observed that:

Whenever there has been a European strike, you will find that the natives are always grumbling, because whenever the white miners strike, they converse with the boys underground, and tell them that they went on strike because of so and so, and got it, and the natives cannot understand why they should remain stationary in their wage, whereas the wage of the white man has always been increased. (33)

As the African workers' wage grievances intensified and as their efforts to secure wage increases and to improve their position met with repeated failure and repression, they became increasingly aware of and opposed to the structure of oppression and exploitation comprised by the exploitation colour bars of the employers, and their grievances and actions broadened to focus upon this structure

- upon the various exploitative labour and wage controls, such as were embodied in the pass system, the contract system, the compound system, the recruiting system and the wage minimisation system, which served to secure the extreme powerlessness and ultra-exploitation of African workers.

We observed this broadening of grievance occurring among African workers on the Rand during the war, and clearly shaping the development of the wage campaign from about 1918 onwards. It was the repression of their wage demands through the operation of the exploitation colour bars, combined with the simultaneous example of white workers freely organising and acting collectively, striking, and successfully securing gains, which more than any other factors 'structuralised' the consciousness and sense of grievance of African workers and their class behaviour.

We see this beginning to crystallise with the strike of African municipal workers on the Rand in 1918, which followed a similar but successful strike by white workers, and in the course of which many African workers were arrested for breaking their contracts. As a government report observed about this strike:

It is noticeable that the failure of this strike was attributed to the existence of the Pass Law and the system of registration of contracts under which they were unable lawfully to leave work at a day's notice as had been the case with certain European employees of the municipality who were on daily contracts. The avowed object of certain of their leaders has since been to abolish passes and contracts with a view to giving them freedom of action to paralyse the industrial world by strikes and to secure the objects they had in view. (34)

And we see the wage campaign of the African workers escalating in 1919 into a campaign against the forced labour system.

This campaign was thus indicative of a growing awareness of and opposition to the exploitation colour bars, which were increasingly seen to be responsible for the degree and continuity of exploitation of African workers. With the repression of the 1918 strike, the coercive contract system, with its criminal sanctions for breach of contract and its long term contracts (one month for non-mine workers, and a minimum of nine months for mine workers), came to be identified and attacked as a key part of the forced labour system. The fact that African workers had been sent to jail for breaking their contracts, an African leader declared, 'made the natives very bitter against the contract system'. (35) 'It is a grievance', a

Congress deputation told the government, 'that a man should not be at liberty to leave an employer when he so desires.' (36) The object of the contract system was 'to obtain cheap and enforced labour'. (37) Only if its coercive elements were abolished could there be 'free trade in labour'. (38) Meetings of African workers on the Rand demanded the abolition of criminal sanctions for breach of contract and of long term contracts. (39)

So also was the pass system identified and opposed as part of the forced labour system. As we observed, the escalation of the wage campaign in 1919 took the specific form of militant passive resistance against the pass system. This system, as was noted earlier on, served to regiment and control the mobility and freedom of African workers in various ways. One of its most unpopular aspects was its effect of reinforcing the many downward pressures on African wage rates by forcing African workers to find and accept employment within a short space of time. When Africans arrived in urban areas, they had to obtain a six day pass to find employment, and if they had not accepted employment within six days they were liable to arrest as 'loafers'. (And when they accepted employment, they had to enter into monthly contracts, the breaking of which constituted a criminal offence; African mine workers had to enter into contracts of a minimum period of nine months, and had to obtain a special pass to leave the mine compounds.)

The pass system thus enabled employers to - among other things - offer minimal wages, 'because', as a Congress leader pointed out, 'the unfortunate native is forced by the Pass Law to take anything that is offered to him'. (40) Because of this and other effects of the pass system, Africans felt that: 'The Pass Law is nothing but slavery and forced labour. It was made to force the natives to work.' (41) The President of the Transvaal Native Congress expressed the general feeling of Africans when he declared that:

> Those who try to beguile us into believing that the Pass Law is for our protection remind me of the blandishments addressed by the spider to the fly. . . . The pass system is a form of slavery. It eliminates all freedom. (42)

Africans also recognised that the African mine workers were constrained by a more extensive system of exploitative labour and wage controls than were the rest of the African workers - being subject as they were not only to the contract system and the pass system, but also to the mining industry's specific wage minimisation system, recruiting system and compound system.

Chapter 4

The wage minimisation system operated by the mining companies - the elimination of competitive wage determination, the standardisation of rates at a very low level, the restriction of piece-work earnings through the maximum average system, and the loafer ticket system of unpaid and extra-contractual labour - was, as we noted earlier, a source of acute grievance to the African mine workers. So too were the recruiting system and the compound system. African mine workers and their representatives attacked the recruiting system as being based on deliberate misrepresentation and the deliberate inducement of indebtedness among Africans. (43) The whole system of commissions, capitation fees and credit advances was seen to constitute a calculated incentive 'to encourage indebtedness' and to 'inducements by misrepresentations or other reprehensible means'. (44) Africans signing up for work in the mines were not informed about such things as the system of wage minimisation - such as having to do unpaid lashing and tramming work and such as the maximum average system, or about the various coercive labour controls. (45) These conditions of employment were not defined in the contract seen and signed by the African worker. (46) And the monopsonisation of recruiting was resented for the downward pressure which it exerted on African wage rates. (47) 'Recruiting', the Congress declared, 'should not be a monopoly for any corporation or group of men.' (48) Instead of being attracted to the mines by good wages and labour conditions, Africans found themselves pushed by economic necessity and pulled by a manipulative recruiting system, as a result of which 'the man is attracted to work under compulsion'. (49) The compound system was likewise attacked as part of an exploitative labour system. Africans often likened the compounds to jails, and the Congress declared that: 'There is no reason why any set of people should be placed in barracks simply because they are working men and single.' (50)

The system of labour exploitation operated by the gold mining companies over their African labour force was thus seen by Africans to be the most extreme and developed form of the general system of forced labour in South Africa, and was characterised by the Congress as something not far removed from slavery.

This object is a relic of the slave trade which civilised countries still practice under modified and conventional forms. Capitalists and others, consciously or unconsciously, are prone to adopt unsavoury methods in the acquirement and mobilisation of labour. Regulations are framed and designed to evade the essential formalities constituting slavery - regulations which in practice are indistinguishable from a traffic-in-human-flesh. Material benefits over-weigh human considerations. ... The labour contracts of the Witwatersrand Native Labour Association and the Native Recruiting Corporation are illustrations of elaborate chains of enforced labour under the pretext that the worker enters into these contracts voluntarily. It passes one's understanding how a man totally ignorant of civilised labour conditions can be said to have voluntarily accepted an intricate contract to which the full meaning, effect and purpose of the various provisions he is utterly dull; because a man agrees to go to work, he is taken to have accepted conditions placing him in the status of a human chattel, to be sold or bought at a price of the recruiter and to be loaded in cattle trucks . . . and then to be compounded in a certain mine . . . under a long contract of labour, and then to be penalised if he should move a yard outside the mining property without a pass. (51)

It was through the operation of the system of forced labour, the Congress declared, that the mining companies were able to keep African wages so low. (52)

As the African workers on the Rand became increasingly aware of and opposed to the forced labour system during this period, so too did they become increasingly conscious and resentful of the specific role played by the officials and armed forces of the State in maintaining and operating this system. African workers were struck by the fact that whenever they threatened or engaged in demonstrations and strike action, government officials and the police or the army - or both - were immediately called in by the employers, and invariably supported and enforced the interests of the employers, whereas this was not the case in the relations between the white workers and the employers. And the Department of Native Affairs, which was supposed to represent the interests of African workers, was increasingly seen and resented by African workers as an agency primarily concerned with protecting the interests of the employers and preserving the existing structure of class relations. 'That Department', a Congress official declared, at a conference with the government in 1919, 'claims to be our protector, but it fails to protect us. It is more concerned with protecting the interests of the employers.' (53) The Department always intervened to implement the coercive labour controls of the forced labour system, which prevented African workers from improving their position. 'The Native Affairs Department claims to be our protector. Yet they cannot help us to improve our position. Then, when we try to enforce our demands, the

Native Affairs Department steps in with its passes and prevents us.' (54) It was not surprising that, as Africans became more opposed to the forced labour system, their opposition should come to be directed as well against those who enforced the system, especially when these officials claimed to be representing their interests.

The growing sense of grievance which was manifesting itself in the unrest among African workers on the Rand during and following the First World War was thus initially and most essentially concerned with wages, but became 'structuralised' and directed against the whole system of forced labour and its exploitation colour bars, which African workers were increasingly identifying as responsible for their wage exploitation. By the end of the war, a marked degree of class consciousness had developed among African workers on the Rand, centred around this growing sense of structural injustice, expressing itself in militant protest and strike actions, and further fostered by the repression of these actions. It is significant that by 1919 the Transvaal Native Congress was defining the problem facing African workers in the following way. Their problem, it declared, was that they were subjugated by a particular economic system 'designed in our view purposely to a) obtain labour cheaply, b) to exploit the labourer's earnings regardless of benefits to himself, c) to retard his advancement as a worker'. (55) The Congress declared that:

> In our continued study we find that all industries are manipulated in such a way as to remain under the exclusive control and guidance of the few. Capital is used as a machinery to make excess profits, to exploit the labour of others, and to do or encourage very little which will relieve humanity or produce better conditions of living for the workers. What is called civilisation, in our view, is a system that 1) causes artificial ways of living, 2) manufactures suffering, 3) perpetuates slumdom, 4) creates a chronic state of poverty and want, 5) brings about cheap and sweated labour, 6) exploits the masses. (56)

This definition of the problem as a structural problem, as a class problem, and as an exploitation problem, was symptomatic of the growing class consciousness of African workers on the Rand, and of their growing sense of class oppression.

2 The African workers and the job colour bar

While the grievances of African mine workers, and of African workers generally on the Rand, centred around wages and the exploitation colour bars of the employers, African workers also felt and expressed grievances against the job colour bar and against the white workers. Grievances against the job colour bar itself came essentially from the minority of Africans possessing some education and skills, and these grievances were usually a form of wage grievance, based on the belief that employment in more skilled work would of itself mean higher earnings. In addition to the opposition of this minority to the job colour bar, there was a fairly widespread sense of grievance among African workers as a whole against the white workers - a discontent that was also closely tied to the issue of wages.

The more skilled and educated African mine workers resented the job colour bar as a restriction on their occupational mobility which they felt curtailed their earnings and status. Such workers, one of them stated, 'feel they would like to have the opportunity of filling some . . . responsible positions', and they wanted access to apprenticeships so that they could acquire skills. (57) An interpreter made a literal translation of one such African's view of the job colour bar:

He puts it this way - it is in the form of cattle put in a kraal and locked up there. They say they think they ought to be let out and go and find pastures somewhere, but the gate is closed. (58)

The justification often given for the job colour bar in the Mining Regulations, that it was a safety measure, was rejected. 'I think the common idea is that they are to protect life', an African leader stated, about the discriminatory Regulations, 'but I am sorry to say that we look upon that as camouflage.' (59) Safety measures, he affirmed, did not require racial discrimination. The more skilled African workers also saw no justification for the Status Quo Agreement, which they had resented during its application. (60)

The Transvaal Native Congress demanded that the job colour bar - 'any restriction or disability, legal or conventional, placed against any individual or section of the community from exercising his skill or ability in any employment to his material benefit' - in the gold mining industry and wherever else it existed should be abolished. (61) What it found particularly objectionable was the incorporation of the job colour bar into the law of the land. 'The State', it claimed, 'should be no party to

obstacles being placed in the way of natives rising to positions to which their industry and ability entitle them.' (62) The Congress declared that:
> Our people have a distinct place in this country: neither the white man nor any foreigner has a right to place an embargo on the native's ability to advance. . . . If the white community are under the idea that the native people will remain contented in the doing of the manual labour for all time, they are mistaken. You cannot give a man the education and then deprive him of the opportunity to improve and utilise his knowledge for his own advancement. (63)

The job colour bar rested, it alleged, on the 'prejudiced and selfish considerations' of the white workers, who 'want us and everybody to believe that there is a divine privilege for a white worker in labour'. (64) It favoured the removal of the job colour bar out of a conviction that this would improve the remuneration, satisfaction and productivity of non-white workers. (65)

While opposition to the job colour bar itself tended to be voiced mainly by the more skilled and educated Africans, there was fairly widespread resentment and hostility towards the white workers among the African mine workers as a whole. What was most resented by the latter was the high level of white wages in contrast to their own wages and in relation to the amount of work performed by white workers and African workers. The African workers had to work very hard, and deeply resented the fact that they received so little pay for this work, while white workers received much higher wages for far less arduous work. In the words of one African mine worker:
> The chief grievance is . . . that the white man does not do the actual work he is sent down for. He leaves the natives to do the work, and he sits on the stoop there, and when pay time comes the white man draws more than the native, who has done the work. . . . The chief trouble is that the natives do the work and that when it comes to pay, two men come to get the money and the man who gets most of the money is the white man and not the native. We do not very much complain about the white man getting more wages, but if he himself puts his own share into that work we would not complain. But why should he get so much pay for what the native does, while the native gets so little? (66)

African workers felt that the high level of white wages was not earned by the white workers, because most of the work was done by African workers.
> At present the white men do not do much work underground; the white men always sit on the boxes and the

natives do the work.

But someone has to direct the natives? - The boss-boys underground direct the natives what to do.

But the boss-boy gets directed again by the white man? - No, in some cases the boss-boy himself directs the native to do the work without the white man, because he knows the work thoroughly himself. (67)

African workers especially resented the fact that new and semi-skilled white workers could enter the industry and immediately receive high wages and be placed in authority over African workers who had been in employment for a long period and acquired certain skills. As one African declared:

> In regard to the point that the European is the overseer of the native, I would ask how it is that the teacher can teach the child when he has not been at school himself. A white man comes straight into the mine to supervise natives who have been working on that mine for years. He does not know as much as my little finger about the mining work, and these boys know it as well as they know their own names. Is not that an extraordinary sort of supervision? (68)

And to African workers, the job colour bar came to be seen as the bulwark of what they felt to be the unearned high level of white wages. As the Congress declared:

> We know that white miners advocate the existence of the colour bar because it helps to maintain the artificial wages for which they do not give equivalent in labour. The colour bar places a certain value on the colour or social class of the man rather than on the skill or efficiency of the worker. In this artificial way, the white miner not above manual labour in efficiency puts himself in a position of an aristocrat who by reason of his birth and money inherently claims to be entitled to all earned and unearned profits. The white miner does not actually earn in labour all the money he gets; he sits on the bucket stool or a stone and points with the fore finger or pipe. We hear of many circumstances where he is taught his work by the black miner under him. This circumstance he calls the 'white standard', by which he means the maintenance of artificial wages, for part of which he does not give or actually render labour. (69)

Another source of discontent among African workers against the white workers, besides the wage differential, was the domineering behaviour of many white workers. African workers complained of being assaulted by whites while working underground, while waiting to work and while coming up from work, and they alleged that this was often done by whites in responsible positions, such as mine captains, and that it was often overlooked by the management. (70) How extensive this behaviour was, it is difficult to ascertain. Reported cases of assault were not very numerous, but such incidents often went unreported. (71) At any rate, it was a fairly prominent grievance of African workers.

Another source of grievance against the white workers lay in the fact that, while the loafer ticket system was initiated and operated by the mining companies, through the Native Recruiting Corporation, it was the white miner who had to mark off shift tickets. This gave the white worker considerable power which, African workers complained, was sometimes abused, with African workers being arbitrarily deprived of shift pay and shift recognition for contract. This power was, according to one report, 'a fruitful source of complaint amongst the native labourers', for it constituted 'a means in the hands of unscrupulous or vindictive miners of "scoring off the native"'. (72) Linguistic differences also contributed to tensions between African and white workers. As the Congress observed:

> The miner has no knowledge of the native language: in giving directions he often points with his finger, speaking English. The native does wrong because he did not understand the directions. The miner gets angry and is tempted to use a blow. Where people work together they must have mutual means of understanding each other. (73)

Not surprisingly, the perpetuation of the job colour bar and of the large differential between white and African wages, together with the domineering behaviour of many white workers, produced antagonism among African workers against the white workers, and discouraged feelings of working class solidarity. African workers came to have no qualms of conscience about undercutting workers who on the whole showed no solidarity with them. Thus when a white trade unionist expressed fears concerning the danger of undercutting of white workers by Africans, an African worker replied: 'We are fighting our own battles and the white man is fighting his own battle. He does not consider us, and we do not consider him in this respect if I may say so.' (74) The white trade unions were looked upon with hostility. 'You say you are fighting those who are injuring you and by that you mean the white trades unionist? - Yes.' (75) 'The main thing', another African stated, 'is we want our people to be employed so as to earn a living, and the trade unions seem to be trying to drive us out gradually.' (76)

African workers thus came to have little sympathy for the protectionist claims of the white workers. The white workers, in their eyes, enjoyed considerable power, but used it in a conservative and selfish manner, and thereby forfeited any right to the sympathy and co-operation of African workers.

After all, what is the position of the white worker? He has behind him all the 20 centuries of civilisation, all the superiority in knowledge, all the assistance and sympathy of capitalists, the whole weapon of the franchise in politics, and the complete support of a selfish white public opinion - and yet in spite of all these fortifications he has the weakness to resort to gagging regulations or customs in order to bolster up an artificial superiority only against an ignorant man. If today in his own superior sphere, he fears the competition of a man just emerging from barbarism with hardly half a century of civilisation in his name or history, then the white man must be conscious that all his fortifications stand on a withering reed. (77)

While this observation ignored the class problems of the white workers, it did express a widespread feeling of African workers that the job colour bar, as it was actually used historically, represented a selfish use of power: a bitterness over the fact that the white workers were merely concerned with protecting themselves against the effects of the forced labour system, and not with helping to liberate African workers from it and thus acting upon the causes of the structural insecurity which they held to justify the job colour bar. It was in response to the conservatism and elitism of the white workers, embodied in their strategy of merely offsetting effects while doing nothing about their causes, that the predominant feelings of African workers about the job colour bar and the white workers were feelings of resentment and hostility.

Summary of part two

Following from, and in the light of, the class analysis of the racial system developed in the first part of the study, the second part went on to look at some important historical events and developments concerning this system and the groups involved in it.

It was particularly concerned with the historical relations and conflict between the two white groups operating the system. This conflict was seen and explained not as a conflict between the forces of economic rationality and social irrationality (as it conventionally has been), but as a class struggle over the specific mode of operation of a class system of racial discrimination, over the relative scope of operation of the class colour bars.

This struggle, which is an on-going feature of South African history since the late nineteenth century, went through a particularly turbulent phase during and following the First World War. We saw how, in response to specific historical developments and class conditions, each group sought to maximise the benefits and minimise the costs which it derived from the racial system, by extending the scope of operation of its own class colour bar and reducing the scope of operation of the other group's. And we observed how and why this led to conflict.

We saw how the white workers, in response to intensifying insecurity, came to extend the job colour bar, in the Status Quo Agreement of 1918. We saw how the mining companies, in response to an intensifying profitability crisis, came to seek to resolve this crisis through a reduction of the scope of the job colour bar and a maximisation of the ultra-exploitation of non-white labour. We saw how this led to the strike and upheaval of 1922. We saw how the companies, emerging victorious from this confrontation, did proceed to reduce the scope of the job colour bar, in a comprehensive reorganisation of labour in the mines. We saw how, in response to this and other threats to their security and livelihood, the white workers came to strengthen their position and to reinforce the job colour bar through political and State measures, with the election of the Pact government, its protectionist labour policies, and the 'Colour Bar Act' of 1926.

The class analysis of the racial system developed in the first part of the study helps us to understand and explain these historical developments. And at the same time, these developments may be said to manifest the class nature and dynamics of the system, and thus in some way to confirm the validity of this analysis. What we are seeing here, as in so much of modern South African history, is a class struggle over the distribution of the various costs and benefits deriving to different white groups from the operation of the different class colour bars, an historical manifestation of the diverse socio-economic roots and functions of the system of discrimination, and of the contradictions built into it.

We then went on to look at the historical behaviour and treatment of the group over which the system operated, the African workers. We observed the growing unrest among African workers on the Rand. We examined the basic grievances underlying this unrest, noting that chief among these were the extremely low wage level, and the employers' system of forced labour which was responsible for this. We observed the effective historical operation of this system, as it helped to resolve the class problems of the mining capitalists by repressing the attempts of African workers to improve their position.

Conclusions

In concluding the study, this section critically examines the school of thought which has predominated in the study of race relations in South Africa and of South African history and society in general, and then reviews the findings and approach of this study.

1

It was observed, in the introduction to the study, that while the system of racial domination in South Africa has not lacked attention as an object of inquiry, the explanation of this system, and of the course of history in South Africa, has, generally speaking, not been taken very far. This, it was suggested, and as we shall now go on to consider, may be said to reflect problems in the approach taken by inquiry.

When we consider the inquiry which has taken place into South Africa, what is important, theoretically, is to elucidate the specific theoretical framework within which inquiry has proceeded, its formal framework ('history', 'economics', 'sociology', etc.) notwithstanding. While such inquiry has pursued various approaches, there is a particular school of thought which has predominated and continues to, and it is to an examination of its specific nature and limitations that we now turn.

When considered analytically, much inquiry may be seen to proceed - with varying degrees of explicitness, and regardless of its formal disciplinary framework - within a common theoretical framework, and to articulate a common general thesis. This thesis may be summarised as the view that the system of racial domination in South Africa is to be seen as some kind of 'dysfunctional' abnormality, which is to be explained essentially by the particular racial and ethnic composition of South Africa. And this framework may be seen to comprise a blend of neo-classical economics and of a kind of ethnological determinism which currently takes the form of 'pluralism'.

This framework is made up of two stages. In the first occurs the initial characterisation of the object of inquiry - the South African social formation and system of racial domination, and in this stage, inquiry proceeds within the theoretical framework of neo-classical economics. The social formation is characterised as having comprised two parts - a harmonious, just, 'functional' part (the system of group relations constituted by the capitalist economic system), and a 'dysfunctional' part (the system of racial domination); and the latter is portrayed as a 'dysfunctional' intrusion upon the former from somewhere outside of it (i.e., the explanation for the system of racial domination is to be found somewhere outside of the economic system), while at the same time the economic system is pictured as fundamentally alien to and subversive of the 'ascriptive' system of racial domination, because of such things as 'market laws' and 'economic rationality'.

While underlying all inquiry within this school of thought, this stage is most explicitly articulated and elaborated in the work of economists (who have written most of what socio-economic history of modern South Africa there has been), such as Horwitz, Hutt, Doxey, Van der Horst, Robinson, Houghton and Wilson. They polarise the social formation into the two compartments - the economic system and the system of racial domination, the 'economy' and the 'polity', the 'economic factor' and the 'political factor', the 'market economy' and 'an administered society', 'free enterprise' and 'étatisme', 'the industrial economy' and 'the racial pattern', and so on. And the relationship between them is pictured as essentially 'dysfunctional'. (1) Thus, as one of these economists puts it:

> The inescapable conclusion . . . is that private enterprise in mining and industry . . . has tended to work wholly for the material advancement (and indirectly the social benefit) of the African people. The intervention of the centralised State, on the other hand, has worked almost entirely in the opposite direction. . . . It is difficult to imagine a better illustration than is provided by South Africa of the truth that the fight against colour injustice is actually against the consequences of planning on the collectivist model. . . . Effective colour bars which have denied economic opportunities and condemned non-whites to be 'hewers of wood

and drawers of water' have all been created in response to demands for State intervention. . . . The dissolution of colour injustice has been continuously assisted by competitive capitalism. (2)

The distinctive theoretical feature of this first stage of the predominant approach is thus the functionalist and dualist nature of its characterisation of the social formation and system of racial domination. The functionalist aspect lies in the portrayal of the system of racial domination as a 'dysfunctional' intrusion upon an allegedly harmonious and just system of group relations constituted by the economic system. This has not been articulated within the formal framework of functionalist sociology, but reflects the functionalist nature of the sociological framework of neo-classical economics. Although formally conceived of as 'economics', neo-classical economics, like any economics, has a specific sociological content, and the specific sociological content of neo-classical economics, comprising as it does a picture of capitalist society as the normal human society and as an objectively harmonious and consensual system of group relations, in which all individuals are equal beneficiaries from the existence and operation of the 'market economy' and from economic growth within such an economy, may be said to be of a functionalist type. It is specifically in virtue of this framework that the system of racial domination is characterised as a 'dysfunctional' abnormality.

Another distinctive feature of this initial stage of the approach is its dualism. The dualism of neo-classical economics refers to its theoretical approach to the phenomenon of regional under-development. This approach pictures the development of the developed sector and the under-development of the under-developed sector as causally unrelated (i.e. the explanation for under-development is to be found outside the economic system of the developed sector), pictures the economic system of the developed sector as a cause of development, and defines the problem of under-development as a lack of integration into and possession of the economic system of the developed sector. Precisely the same tendency characterises the first stage of the predominant approach towards the analysis of race relations in South Africa. The 'under-development' of the non-whites is pictured as causally unrelated to the capitalist economic system, the latter is pictured as an agent of development, and the problem of the 'under-development' of the non-whites is defined as a lack of sufficient integration into and participation in this economic system, because of the 'dysfunctional' intervention of 'the political factor' of the system of racial domination.

This school of thought thus proceeds initially within the analytical framework of neo-classical economics, and involves a functionalist and dualist initial characterisation of the social formation and racial system. Needless to say, this determines and circumscribes the direction of further inquiry. The fundamental limitations of this stage of the approach will be considered shortly.

Having progressed through this stage, inquiry has then been faced with the problem of providing a specific explanation of the very evident 'peculiar' - and allegedly 'dysfunctional' - feature of the situation: the system of racial domination. Given the functionalist nature of the sociological framework of neo-classical economics, inquiry proceeding within it has been unable to explain the fundamentally conflictual, coercive and non-consensual system of group relations constituted by the system of racial domination. All that inquiry has done in this first stage is to circumscribe the area of possible explanation, by saying where the explanation for this system is not to be found - it is not to be found in the economic system, it is a 'dysfunctional' intrusion upon the economic system from somewhere outside of it. Where, then, is it to be found? How has inquiry then proceeded to explain this system?

There has been no one single answer to this question. But there has been a general tendency towards a particular type of explanation, and this has been dominated by a specific outlook, which constitutes the second stage of the predominant approach.

The general tendency has been towards an idealist type of explanation - that is, explanation of social structure and social change essentially in terms of subjective attitudes and beliefs. This has expressed itself in a general preoccupation with such areas as individual and social psychology, ideology and ethnicity - a preoccupation with such factors as prejudice, racism and nationalism. Within this general approach, a specific tendency has predominated - the tendency to 'explain' the system of racial domination in terms of what amounts to a kind of ethnological determinism, which currently takes the form of 'pluralism' - specifically, the concept of 'social and cultural pluralism'.

Leading exponents of the pluralist approach towards the analysis of group relations in South Africa, such as Van den Berghe and Rex, recognise that the functionalist model of society, with its concept of consensual and harmonious social stratification, is not only of limited value for the analysis of those societies to which it has been applied, but is quite definitely inadequate for the explanation of social systems - such as the one in South Africa - characterised by extremely coercive, non-consensual and conflictual group differentiation and stratification. (3) The concept of social and cultural pluralism is then proposed as a more adequate means of explaining the system of group relations in South Africa. Space does not permit any comprehensive discussion of pluralism here; what is specifically intended is a brief assessment and critique of the analytical role which it plays in the school of thought which we are considering.

The concept of social and cultural pluralism (as opposed to the 'equilibrium' concept of pluralism prevalent in political science) comprises the model of a particular type of society. Societies characterised by social and cultural pluralism, according to Kuper and Smith, are

societies possessed of a minimum of common values . . . maintained more by coercion than by consent . . . divided by sharp and persistent cleavages, which threaten their dissolution. . . . The terms refer to societies with sharp cleavages between different population groups brought together within the same political unit. The characteristic expressions of pluralism . . . take the form of dissension and of conflict between racial, tribal, religious and regional groups; and the system is maintained by domination, regulation and force. (4)

Certain societies are thus said to be 'plural' societies - societies which are extensively segmented into institutionally distinct groups along racial or ethnic lines in a dominational system of group relations. (5) Because South Africa fits this description, it is therefore defined and described as a plural society, characterised by compartmentalisation into four institutionally distinct 'colourcastes' and by a racist ideology. (6)

Where precisely does the concept of social and cultural pluralism get us, as far as explanation is concerned? Just what the explanatory value of this concept is supposed to be is by no means obvious. What we are confronted with essentially, in this concept, is an extensive definition, description and classification of a particular type of society. The problem is not that societies of this type do not exist. They obviously do, and one such society was and is certainly to be found in South Africa. The problem is, what has describing a society as a 'plural' society explained? What is the nature of the explanation advanced by the concept of social and cultural pluralism?

The significant phrase in the above-cited definition of social and cultural pluralism is the phrase 'racial, tribal, religious and regional groups', and, more generally, the statement that 'the characteristic expressions of pluralism . . . take the form of dissension and of conflict between racial, tribal, religious and regional groups'. The distinctive theoretical feature of the concept of social and cultural pluralism is not its preoccupation with social heterogeneity and conflict (despite the stress which is laid on this, to differentiate it from functionalist sociology). For in the general spectrum of social theory, such a preoccupation is in itself, of course, no innovation at all. It is this preoccupation with 'racial, tribal, religious and regional groups' which is notable, and it is this insistent implication that there is some kind of necessary causal connection between the characteristics described as typical of the plural society and 'racial, tribal, religious and regional groups' which constitutes the theoretical specificity of the concept of social and cultural pluralism. And when we examine the nature of pluralist explanation, we may observe that it is characterised by a kind of ethnological determinism, and is of a tautological nature.

This is what we find in the pluralist analysis of South Africa - in Van den Berghe's analysis of South Africa, for instance, which is a good example of the school of thought we are considering, and of its pluralist type of explanation. South African society is said to be a society of 'colour-castes', which are said to be 'based' (what this means is unclear) on 'conflict', and the cause of the lack of consensus is said to be 'racism'. This conflict is said to be about 'power', and this conflict over power 'cannot be dissociated from' (what this means is unclear) certain ethnic and racial groups in the situation - Afrikaners, English and Africans. South African society is said to comprise 'a triangle of forces in which the Afrikaners, the English and the Africans represent the three antagonistic poles', and these groups constitute 'the basic triangle of forces in the South African power struggle'. We thus have both 'colour-castes' 'based' on 'conflict', and 'ethnic forces' at different 'antagonistic poles'. It is these groupings which are said to be the analytically significant forms of group differentiation for the explanation of the social system. Classes 'in the Marxian sense of relationships to the means of production . . . are not meaningful social realities'. Then what is characterised as the 'political and economic dualism' of South Africa (the neo-classical element of the predominant approach) is analysed and explained as the product of this 'social and cultural pluralism' of 'colour-castes' and 'ethnic forces'. The system of group relations and racial domination in South Africa is thus ultimately 'explained' by the existence of 'social and cultural pluralism', which, it is said, 'often fosters acute conflict'. (7)

This 'explanation' does not, however, really take us very far. When considered critically, this pluralist type of explanation may be said to amount not to an explanation at all but merely to a tautological redescription of the phenomenon to be explained, which treats as given and as an explanation precisely what needs to be explained - the specific form and system of 'social and cultural pluralism' in South Africa. Characterising the South African social system as a 'plural' society and as a 'caste' society does not explain anything. It is merely an extended description of what needs to be explained. Why are there what are referred to as 'colour-castes'? It cannot be 'because there are colour-castes'.

This is the problem which runs right through the 'analytic framework' of pluralism. Conditions are extensively defined and described but not explained. A complex descriptive model is developed which has little if any explanatory value. Thus we are told that a characteristic feature of a 'plural' society is that 'always, wherever differential incorporation prevails, one institutionally distinct sector dominates the others', (8) and that a definitive feature of such a society is that it is made up of racial, tribal, religious or regional groups, and that classes 'are not meaningful social realities'. But how is the former condition to be explained? And what is the analytical justification and significance of the latter standpoint? The important issue is not the observation of 'domination by an institutionally distinct group' but the explanation of this condition: why has a specific institutionally distinct group become dominant in a specific situation at a specific time? And the important issue is not the observation of coercive racial and ethnic group differentiation, but the explanation of such differentiation: why have such forms of group differentiation become 'meaningful social realities' in specific situations at specific times?

But the 'analytic framework' of pluralism is incapable of answering these crucial questions, because nowhere within it is there to be found any social theory capable of answering them and of giving its analytical model explanatory power. Pluralist analysis essentially comprises extensive definition, classification and description. All that it offers in the way of explanation is a tautological redescription of the phenomenon to be explained, in terms of a kind of ethnological determinism. Of course it goes without saying that such criteria of group differentiation as race and ethnicity may be significant causal determinants in their own right in a specific social formation for specific reasons. But it is these specific reasons and the specific nature of the social formation which require elucidation. What is invalid about the approach of 'social and cultural pluralism' - and about the analytically equivalent tendency which has long preceded the advent of the concept of 'social and cultural pluralism' - is the treatment of ethnic and racial forms of group differentiation as given and as the key explanatory variable, and the substitution of tautological redescription for explanation. It is not South Africa's 'social and cultural pluralism' which explains its system of group relations - they are the same thing; it is South Africa's 'socially and culturally pluralist' system of group relations which needs to be explained.

The theoretical framework of the school of thought we are considering may thus be said to comprise a particular synthesis of two specific approaches - that of neo-classical functionalism and dualism, and that of pluralism (or its analytical equivalent). There have been other tendencies as well, of course, but these have been dominant. And while they may be distinguished from each other for purposes of analysis, they invariably occur together in the particular blend which this school of thought comprises.

Thus the 'sociological' analysis of a sociologist like Van den Berghe partly comprises a typical articulation of neo-classical functionalism and dualism. A chapter suitably entitled 'The economic system and its dysfunctions' pictures South Africa as initially a 'normal', capitalist, industrialising society, which 'deviated' from the norm, because of the 'dysfunctional' operation of the system of racial domination 'in a maladjusting direction', so that the South African social system came to be - and is to be seen and explained as - 'an equilibrium system that has run amok'. (9) Similarly, the 'economic' analysis of the economists involves a typical articulation of the pluralist type of explanation. The system of domination in South Africa is, according to Horwitz, to be explained essentially by the ethnic and racial differentiations in South Africa. For Horwitz, as for this whole school of thought, the key explanatory factor is 'Afrikanerdom'; virtually everything is to be explained by 'Afrikanerdom'. (10) The main explanation of the system of domination, according to Van der Horst, is to be found in cultural differentiations and race attitudes, and their specific reflections in prejudice and law. (11)

This blend is, of course, only to be expected, for the two tendencies well complement each other, in the internal dynamic of this school of thought. The basic picture of the social formation is rooted and articulated within the functionalist and dualist framework of neo-classical economics, in terms of which the system of racial domination is characterised as a 'dysfunctional' intrusion upon the harmonious system of group relations constituted by the capitalist economic system. This framework is unable, however, specifically to explain the coercive and non-consensual system of group differentiation constituted by the system of racial domination; but what it does do is to locate the explanation somewhere outside of this economic system. At this point, recourse is made to a pluralist type of explanation, which provides an 'explanation' which does recognise the coercive nature of the system of group differentiation and which does locate the explanation outside of the economic system, in South Africa's 'social and cultural pluralism'.

2

The fact that inquiry has been so unsuccessful in relation to the problem of explanation may be attributed in large measure to the fact that this school of thought, within which most inquiry has proceeded, does not provide and is unable to provide an adequate explanation of the system and history of group relations in South Africa, nor, in particular, of the genesis, nature, dynamics and continuity of the system of racial domination.

We have noted that the pluralist type of explanation which it eventually produces does not in fact provide an explanation at all, but merely amounts to a tautological redescription of the phenomenon to be explained. We may go on to observe that the explanatory inadequacy of this approach may be traced back to, and is rooted in, its initial, neo-classical stage. The initial characterisation of the social formation and system of racial domination within and in terms of the functionalist and dualist analytical framework of neo-classical economics is profoundly inaccurate. And no successful explanation can follow from such an inaccurate initial characterisation of the object of inquiry.

Just why inquiry has initially proceeded in this way is an interesting question. For this initial delineation of the object of inquiry could hardly be further removed from the salient features of the empirical evidence. Of these features, we may note the following: the enormous economic expansion which has taken place in the allegedly 'dysfunctional' social system, the continuity of the system of racial domination in the midst of this economic expansion, and the extensive involvement of property owners in the system of racial domination. These are features of South African history which, it must be agreed, stand out with considerable prominence. These features do not accord, however, with the predominant picture, and they suggest very strongly that the nature of the relationship between the system of racial domination and the economic system has been altogether different from that portrayed by this picture.

Given the vast economic growth and industrialisation which have taken place in South Africa during the twentieth century, and given the concomitant continuity and consolidation of the system of racial domination, it clearly makes little sense to begin by characterising the relationship between this system and the economic system as essentially 'dysfunctional'. Still less sense does this make in view of the extensive determination of the system of racial domination by property owners, notably in such forms of racial discrimination as the coercive labour controls of the contract system, the pass system and the compound system, and the various discriminatory property laws.

These salient features require explanation, and are vital clues in the search for the explanation of the system of racial domination. They suggest very strongly that there has been something highly functional and causally significant about the relationship between the economic system and the system of racial domination. But these clues, with all that they suggest, are not taken up by an approach which begins by insisting, in terms of a functionalist and dualist framework, that the relationship is essentially 'dysfunctional'. What is obviously required is an approach which begins by recognising these features and their importance, and which sets out to explain them and to elucidate their significance for the explanation of the system of racial domination. But the predominant approach does not constitute such an approach, and its initial characterisation of the situation provides a fundamentally inaccurate picture of it.

Thus, for instance, it is only within the initially functionalist framework of this approach that it could be said, of the relations between capital and non-white labour in South Africa, that 'white capital and entrepreneurship cooperate with non-white labour', (12) or that the ultra-low level of non-white wages could be explained as having been due to 'the market realities of demand, supply and marginal productivity', (13) or that the deprivations suffered by non-whites in South Africa in the twentieth century could be explained in such terms as:

'The Government was, however, so concerned with the poor white problem that little attention was paid to the poverty of other races.' (14)

And it is this initial characterisation of the situation which accounts for the marked preoccupation of the predominant approach with the job colour bar. For once it is assumed that economic growth within the capitalist economic system would have been synonymous with economic development (in the sense of the maximisation of social justice) had it not been for the 'dysfunctional' operation of the system of racial discrimination, it follows logically that the latter is assessed essentially in terms of its alleged 'dysfunctionality' for economic growth and 'economic rationality', and its most important aspect is thus defined as the job colour bar (because of its effect of preventing employers from making the most productive and profitable utilisation of ultra-cheap (non-white) labour).

Thus it is a characteristic and distinctive feature of this school of thought that it invariably defines and refers to the job colour bar simply as 'the colour bar'. And in its assessment of the economic operation of the system of racial discrimination, it is 'the colour bar' which receives virtually all attention. Attention is focused on 'the industrial colour bar', 'the economics of the colour bar', the effects of 'the colour bar' on economic growth, 'the colour bar' and 'rigidities in the labour market', 'the colour bar' as a cause of ultra-low non-white wages, 'the colour bar' as the primary problem and grievance of non-white workers, and so on. (15) And the particular historical situation with which this study has been concerned is seen essentially in these terms - as a conflict about the job colour bar, as a conflict between the forces of 'economic rationality' (allegedly represented by the mining companies in their attack against the job colour bar), and those of 'irrational colour prejudice' (allegedly represented by the white workers in their operation of the job colour bar). (16)

What is always of cardinal importance for this school of thought, in its assessment of the system of racial domination, is thus the tendency of 'the colour bar' to 'prevent the development and full use of one of South Africa's greatest resources, the labour of her native population'. (17) It is 'the colour bar' which is defined as the main problem and as the most significant part of this system, because of its effect of 'holding back an otherwise attainable increase in productivity of black workers'. (18)

But this preoccupation with the job colour bar is far from justified, and is a manifestation of the kind of distortion produced in the neo-classical stage of the predominant approach. In its concentration of attention on the involvement of the white workers in the system of racial domination, and in its obliviousness to the extensive determination and operation of the system by the capitalist class, this preoccupation comprises a thoroughly inaccurate picture of the system of racial domination. And the degree of importance which it attributes to the job colour bar as a problem, both as an obstruction of economic growth and as a form of social injustice, is unwarranted. The job colour bar has certainly not prevented an enormous amount of economic expansion from taking place in South Africa. And non-white workers have suffered far more from the exploitation colour bars of the employers than from the job colour bar of the white workers, and their grievances have always centred not around the job colour bar and their more productive employment in the prevailing system of production, but around the forced labour system and their ultra-exploitable position in, and ultra-exploitation by, that system of production. The long established and still predominant preoccupation with the job colour bar and the more productive employment of non-white labour may be said to be a preoccupation with the interests not of non-white workers but of employers, a preoccupation not with social justice but with capital accumulation.

As if in recognition of the incongruity of the predominant approach with the salient features of the evidence, Van den Berghe ends his analysis of 'the economic system and its dysfunctions' with 'an obvious question that seems to invalidate our analysis', namely: 'If the South African economy is so ridden with conflict and malfunction, why does it, far from collapsing, even continue to expand?' The answer to this question is said to reside in such factors as geology and geography, 'a mild Mediterranean climate', cheap labour, and the willingness of business and the government 'to compromise', all of which mean that 'the apparent contradiction just raised is thus easily resolved'. (19) The apparent contradiction is, however, not so easily resolved, and is as substantial as it is apparent. A factor like 'cheap labour', which is so fleetingly referred to despite its salience in the situation, is a factor which requires systematic attention, pointing, as do those features already mentioned, to the 'functionality' of the system of racial domination for the capitalist system in South Africa. But such attention is not forthcoming from an approach which insists on portraying the system of racial domination as a 'dysfunctional' intrusion upon the capitalist system from somewhere outside of it.

215 Conclusions

The explanatory inadequacy of the school of thought we are considering may thus be said not only to reside in its pluralist type of explanation, but to be rooted in its underlying neo-classical characterisation of the object of inquiry. The neo-classically functionalist and dualist characterisation of the social formation and system of racial domination is empirically inaccurate and analytically undynamic. It precludes any systematic recognition and investigation of certain salient features of the evidence - features which are important clues for the explanation of the system of racial domination, and it leads inquiry completely away from what will be suggested is the most important causal determinant of the system of racial domination, namely, the system of production and its constituent class structure.

3

The prevailing, 'liberal' approach to the history and social system of South Africa is thus seriously inadequate, and does not provide an accurate account or valid explanation of the system of racial domination. A more valid and fruitful approach would seem to lie in the one pursued in this study. This sees and explains the racial system not as some dysfunctional intrusion on the economic system from such outside, non-material factors as prejudice, racism and 'social and cultural pluralism', but as a system generated and determined by the economic system of which it formed a part.

Focusing on the South African racial system as it developed and was institutionalised in the gold mining industry, the study analysed and explained this system as a class system - as a system of class instruments, produced and determined in its specific form, nature and functions, by the capitalist system of production and its constituent class structure, and it examined and explained the turbulent course of historical events around the time of the First World War in terms of this class analysis.

In its first part, the study thus found and elucidated a definite set of linkages between the capitalist system of production, of which the groups operating the system of racial discrimination formed a part, the specific class problems and interests deriving to these groups from their specific positions in this system and the South African social formation, and the specific involvement of these groups in racial discrimination. The system of racial discrimination was seen to be generated by this system of production, via these group positions, problems and interests. And the various forms of discrimination were seen and identified as instruments, referred to as class colour bars, of the groups operating them (the capitalists and the white workers), which served to resolve these class problems, and which also were seen to have the effect of both extending and mediating class contradictions.

Following from and in the light of this structuralist Marxist class analysis of the system of racial discrimination, the study then went on to examine and explain the historical behaviour and relations of the groups operating the system (capitalists and white workers) and the group over which it operated (non-white workers), during a period when this system was itself the object of acute historical tension and conflict (during and following the First World War). These historical developments were seen to manifest and to confirm the class nature of the system of racial discrimination, especially the conflict between the two white 'operator' groups. This conflict, which is conventionally seen as a conflict between the forces of 'economic rationality' and 'irrational colour prejudice, racism and discrimination', was seen and explained as a class struggle over the specific mode of operation of the class system of racial discrimination, over the relative scope of operation of the different and contradictory class colour bars, over the distribution of the costs and benefits accruing to these groups from the system. This class struggle (as well as the historical behaviour of and treatment of the African workers during this period) were seen as a particularly clear historical manifestation of the specific, class nature of the involvement of these groups in racial discrimination, and thus of the specific, class nature of this system.

The specific nature of the racial system, its specific class nature, was thus deciphered and elucidated by analysis both of the structure of social relations and of the course of historical events, by analysis of structural relations and contradictions, and of their historical manifestation in historical events and conflict.

In conclusion, I hope that this study may demonstrate the value of a Marxist approach in the 'race relations' and minority groups area. Whatever else it may or may not do, this approach certainly elucidates a level of social reality and a kind of causal determination (at the level of the specific system of production within which the phenomena to be explained are situated) which are clearly very important, but which are neglected by the prevailing approach, in ways already observed.

Since the 'Marxist' approach is often perceived and

practised in a simplistic manner, however, it is important to distinguish what this work is and is not saying about it. Because it is saying that racial discrimination in South Africa has had a lot to do with capitalism, it is not saying that the Marxist approach just amounts to some kind of simple linking of all minority group phenomena to capitalism. This study has definitely been concerned with capitalism. It has sought to bring to light a whole system of linkages between capitalism and its constituent groups, on the one hand, and a system of racial domination, on the other, and to decipher historical events in these terms. But this has been an implementation of a more general concern, a concern not with capitalism per se but with capitalism as a system of production.

It is a crude and untenable position to try to analyse and explain all minority group phenomena, such as racial discrimination, simply in terms of capitalism, colonialism and imperialism. Certainly these have been decisive factors, which were ignored by inquiry, and had to be and still have to be emphasised, and their decisiveness emphasised, as this study has done. (Though their role has to be carefully unravelled rather than dogmatically asserted.) But therein does not reside the theoretical specificity of Marxist social science. This is to be found in its dialectical and historical materialism, and its general theory about the nature and significance of the system of production in any given social formation.

Such a system of production may be post-capitalist as well as capitalist and pre-capitalist. The principles of dialectical and historical materialism do not suddenly lose their relevance and power when no longer having to do with capitalism and class (despite the implication of some Marxist work). And social inequality and minority group forms of it are not confined to pre-capitalist and capitalist systems (although extensively involved with them). They are to be found in post-capitalist societies. The road which passes through the South African gold mines also passes through the Siberian labour camps. And those who travel this road in pursuit of understanding must travel the whole road. This road does present some difficult problems of explanation for Marxist (as well as non-Marxist) science, problems which are not insurmountable nor insurmounted, but which do require more than a simplistic characterisation of Marxist sociology in terms of capitalism and class. Like capitalism, class is a secondary concept, deriving from a more fundamental theoretical level. Marxist science arrives at capitalism and class, it does not begin with them. And while dialectical and historical materialism may assume the specific form of class analysis, it is not necessarily confined to that, and is re-articulable in more general structuralist and other terms.

A quasi-Marxist, quasi-structuralist approach may hopefully contribute something of value in the 'race relations' and minority groups area, where there has been and remains a need for it to be more fully explored. But it is not perfect or infallible, and is merely one of many paths into the great complexity of social life, all of which should be pursued.

Notes

INTRODUCTION

1 In this study, the terms 'white' and 'non-white' are used historiographically, i.e. as they were (and are) used in South Africa, and of course not in any literal sense. Because of frequency, however, they are not placed in inverted commas throughout, as they are above, although this is the sense, be it here noted, in which they are being used in this work.

2 E.g. A. Jensen, 'Genetics and Education' (London: 1972); H. Eysenck, 'Race, Intelligence and Education' (London: 1971). In critique, e.g. K. Richardson, D. Spears and M. Richards (eds), 'Race, Culture and Intelligence' (London: 1972).

Much of the former kind of work may be interpreted as a form of, rather than refutation of, socio-environmental explanation. For example, serious socio-environmental deprivation may have all kinds of relatively deep and permanent ill-effects on individuals (including biological effects, as nutritional research is bringing to light), negatively affecting the development of intelligence and other faculties, and showing up in such things as low IQ scores. And obviously in so far as such deprivation is the common experience of a given group, e.g. racial group, so would such effects be common in that group. Data about such things as 'intelligence' in individuals and groups may thus validly be interpreted as socio-environmental effects, as a manifestation of socio-environmental factors, rather than being, as the genetic determinists conclude, signs of innate group differences and inequalities (a scientifically quite unjustified leap, all the odder from people who insist that they, unlike environmentalists, are really scientists). But as long as such work parades about in the guise of genetic determinism, it does present some kind of formal (and political) challenge to environmentalism, despite this actual compatibility with it.

3   In other work I have analysed South Africa today in terms of this approach, and developed a critique of the conventional wisdom that 'economic growth is making nonsense of apartheid and bringing social justice to South Africa'. See F.A. Johnstone, White prosperity and white supremacy in South Africa today, 'African Affairs', vol.69, no.275, 1970; and F.A. Johnstone, Economic growth, apartheid and social injustice in South Africa (forthcoming). See also the work of M. Legassick and H. Wolpe.

CHAPTER 1

(A) The mining companies and the system of racial discrimination

1   On the rise and importance of the gold mining industry, see such works as S.H. Frankel, 'Capital Investment in Africa' (London: 1938); L. Katzen, 'Gold and the South African Economy: The Influence of the Gold Mining Industry on Business Cycles and Economic Growth in South Africa, 1886-1961' (Cape Town: 1964); C.W. de Kiewiet, 'A History of South Africa: Social and Economic' (London: (1941) 1966); D.H. Houghton, 'The South African Economy' (Cape Town: (1964) 1967); 'Report No. 11 of the Social and Economic Planning Council, Economic Aspects of the Gold Mining Industry' (Pretoria: 1948, UG 32/48).
2   Frankel, op. cit., p.81.
3   'Report of the Witwatersrand Mine Natives' Wages Commission' (Pretoria: 1944, UG 21/44), p.3.
4   Ibid.
5   Frankel, op. cit., pp.76-7.
6   M.R. Graham, The gold mining finance system in South Africa (Ph.D. thesis, University of London: 1964), pp.49-50.
7   Frankel, op. cit., p.102.
8   Speech of the President, annual general meeting of the Chamber, March 1910, 'Annual Report of the Transvaal Chamber of Mines for the Year 1909' ('ARTCM 1909') (Johannesburg: 1910), p.lviii.
9   Sir T. Gregory, 'Ernest Oppenheimer and the Economic Development of South Africa' (Cape Town: 1962), p.15.

Notes to chapter 1

10 Services in such areas as research, statistics and information, Parliamentary and legal affairs and evidence to Commissions, gold refining and by-products, technological innovation, accounting and taxation, labour conditions, the administration of the Mining Regulations, and collective buying.
11 Tvl Ch. of Mines, 'The Transvaal Chamber of Mines and its Subsidiary Organisations' (Johannesburg: 1936), p.5.
12 Professor H. Clay (of the Economic and Wage Commission of 1925-6), quoted in Frankel, op. cit., pp.81-2.
13 Tvl Ch. of Mines, 'The Gold of the Rand: A Great National Industry, 1887-1927' (Johannesburg: 1927), pp.14-15.
14 Tvl Ch. of Mines, 'Statements of Evidence to the Mining Industry Arbitration Board' (Johannesburg: 1927), Statement no. 1, p.52, para.23.
15 Gregory, op. cit., p.492.
16 Tvl Ch. of Mines, 'Statements of Evidence to the Mining Industry Arbitration Board', Statement no. 1, p.52, para.24.
17 Speech of the President, annual general meeting of the Chamber, March 1927, 'ARTCM 1926', p.58.
18 De Kiewiet, op. cit., p.180.
19 Ibid., p.203.
20 J.F. Herbst, Memorandum on native labour in South Africa, p.6; Herbst Papers, Archs of the Univ. of Cape Town.
21 Act 27, 1913, Section 1.
22 Transvaal: Law 15, 1898, Articles 59, 133; Law 32, 1908, Art. 130.
23 Law 15, 1898, Arts 148, 149; Law 32, 1908, Arts 113, 114.
24 Law 32, 1908, Art. 131.
25 Law 15, 1898, Art. 92.
26 Law 15, 1898, Art. 133.
27 E.g., Cape: Act 25, 1894; OFS: Ordinance 2, 1871.
28 E.g., Cape: Act 6, 1876; Act 8, 1878; Act 37, 1884; Act 33, 1892; Act 30, 1899; Act 32, 1909; Natal: Laws of the Volksraad of Emigrant Farmers, in the 1840s; Ordinance 2, 1855; Transvaal: Law 11, 1887; Law 21, 1895; OFS: Law 4, 1895; Union: Act 27, 1913; Act 26, 1926.
29 Cape: Act 15, 1856; Act 18, 1873; Act 7, 1875; Act 30, 1889; Act 20, 1892; Natal: Ordin. 2, 1850; Act 40, 1894; Act 35, 1899; Act 50, 1891; Act 49, 1901; Act 3, 1904; Transvaal: Law 13, 1880; Proclamation 37, 1901; Ordin. 27, 1903; Act 27, 1909;

Notes to chapter 1

OFS: Ordin. 1, 1873; Law 4, 1895; Ordin. 7, 1904; Ordin. 9, 1906; Union: Act 27, 1913; Act 26, 1926.
30 Cape: Act 22, 1867; Natal: Law 49, 1901; Law 3, 1904; Transvaal: Law 4, 1873; Law 1, 1883; Laws 22 and 23, 1895; Law 31, 1896; Law 23, 1899; Proc. 37, 1901; Ordin. 43, 1902; Ordin. 27, 1903; OFS: Law 8, 1893; Ordin. 9, 1906.
31 A discriminatory system of government, which excluded the majority of the people from the franchise and other government rights, had developed, in various forms, in the various Provinces before their union in 1910, and was instituted in the constitution of the Union of South Africa by the South Africa Act of 1909.
32 Speech of the President, ordinary general meeting of the Chamber, September 1906, 'ARTCM 1906', p.481.
33 Speech of the President, annual general meeting of the Chamber, March 1912, 'ARTCM 1911', p.lxxi.
34 Ibid.
35 Ibid.
36 Ibid.
37 Evidence of the Native Mine Clerks' Association (Mr A.W.G. Champion) to the Mining Industry Board, Evid. of the Min. Ind. Board (1922), p.3038; Nat. Archs.
38 Evidence of Mr D.D.T. Jabavu to the Mining Industry Board, ibid., p.4814.
39 Ibid., p.4825.
40 Evidence of the Native Mine Clerks' Association (Mr E. May) to the Mining Industry Board, ibid., p.3037.
41 Ibid.
42 Evidence of the Consulting Engineer of the East Rand Proprietary mine to the Low Grade Mines Commission, Evid. of the Low Grade Mines Comm. (1919-20), p.343, paras 2397-8; Nat. Archs.
43 'ARTCM 1911', p.421.
44 Speech of the President, annual general meeting of the Chamber, March 1912, ibid., p.lxx.
45 Ibid., p.lxxi.
46 Ibid., p.xliv.
47 Ibid., p.lxxi.
48 Speech of Mr L. Albu, annual general meeting of the Van Ryn Gold Mines and Estates Ltd in London, December 1911, 'South African Mining Journal', 30 December 1911, p.600.
49 Speech of the President, annual general meeting of the Chamber, March 1912, 'ARTCM 1911', p.lxxiii.
50 Report of the Executive Committee of the Chamber, 'ARTCM 1912', p.xl. This included all the gold mining companies except a few belonging to the J.B.

Notes to chapter 1

Robinson Group which later joined. Its scope of operations comprised the Union and the High Commission Territories.

51 Evidence of the Tvl Ch. of Mines (Mr A. French) to the Low Grade Mines Commission, Evid. of the Low Grade Mines Comm. (1919-20), p.1074, para.8659; Nat. Archs.
52 Letter from the President of the Tvl Ch. of Mines to the Director of Native Labour, 8 October 1914; Archs of the Dept of Native Affairs, File NA 2782/13/F473; Nat. Archs.
53 Report of the Executive Committee of the Chamber, 'ARTCM 1924', p.35.
54 Report of the Complements Committee, 11 September 1915, 'ARTCM 1915', p.5.
55 Report of the Executive Committee of the Chamber, ibid., p.xli.
56 Statement of the Complements Committee of the Tvl Ch. of Mines to the Low Grade Mines Commission; Archs of the Low Grade Mines Comm. (1919-20), Misc. Files; Nat. Archs.
57 Speech of the President, annual general meeting of the Chamber, March 1913, 'ARTCM 1912', p.lxvi.
58 Speech of the Chairman of the Native Recruiting Corporation, 'South African Mining Journal', 25 October 1919, p.145.
59 Speech of the President, annual general meeting of the Chamber, March 1912, 'ARTCM 1911', p.lxx.
60 Tvl Ch. of Mines, Employment of East Coast natives in the mines, 'ARTCM 1922', p.77.
61 Ibid.
62 Tvl Ch. of Mines, 'Party Programmes and the Mines: A Business Statement' (Johannesburg: 1924), p.2.
63 Evidence of the Tvl Ch. of Mines (Mr A. French) to the Low Grade Mines Commission, Evid. of the Low Grade Mines Comm. (1919-20), p.1053, para.8484; Nat. Archs.
64 A. Gorz, Immigrant labour, 'New Left Review', 61 (1970), p.28.
65 Tvl Ch. of Mines, Employment of East Coast natives in the mines, 'ARTCM 1922', p.77.
66 J.F. Herbst, Memorandum on the Master and Servant Laws of the various Provinces of the Union, pp.1-18; Herbst Papers, Archs of the Univ. of Cape Town.
67 Act 15, 1911, Section 14.
68 Statement of the Director of Native Labour to the Low Grade Mines Commission, p.5; Archs of the Low Grade Mines Comm. (1919-20), Misc. Papers File; Nat. Archs.

224 Notes to chapter 1

69 Evidence of Mr F.H.P. Creswell to the Low Grade Mines Commission, Evid. of the Low Grade Mines Comm. (1919-20), p.847, para.6893; Nat. Archs.
70 This extension reflected the stronger market position of the mining companies after the 1922 strike and labour reorganisation ('ARTCM 1925', p.55).
71 Act 15, 1911, Section 23 (4).
72 Speech of the President, ordinary general meeting of the Chamber, December 1924, 'ARTCM 1924', p.195.
73 The Pass Laws (a study made by government officials), p.38; Archs of the Dept of Native Affairs, File NA 658/18/F473; Nat. Archs.
74 Ibid., p.1.
75 Ibid., p.38.
76 Evidence of the Deputy Commissioner of Police, Johannesburg District, to the Native Grievances Inquiry, 6 March 1914, p.6; Evid. of the Nat. Grievs Inq. (1913-14), Archs of the Dept of Native Affairs, File NA 2782/13/F473; Nat. Archs.
77 Ibid., p.4.
78 Evidence of the Director of Native Labour to the Native Grievances Inquiry, 2 February 1914, p.65; ibid.
79 G.V. Doxey, 'The Industrial Colour Bar in South Africa' (Cape Town: 1961), p.51.
80 'Report of the Economic and Wage Commission' (Cape Town: 1926, UG 14/26), p.38.
81 N. Franklin, 'Economics in South Africa' (London: 1954), p.154.
82 Speech of the President, annual general meeting of the Chamber, March 1926, 'ARTCM 1925', p.55.
83 Evidence of Mr S. Msimang (of the Tvl Nat. Cong.) to the Mining Industry Board, Evid. of the Min. Ind. Board (1922), p.2779; Nat. Archs.
84 Statement of the Tvl Nat. Cong. to the Low Grade Mines Commission, pp.14-15; Archs of the Low Grade Mines Comm. (1919-20), Misc. Papers File; Nat. Archs.
85 Ibid.
86 Evidence of the National Native Congress (Mr S. Msane) to the Low Grade Mines Commission, summary, p.3; ibid.
87 Evidence of the Chief Induna of the Crown Mines (Mr E.W. Nogaga) to the Mining Industry Board, Evid. of the Min. Ind. Board (1922), p.2766; Nat. Archs.
88 NRC Ltd, Schedule of rates of pay, 'Report of the Mining Industry Board' (1922), p.48.
89 Ibid.
90 Ibid., p.51.

Notes to chapter 1

91 Resolutions of the Executive Committee of the Chamber of Mines, 'ARTCM 1909', p.14.
92 Letter from the Director of Native Labour to the Secretary of Native Affairs, 10 May 1918; Archs of the Dept of Native Affairs, File NA 1117/17/F473; Nat. Archs.
93 NRC Ltd, op. cit., p.46.
94 The ultra-cheapness of African labour was also secured through discriminatory compensation rates. The compensation rates for African workers for accident, death and phthisis were negligible compared with those for white workers. African workers were entitled to between £1 and £20 for partial incapacitation, and between £30 and £50 for total incapacitation or to dependents in the event of death. White workers, by contrast, were entitled to £375 for partial incapacitation, three years wages for total incapacitation, two years wages to dependents in the event of death, and half pay for temporary incapacitation. African workers were not entitled to any phthisis compensation until 1916, and then only to the same rates as for accident and death, whereas white workers were entitled to far more substantial phthisis compensation (Statement of the Tvl Nat. Cong. to the Low Grade Mines Commission, pp.23-4; Archs of the Low Grade Mines Comm. (1919-20), Misc. Papers File; Nat. Archs).
95 Evidence of the Chairman of the Native Recruiting Corporation to the Native Grievances Inquiry, 3 March 1914, p.12, and, e.g., Evidence of the Manager of the Modder B mine to the Native Grievances Inquiry, 5 February 1914; Evid. of the Nat. Grievs Inq. (1913-14), Archs of the Dept of Native Affairs, File NA 2782/13/F473; Nat. Archs. Also, e.g., 'Report of the Native Grievances Inquiry' (Cape Town: 1914, UG 37/14), p.37, paras 263-6.
96 'Report of the Native Grievances Inquiry' (1914), p.37, para.265.
97 Ibid., para.266.
98 Evidence of the Chairman of the NRC to the Native Grievances Inquiry, 3 March 1914, p.14; Evid. of the Nat. Grievs Inq. (1913-14), Archs of the Dept of Native Affairs, File NA 2782/13/F473; Nat. Archs.
99 Evidence of the General Superintendent of the NRC to the Native Grievances Inquiry, 6 February 1914, p.5; ibid. Another reason given by the companies for the maximum average system was the difficulty of fixing wage rates according to volume of output, because of the great variation in conditions between different

mines, which were reflected in variations of average output ranging between 1.37 tons per African worker per shift to 4.80 tons. If African workers were paid at different rates, it was alleged, they would expect the highest rates, and thus 'it was in order to give all boys throughout the Rand an equal chance on tramming and shovelling that we fixed the maximum average' (Evidence of the Technical Adviser of the NRC to the Native Grievances Inquiry, 6 March 1914, p.12; ibid.). The standardisation of rates might be partly explained by this factor, but not their ultra-low level.

100 Evidence of the Chairman of the NRC to the Mining Industry Board, Evid. of the Min. Ind. Board (1922), p.1383; Nat. Archs.
101 Interestingly enough, as we shall have occasion to observe, the white workers were to be concerned to challenge the prevailing restriction of the term 'colour bar' to the job colour bar, and to identify the measures of racial discrimination operated by the employers as colour bars.
102 Tvl Ch. of Mines, 'Statements of Evidence to the Economic and Wage Commission', Statement no. 5, p.6.
103 Tvl Ch. of Mines, 'Party Programmes and the Mines', p.2.
104 'South African Mining Journal', 19 September 1925, p.69.
105 Evidence of the Superintendent Engineer of the New Consolidated Gold Fields to the Mining Industry Board, Evid. of the Min. Ind. Board (1922), pp.1225-6; Nat. Archs.
106 D.W. Gilbert, The economic effects of gold discoveries upon South Africa, 'Quarterly Journal of Economics' (1933), p.579. (The £50 figure refers to wages plus food and lodging.)
107 Evidence of the Consulting Engineer of the Rand Group to the Low Grade Mines Commission, Evid. of the Low Grade Mines Comm. (1919-20), p.371, para.2609; Nat. Archs.
108 Certain illustrations of the extreme dependence of the profitability of the mining companies on the ultra-exploitation of non-white labour appear elsewhere - e.g., Table 2, and the statement of the Chamber of Mines at the time of the strike by African workers in 1920.

Notes to chapter 1

(B) The white workers and the system of racial discrimination

1. W.M. MacMillan, 'The South African Agrarian Problem and its Historical Development' (Johannesburg: 1919), p.33; C.W. de Kiewiet, 'A History of South Africa: Social and Economic' (London: (1941) 1966), p.191.
2. De Kiewiet, op. cit., p.187.
3. MacMillan, op. cit., pp.68-77.
4. Ibid., pp.63-4.
5. 'Report of the Transvaal Indigency Commission' (Pretoria: 1908, TG 13/08), p.11, para.21. The railway from the Rand to the Cape was completed in 1892, and to Natal and to Delagoa Bay in 1895.
6. Ibid., para.22.
7. Ibid., p.12, para.24.
8. Ibid.
9. De Kiewiet, op. cit., p.196.
10. H.A. Shannon, Urbanisation, 1904-36, 'South African Journal of Economics', 5, 1937, Table VII, p.184.
11. 'Final Report of the 1926 Census of the Union of South Africa' (Pretoria: 1931, UG 4/31), Table XIV, p.16.
12. 'Urban and Rural Population of South Africa, 1904-60' (Pretoria: 1968, Report no. 02.02.01 of the South African Bureau of Statistics), Table III, p.xxx.
13. Compared with negligible changes in the urban population of the other provinces. 'Report of the 1911 Census of the Population of the Union of South Africa' (Pretoria: 1912, UG 32/12), p.xxxiii.
14. Ibid., p.xxxiv.
15. 'Urban and Rural Population of South Africa, 1904-60', pp.90-1.
16. 'Final Report of the 1926 Census ...', p.17.
17. Thus between 1904 and 1921, the population of Benoni rose from 6,000 to 54,000; that of Boksburg from 16,000 to 39,000; that of Brakpan from 1,000 to 25,000; that of Springs from 7,000 to 23,000; and that of Randfontein from 4,000 to 28,000 (ibid., Table 3.3.1., p.86).
18. Ibid.
19. Ibid., p.19.
20. De Kiewiet, op. cit., p.204.
21. MacMillan, op. cit., p.63.
22. W.M. MacMillan, 'The Land, the Native and Unemployment' (Johannesburg: 1924), p.12.
23. 'Report of the 1918 Census of the European or White Races of the Union of South Africa' (Cape Town: 1919, UG 50/19), Table 11, pp.16-17; 'Report of the 1926

228   Notes to chapter 1

Census of the European Population of the Union of South Africa' (Pretoria: 1930, UG 27/30), pp.30, 56, 124-6, 169.
24 Report of the Inspector of White Labour to the Secretary of Mines and Industries, 30 January 1914; Archs of the Dept of Mines and Industries, File MM 1293/14; Nat. Archs.
25 Ibid.; and Evidence of the South African Mine Workers' Union (SAMWU) to the Mining Industry Board, Evid. of the Min. Ind. Board (1922), pp.3208-9; Nat. Archs.
26 The term 'structural insecurity' is used to refer to a condition of insecurity that stems not from any personal attributes or qualities of the individual experiencing the condition, but from the specific nature of the specific structure and system of human relations of which that individual forms a part - in this case, the specific nature of a specific class structure and system of production.
27 Evidence of Mr H. Sampson (of the Typographical Union and the Labour Party) to the Low Grade Mines Commission, Evid. of the Low Grade Mines Comm. (1919-20), p.1011, para.8200; Nat. Archs.
28 Evidence of the Consulting Engineer of the Consolidated Gold Fields to the Low Grade Mines Commission, ibid., p.102, para.765.
29 'Report of the Transvaal Indigency Commission' (1908), p.25, para.48.
30 Ibid., p.36, para.68.
31 'Report and Minutes of Evidence of the Select Committee of the House of Assembly on European Employment and Labour Conditions' (Cape Town: 1913, SC 9/13), p.120, para.900.
32 'Report of the Transvaal Indigency Commission' (1908), p.35, para.67; p.197, para.407.
33 Report of the Inspector of White Labour on Factories, Trades and Industries, 9 December 1918, p.2; Archs of the Dept of Mines and Industries, File MM 3066/18; Nat. Archs.
34 W.H. Hutt, 'The Economics of the Colour Bar' (London: 1964), p.35.
35 'Annual Report of the Dept of Mines and Industries and the Government Mining Engineer for 1923' (Pretoria: 1924), p.55.
36 E.J.C. Stevens, 'White and Black: An Inquiry into South Africa's Greatest Problem' (Cape Town: 1914), p.210.
37 'Report of the Transvaal Indigency Commission' (1908), p.4.

Notes to chapter 1

38 'Second Interim Report of the Unemployment Commission' (Cape Town: 1921, UG 34/21), p.7.
39 MacMillan, 'The South African Agrarian Problem . . .', p.11.
40 Report of the Government Adviser on Technical Education, 1917; Archs of the Dept of Mines and Industries, File MM 1320/17, p.1; Nat. Archs.
41 Ibid., Diagram VI.
42 'Second Interim Report of the Unemployment Commission' (1921), p.7.
43 Report of the Government Adviser on Technical Education, 1917; Archs of the Dept of Mines and Industries, File MM 1320/17, Table VIII; Nat. Archs.
44 'Report of the Select Committee . . . on European Employment and Labour Conditions' (1913), p.xii, para. 31.
45 'Report of the Transvaal Indigency Commission' (1908), p.4, p.49.
46 'Report of the Carnegie Commission on the Poor White Problem in South Africa' (Stellenbosch: 1932), Joint findings and recommendations, pp.xviii-xix, para.61.
47 'Second Interim Report of the Unemployment Commission' (1921), para.20.
48 Ibid.
49 'Report of the Select Committee . . . on European Employment and Labour Conditions' (1913), pp.xiii-xiv, paras 33-4.
50 Law No. 12, 1898, Section 104.
51 Ordinance No. 54, 1903, Section 153.
52 'Final Report of the Transvaal Mining Regulations Commission' (Pretoria: 1910), Draft Regulation No. 189.
53 Memorandum on the Colour Bar by the Government Mining Engineer to the Minister of Mines and Industries, 3 March, 1925, p.1; Archs of the Dept of Mines and Industries, File MM 2759/14; Nat. Archs.
54 Ordinance 54, 1903, Regulations 92-5.
55 'Final Report of the Transvaal Mining Regulations Commission' (1910), Draft Regulation 95.
56 Memorandum on the Colour Bar . . ., p.2.
57 Ordinance 17, 1904, Article 9, Schedule I.
58 Ordinance 17, 1904, Interpretation of Terms.
59 'Final Report of the Transvaal Mining Regulations Commission' (1910), p.220.
60 Evidence of the Mining Regulations Commission (1907-10), 22 February 1908, pp.34-5; Nat. Archs.
61 The Mines, Works and Machinery Act, Act 12, 1911; The Mines, Works, Machinery and Certificates Regulations (GN 1922, 'South African Government Gazette

Extraordinary', 21 November 1911, pp.1168-240).
62 Regulation 285. The discriminatory provisions were contained in: Interpretation of Terms, Regulations 30(1), 39, 75(1), 76(4), 91(1)(a)(b), 99(1)(a)(b), 99(2), 100(1)(2), 106, 146, 158(1)(g), 161, 162, 180 (1), 285.
63 There was no pressing reason for the government to change this, and changing it, by introducing racial discrimination into the Act, held out the possibility of a storm of conflict and controversy in Parliament, as did occur, as we shall see, when the Pact government set about doing this in 1925 and 1926.
64 E.g., 'ARTCM 1910', p.43; Interview with the General Secretary of the South African Engine Drivers' and Firemen's Association (SAEDFA), 'Rand Daily Mail', 25 November 1911.
65 E.g., Evidence of the SAEDFA to the Mining Regulations Comm., 23 July 1907, p.44; 10 October 1907, p.50; Evid. of the Min. Regs Comm. (1907-10); Nat. Archs.
66 Letter from the Government Mining Engineer to the Secretary of Mines and Industries, 13 December 1911; Archs of the Dept of Mines and Industries, File MM 3277/11; Nat. Archs.
67 Letter from the General Secretary of the SAEDFA to the Prime Minister, 1 December 1911; Minutes of conferences between representatives of the white mine workers and the Minister of Mines and other government officials, 22 December 1911, 4 May 1912; Letter from the Government Mining Engineer to the Secretary of Mines and Industries, 18 February 1913; Archs of the Dept of Mines and Industries, File MM 3277/11; Nat. Archs. 'Government Gazette', 31 October 1913, GN 1675, Regulations 41-2, 158(10), 306-24.
68 Letter from the Secretary of the Chamber of Mines to the Secretary of Mines and Industries, 19 January 1914; Archs of the Dept of Mines and Industries, File MM 1211/14; Nat. Archs. Also, e.g., Transvaal Chamber of Mines, Statement on the Job Colour Bar in the Mines, 8 May 1914, p.2; Merriman Papers, 1914 (South African Public Library, Cape Town).
69 Evidence of the SAMWU to the Mining Industry Board, Evid. of the Min. Ind. Board (1922), p.3571; Nat. Archs.
70 Comment of Sir C. Beattie, of the Mining Industry Board, Evidence of the SAMWU to the Min. Ind. Board, ibid., p.3574; Nat. Archs.
71 Evidence of the SAMWU (Mr D. Reich) to the Mining Regulations Commission, pp.630-1, Evid. of the Min.

Notes to chapters 1 and 2

Regs Comm. (1924-5); Nat. Archs.
72 Comment by a trade union representative (Mr B. Pohl) on the Low Grade Mines Commission, Evidence of the Low Grade Mines Comm. (1919-20), p.1892, para.14373; Nat. Archs.
73 Statement of the mining unions to the Mining Industry Board (1922), p.1; Archs of the Trade Union Council of South Africa (TUCSA).
74 Ibid., p.30.
75 Ibid., p.32.
76 Ibid., p.3.
77 Statement of the SAMWU to the Low Grade Mines Commission, Evid. of the Low Grade Mines Comm. (1919-20), p.1926; Nat. Archs.
78 Evidence of the SAMWU (Mr W.P. Whitney) to the Low Grade Mines Commission, ibid., pp.1953-4, para.14657; Nat. Archs.
79 Evidence of Mr F.H.P. Creswell to the Low Grade Mines Commission, ibid., p.863, para.7003.
80 Statement of European mine workers of the Transvaal and Orange Free State to the Mining Industry Board (1922), p.13; Archs of the South African Boilermakers', Iron and Steel Workers', Shipbuilders' and Welders' Society.
81 Ibid., pp.13, 17.
82 Evidence of the SAMWU (Mr G.H. Gillman) to the Low Grade Mines Commission, Evid. of the Low Grade Mines Comm. (1919-20), p.2017, para.15006; and Statement of the SAMWU to the Low Grade Mines Comm., ibid., p.1926; Nat. Archs.
83 Supplementary statement of the mining unions to the Mining Industry Board (1922), p.3, para.17; TUCSA Archs.

CHAPTER 2

1 Dialogue between the representative of the Transvaal Chamber of Mines on the Low Grade Mines Commission and representatives of the Compound Managers' Association, Evidence of the Compound Managers' Association to the Low Grade Mines Commission, Evid. of the Low Grade Mines Comm. (1919-20), pp.1788-9, paras 13636-40; Nat. Archs.
2 Evidence of the General Superintendent of the Native Recruiting Corporation to the Native Grievances Inquiry, 6 February 1914, p.34; Evid. of the Nat. Grievs Inq. (1913-14), Archs of the Dept of Native Affairs, File NA 2782/13/F473; Nat. Archs.

3 Statement of Evidence of the Director of Native Labour to the Low Grade Mines Commission, pp.11-12; Archs of the Low Grade Mines Comm. (1919-20); Nat. Archs.
4 Report of the Executive Committee of the Chamber, 'ARTCM 1903', p.30.
5 Speech of Sir G. Farrar to white mine workers at Boksburg, 'Further Correspondence relating to the Affairs of the Transvaal and the Orange River Colony' (London: 1904, Cd. 1895), p.13.
6 Speech of the President, monthly meeting of the Chamber, September 1906, 'ARTCM 1906', p.482.
7 Recommendations of the Transvaal Chamber of Mines on the Draft Mines and Works Act and Regulations to the Secretary of Mines and Industries, 4 February 1911, and related correspondence; Archs of the Dept of Mines and Industries, File MM 2570/10; Nat. Archs.
8 'ARTCM 1910', p.43.
9 Speech of the President, annual general meeting of the Chamber, March 1912, 'ARTCM 1911', p.lxii. The Chamber of Mines considered that competition was 'healthy' amongst workers but not amongst employers.
10 Letter from the Chairman of the London Board of Directors of the Village Main Reef Co. (Mr P. Tarbut) to Mr F.H.P. Creswell, 2 July 1902; Archs of the Economic and Wage Commission (1925-6), vol.11; Nat. Archs.
11 Report of the Consulting Engineer of the Village Main Reef Co. (Mr A.M. Robeson) on the Creswell experiments in the Village Main Reef mine in 1899 and 1902-3; 'South African Mining Journal', 18 November 1922, p.248.
12 'Report of the Transvaal Mining Industry Commission' (Pretoria: 1908), Majority Report.
13 Speech of a company director, monthly meeting of the Chamber, September 1907, 'ARTCM 1907', p.449.
14 Speech of the President, monthly meeting of the Chamber, May 1908, 'ARTCM 1908', p.499.
15 Speech of the President, monthly meeting of the Chamber, March 1908, ibid., p.478.
16 Letter from the President of the Chamber to the Administrator of the Transvaal, 28 September 1914, 'ARTCM 1914', p.96.
17 Speech of the President, monthly meeting of the Chamber, September 1906, 'ARTCM 1906', pp.481-2.
18 Speech of the President, quarterly meeting of the Chamber, December 1925, 'ARTCM 1925', pp.170-1.
19 The white labour bogey again, 'South African Mining Journal', 18 November 1922, p.247.

233 Notes to chapter 3

CHAPTER 3

1. The post-war profitability crisis

1   V. Bosman (ed.), 'Industrial Development in South Africa' (Pretoria: 1936), Table 3, p.6.
2   S.H. Frankel, 'Capital Investment in Africa' (London: 1938), p.95.
3   Bosman, op. cit., Table 3, p.6.
4   'Report of the Low Grade Mines Commission' (Cape Town: 1920, UG 34/20), p.6.
5   'Report of the Select Committee of the House of Assembly on the Gold Mining Industry' (Cape Town: 1918, SC 3/18), p.vi.
6   'Interim Report of the Low Grade Mines Commission' (Cape Town: 1919, UG 45/19), p.3.
7   Text of agreement between the Bank of England and the mining companies, and statements concerning the new arrangement, 'ARTCM 1919', pp.291-3.
8   Speech of the President, annual general meeting of the Chamber, ibid., p.60.
9   'Report of the Low Grade Mines Commission' (1920), pp.6-7.
10 'First Interim Report of the Unemployment Commission' (1921), (Cape Town: 1921, UG 16/21), p.3.
11 'Report of the Low Grade Mines Commission' (1920), p.8.
12 Ibid.
13 Comparison of certain costs incurred in the gold mines, 'ARTCM 1921', p.151.
14 This included, besides the increased cost of supplies (£4 million), increased gold realisation charges (£0.4 million), a war-time wage bonus (£1 million), allowances to employees on active service (£0.2 million), and a special government war levy (£0.4 million) ('ARTCM 1918', p.68).
15 'ARTCM 1917', p.452.
16 Speech of the President, annual general meeting of the Chamber, 'ARTCM 1918', p.69.
17 Tvl Ch. of Mines, Statement in regard to the native labour supply of the Witwatersrand gold mines, 30 July 1919; 'ARTCM 1919', p.223.
18 Tvl Ch. of Mines, Statement to the select committee on the gold mining industry, 'ARTCM 1918', p.203.
19 'Report of the Low Grade Mines Commission' (1920), p.22.
20 Tvl Ch. of Mines, Statement to the select committee . . ., 'ARTCM 1918', p.203.
21 Bosman, op. cit., Table 4, pp.8-9.

Notes to chapter 3

22 Ibid., Table 6, p.11.
23 Speech of the President, monthly meeting of the Chamber, 24 September 1917, 'ARTCM 1917', p.458.
24 Statement of the Director of Native Labour to the Low Grade Mines Commission, pp.21-5, Evid. of the Low Grade Mines Comm. (1919-20); Nat. Archs.
25 'House of Assembly Debates', 8 May 1913, col. 2230.
26 Letters from the Tvl Ch. of Mines to the Minister of Native Affairs, e.g. 3 December 1917, Archs of the Dept of Mines and Inds, File MM 2591/17; Nat. Archs.
27 'Report of the Low Grade Mines Commission' (1920), p.8. Average earnings per shift of African workers were £1 11s. 7d. in 1914 and £2 0s. 2d. in 1919, a variation of seven-tenths of a penny (ibid.).
28 E.g., the Miners Phthisis Act of 1919 raised the annual compensation liability of the mining companies by £2.3 million, to £3.6 million (ibid.).
29 Tvl Ch. of Mines, Statement on the increase in the cost of production of the Witwatersrand gold mines, 1914-1919, 15 August 1919, 'ARTCM 1919', p.232.
30 Tvl Ch. of Mines, Addendum to statement on the increase in the cost of production . . ., ibid., p.232. Tons handled per 26 African tramming and shovelling shifts were 52.7 in 1918 (first half) compared with 62.3 in 1914 (first half) (ibid.).
31 Speech of the President, annual general meeting of the Chamber, 'ARTCM 1926', p.58.
32 Statement of the Consulting Engineer of the Simmer Deep mine (Mr C.D. Leslie) to the Low Grade Mines Commission, pp.1-9, Evid. of the Low Grade Mines Comm. (1919-20); Nat. Archs.
33 Ibid. E.g., evidence of the Manager of the Village Deep mine, evidence of the representatives of the East Rand Proprietary mine, etc.
34 See, e.g., 'Report of the Committee of Inquiry: Into the Simmer Deep and Jupiter Gold Mines' (UG 44/20); 'Into the Closing Down of the Princess Estate Mine' (UG 39/20); 'Into the Closing Down of the Knights Deep Mine' (UG 63/20); 'Into the Probable Closing Down of the Roodepoort United Main Reef Mine' (UG 51/20).
35 Minutes of a conference between the Tvl Ch. of Mines and the mining unions, 15 December 1921, p.8; SAEDFA (South African Engine Drivers' and Firemen's Association) Archs.
36 'Report of the Low Grade Mines Commission' (1920), p.7.
37 Letter from the Tvl Ch. of Mines to the SAIF (South African Industrial Federation), 23 December 1921,

235 Notes to chapter 3

pp.1-2; SAEDFA Archs.
38 Tvl Ch. of Mines, The ore contents of the Witwatersrand (Statement to the Mining Industry Board, 11 July 1922), 'ARTCM 1922', p.101.
39 Evidence of the Manager of the East Rand Proprietary mine (Mr Clifford) to the Low Grade Mines Commission, Evid. of the Low Grade Mines Comm. (1919-20), p.365, para.2560; Nat. Archs.
40 President of the South African Reduction Workers' Association (SARWA) (Mr J. George), Minutes of a conference between the Tvl Ch. of Mines and the SAIF, 5 July 1921, p.62; TUCSA (Trade Union Council of South Africa) Archs.
41 Speech of the President, annual general meeting of the Chamber, 'ARTCM 1916', p.59.
42 'Report of the Low Grade Mines Commission' (1920), p.11.
43 Letter from the Tvl Ch. of Mines to the General Recruiting Committee, Johannesburg, 10 April 1916, 'ARTCM 1916', p.127.
44 Telegram from Minister of Defence to Tvl Ch. of Mines, 10 March 1916, ibid., p.127.
45 Letter from the Tvl Ch. of Mines to the Gen. Rec. Cttee, Johannesburg, ibid., p.128.
46 Workers who left with the permission of their employer continued to receive some pay and a right to their job, but this attempt to control the outflow of workers also constituted an additional cost for the companies.
47 'Report of the Martial Law Inquiry Judicial Commission' (Pretoria: 1922, UG 34/22), para.96.
48 Evidence of the Consulting Engineer of the Simmer Deep mine (Mr C.D. Leslie) to the Low Grade Mines Commission, Evid. of the Low Grade Mines Comm. (1919-20), p.67, paras 475-8; Nat. Archs.
49 Ibid., p.34, para.199.
50 Letter from Dr J. Fehrsen to J.X. Merriman, 26 May 1920; Merriman Papers (1920).
51 The Chamber of Mines estimated that about 70 per cent of the African workers from Portuguese Africa had previous experience of work in the mines (Evidence of the Tvl Ch. of Mines (Mr A. French) to the Low Grade Mines Commission, Evid. of the Low Grade Mines Comm. (1919-20), p.1055, para.8504; Nat. Archs).
52 Evidence of the Consulting Engineer of the Simmer Deep mine (Mr C.D. Leslie) to the Low Grade Mines Commission, ibid., pp.63-4, paras 445-50.
53 'Report of the Mining Industry Board' (1922), p.5, para.14.

54 Report of the Inspector of White Labour to the Secretary of Mines and Industries, 6 January 1917, Archs of the Dept of Mines and Inds, File MM 1212/17; Nat. Archs.
55 Report of the Government Mining Engineer to the Secretary of Mines and Industries, 6 January 1917, ibid.
56 Ibid.
57 Report by the Resident Magistrate of Boksburg into the cessation of work at the Van Ryn Deep mine, 1 February 1917, pp.1, 7, ibid., File MM 1250/17; Nat. Archs.
58 Ibid., p.7.
59 Ibid., pp.6-7.
60 Letter from R.A. Barry to J.X. Merriman, 18 January 1917; Merriman Papers (1917).
61 Tvl Ch. of Mines, Statement in regard to matters discussed at a conference between representatives of the Chamber and of SAMWU, 24 February 1917, para.3; Archs of the Dept of Mines and Inds, File MM 2005/16; Nat. Archs. The union also demanded a maximum limit on the number of machines and non-white workers per white worker, which the Chamber also rejected, on the grounds that it would be too difficult to arrange.
62 Ibid.
63 Tvl Ch. of Mines, Statement in regard to the demands put forward in July 1917 by the SAMWU, 4 August 1917, pp.4, 8; Archs of the Boilermakers' Society.
64 Ibid., p.4.
65 Ibid.
66 'ARTCM 1917', p.466.
67 Letter from the SAIF to the Tvl Ch. of Mines, 20 June 1918 and 8 July 1918; SAIF, 'Copies of Memoranda and Correspondence Exchanged between the Chamber of Mines and the Federated Trade Unions during the Negotiations of July-August 1918', p.1; Archs of the Boilermakers' Society.
68 Tvl Ch. of Mines, Statement in regard to the demands submitted to the Chamber by the SAIF on 8 July 1918, 17 July 1918, ibid., p.4.
69 Letter from the SAIF to the Tvl Ch. of Mines, 29 July 1918, ibid., pp.7-8.
70 Letter from the Tvl Ch. of Mines to the SAIF, 2 August 1918, ibid., p.10.
71 Tvl Ch. of Mines, Circular of the Chamber to the mining companies, 24 September 1918, 'ARTCM 1918', p.135.
72 Supplementary statement of the mining unions to the Mining Industry Board (1922), p.1, para.1; TUCSA Archs.

237 Notes to chapter 3

73 Ibid.
74 Supplementary statement of the mining unions to the Mining Industry Board (1922), p.1, para.6; ibid.
75 SAIF, The present strike in the industries of the Transvaal (statement issued during the 1922 strike), p.4; ibid.
76 Ibid.
77 Evidence of the Amalgamated Society of Woodworkers (ASW) (Mr W.K. Jolly) to the Mining Industry Board, Evid. of the Min. Ind. Board (1922), p.2893; Nat. Archs.
78 Evidence of the SAIF (Mr A. Crawford) to the Mining Industry Board, ibid., p.5189.
79 Evidence of the SAMWU to the Mining Industry Board, ibid., pp.3219, 3224-5.
80 Supplementary statement of the mining unions to the Mining Industry Board (1922), p.1, para.5; TUCSA Archs.
81 Ibid., p.1, para.2.
82 Speech of the President, ordinary general meeting of the Chamber, September 1918, 'ARTCM 1918', p.489.
83 Speech of the President, annual general meeting of the Chamber, March 1917, 'ARTCM 1917', p.64.
84 Ibid.
85 Speech of the President, annual general meeting of the Chamber, March 1918, ibid., p.63.
86 Speech of the President, annual general meeting of the Chamber, March 1919, 'ARTCM 1918', p.65.
87 Ibid., p.62.
88 Ibid.
89 Ibid., p.67.
90 Speech of the President, annual general meeting of the Chamber, March 1918, 'ARTCM 1917', p.64.
91 Ibid.
92 Speech of the President, annual general meeting of the Chamber, March 1919, 'ARTCM 1918', p.62.
93 Ibid.
94 Ibid., pp.65-6.
95 Ibid.
96 Speech of the President, ordinary general meeting of the Chamber, September 1918, ibid., p.489.
97 Evidence of the Manager of the Village Deep mine (Mr J. Whitehouse) to the Low Grade Mines Commission, Evid. of the Low Grade Mines Comm. (1919-20), p.217, paras 1504-5; Nat. Archs.
98 'Report of the Mining Industry Board' (1922), p.20.
99 Ibid.
100 'Report of the Low Grade Mines Commission' (1920), p.11.

238 Notes to chapter 3

101 Tvl Ch. of Mines, Statement on the increase in the cost of production . . ., 'ARTCM 1919', p.232.
102 Speech of the President, ordinary general meeting of the Chamber, December 1917, 'ARTCM 1917', p.469.
103 Speech of the President, ordinary general meeting of the Chamber, December 1918, 'ARTCM 1918', p.495.
104 Report of the Inspector of White Labour to the Secretary of Mines and Industries, 6 February 1917, Archs of the Dept of Mines and Inds, File MM 1384/17; Nat. Archs.
105 Report by an official (unnamed) of the Dept of Mines and Inds to the Secretary of Mines and Industries, 1 May 1917, ibid., File MM 1791/17; Nat. Archs.
106 Telegram from Government Mining Engineer to Minister of Mines and Industries, 7 June 1917, ibid., File MM 1856/17; Nat. Archs.
107 Confidential minute of the Secretary of Mines to the Minister of Mines and Industries, 10 January 1917, para. 1; Archs of the Dept of Justice, File 3/20/17/232; Nat. Archs.
108 Ibid., paras 3, 5.
109 Ibid., para.8.
110 Ibid., para.9.
111 Confidential minute from the Secretary of Justice to the Commissioner, South African Police (SAP), 16 January 1917; Archs of the Dept of Justice, File 3/20/17/232; Nat. Archs.
112 Report of the District Commandant, SAP, Boksburg, to the Commissioner, SAP, 30 January 1917; ibid.
113 Ibid.
114 Letter from the Secretary of Mines and Industries to the Governor-General, 12 March 1917; Archs of the Dept of Mines and Inds, File MM 2005/16; Nat. Archs.
115 Report by the Secretary of Mines and Industries on industrial unrest on the Rand in 1917; Archs of the Dept of Mines and Inds, File MM 1856/17; Nat. Archs.
116 Letter from the Commissioner, SAP, to the Secretary of Justice, 16 June 1917; Archs of the Dept of Justice, File 3/20/17/232; Nat. Archs.
117 Minute of the Minister of Justice on ibid., 22 June 1917, and letter from the Secretary of Justice to the Commissioner, SAP, 28 June 1917; ibid., File 3/20/17/232.
118 Letter from the Commissioner, SAP, to the Secretary of Justice, 15 August 1917; ibid., File 3/20/17/232.
119 Letter from the Secretary of Justice to the Commissioner, SAP, 17 August 1917, and from the Commissioner, SAP, to the Secretary of Justice, 17 October 1917; Archs of the Dept of Justice, File 3/20/17/232; Nat. Archs.

Notes to chapter 3

120 Evidence of the Consulting Engineer of the Simmer Deep mine (Mr C.D. Leslie) to the Low Grade Mines Commission, Evid. of the Low Grade Mines Comm. (1919-20), p.27, para.144; Nat. Archs.

2. The offensive of the mining companies against the white workers

1 Speech of the President, annual general meeting of the Chamber, March 1920, 'ARTCM 1919', pp.60, 61.
2 Ibid., p.60.
3 Ibid., p.61.
4 Ibid., p.64.
5 Ibid., p.61.
6 'Report of the Low Grade Mines Commission' (1920), p.10.
7 Tvl Ch. of Mines, Statement in regard to the native labour supply of the Witwatersrand gold mines, 30 July 1919, 'ARTCM 1919', p.224.
8 Ibid.
9 Statement of the Association of Mine Managers to the Low Grade Mines Commission, Evid. of the Low Grade Mines Comm. (1919-20), p.2037; Nat. Archs.
10 The Regulations involved were Reg. 100(11) (no member of a gang to enter a work place until instructed to do so by the white ganger); Reg. 106(7)(a) (examination of working places to be carried out by the white ganger and by members of his gang working under his direct personal supervision); and Reg. 158(12)(a) (no non-white workers to go to their working places until taken in charge by their gangers).
11 Statement of the Association of Mine Managers to the Low Grade Mines Commission, Evid. of the Low Grade Mines Comm. (1919-20), p.2037; Nat. Archs.
12 Ibid.
13 Evidence of the Tvl Ch. of Mines (Mr A. French) to the Low Grade Mines Commission, ibid., p.1031, para. 8343.
14 Statement of the Association of Mine Managers to the Low Grade Mines Commission, ibid., p.2037.
15 Evidence of the Tvl Ch. of Mines (Mr A. Brett) to the Low Grade Mines Commission, ibid., p.1060, paras 8545-6.
16 Ibid., p.1047, para.3439; p.1052, paras 8476-7.
17 Evidence of the Association of Mine Managers (Mr J.J. Wessels, President of the AMM) to the Low Grade Mines Commission, ibid., p.2079, para.15370.

240 Notes to chapter 3

18 Evidence of the Tvl Ch. of Mines (Mr A. French) to the Low Grade Mines Commission, ibid., p.1047, para. 3439.
19 Ibid. (Mr A. Brett), p.1065, paras 8584-90.
20 Evidence of the Manager of the Village Deep mine (Mr J. Whitehouse) to the Low Grade Mines Commission, ibid., pp.189-90, paras 1276-89; Nat. Archs.
21 Comment by Mr Gemmill of the Tvl Ch. of Mines, Evidence of the SAMWU to the Mining Regulations Commission, Evid. of the Min. Regs Comm. (1924-5), p.542; Nat. Archs.
22 'Report of the Mining Industry Board' (1922), p.7.
23 Tvl Ch. of Mines, Statement in regard to the native labour supply of the Witwatersrand gold mines, 30 July 1919, 'ARTCM 1919', p.224.
24 Ibid.
25 Ibid.
26 Evidence of the Manager of the East Rand Proprietary mine to the Low Grade Mines Commission, Evid. of the Low Grade Mines Comm. (1919-20), p.346, paras 2416-17; Nat. Archs.
27 Ibid., p.328, para.2274.
28 Evidence of the Tvl Ch. of Mines (Mr A. Brett) to the Low Grade Mines Commission, ibid., p.1067, para.8604.
29 Evidence of the Manager of the East Rand Proprietary mine to the Low Grade Mines Commission, ibid., p.323, para.2237; Nat. Archs.
30 Memorandum from the Tvl Ch. of Mines to the SAIF, 27 June 1921, p.3; Archs of the Boilermakers' Society.
31 Letter from the Prime Minister to the Minister of Mines and Industries, 20 October 1919; Archs of the Dept of Mines and Inds, File MM 2028/19; Nat. Archs.
32 'Official Yearbook of the Union of South Africa, No. 6, 1910-22' (Pretoria: 1924), p.313.
33 Ibid., pp.310-11.
34 I.L. Walker, Labour conditions in South Africa, in V. Bosman (ed.), 'Industrial Development in South Africa' (Pretoria: 1936), p.30.
35 R.K. Cope, 'Comrade Bill: The Life and Times of W.H. Andrews, Workers' Leader' (Cape Town: 1943), p.201.
36 Notes of a meeting between the Minister of Mines and Industries and a deputation of the SAIF, 4 June 1920, p.8; Archs of the Dept of Mines and Inds, File MM 3024/20; Nat. Archs.
37 Report on the meeting of unemployed workers, 17 October 1920; Archs of the Dept of Mines and Inds, File MM 2882/20; Nat. Archs.
38 'Rand Daily Mail', 18 October 1920, p.5.
39 Letter from the Tvl Ch. of Mines to the SAIF, 18 May 1921; TUCSA Archs.

Notes to chapter 3

40 Letter from the Tvl Ch. of Mines to the SAIF, 27 May 1921; Archs of the Boilermakers' Society.
41 Letter from the Tvl Ch. of Mines to the SAIF, 4 June 1921; ibid.
42 Memorandum from the SAIF to the Tvl Ch. of Mines, 29 May 1921; TUCSA Archs.
43 Letter from the Tvl Ch. of Mines to the SAIF, 27 June 1921; Archs of the Boilermakers' Society.
44 Minutes of the conference between the Tvl Ch. of Mines and the SAIF, 5 July 1921, p.2; SAEDFA Archs.
45 Minutes of the conference between the Tvl Ch. of Mines and the SAIF, 2 August 1921; and correspondence between the Tvl Ch. of Mines and the SAIF, 6 July, 21 July, 9 August, 15 August, 26 August 1921; TUCSA Archs.
46 Minutes of the conference between the Prime Minister and representatives of the Tvl Ch. of Mines and the white workers, 10 November 1921, SAEDFA Archs.
47 Minutes of conferences between the Tvl Ch. of Mines and the SAMWU, March-May 1920; Memorandum of the Tvl Ch. of Mines to the SAIF, 27 June 1921, p.4; Archs of the Boilermakers' Society.
48 Telegram from the Prime Minister (General Smuts) to the Acting Prime Minister, 18 June 1921; Archs of the Dept. of Mines and Inds, File MM 3261/20; Nat. Archs.
49 Telegrams between the Government Mining Engineer, the Secretary of Mines and Industries and the Prime Minister, 22 and 29 June 1921; ibid.
50 Letter from the Secretary of Mines and Industries to the SAMWU, 27 October 1921; Smuts Papers, Box CXV, vol.27; Nat. Archs.
51 Ibid.
52 Letter from the SAMWU to the Secretary of Mines and Industries, 28 October 1921; ibid.
53 Minutes of the conferences between the Prime Minister and representatives of the Tvl Ch. of Mines and the white workers, 10 November and 15 November 1921; SAEDFA Archs.
54 Ibid., conference of 10 November, pp.22-3.
55 Ibid., pp.25-6.
56 Ibid., conference of 15 November, p.45.
57 Statement of the Tvl Ch. of Mines on the basis upon which the gold mines can restart operations, 'ARTCM 1921', p.156.
58 Letter from the Tvl Ch. of Mines to the SAIF, 8 December 1921; ibid., pp.145-6.
59 Minutes of a conference between the Tvl Ch. of Mines, the SAMWU and the SAIF regarding the proposals of the

Chamber, 15 December 1921, pp.2-6; SAEDFA Archs.
60 Minutes of a conference between the Tvl Ch. of Mines, the SAMWU and the SAIF regarding the proposals of the Chamber, 15 December 1921, pp.16-17, 26, 38; ibid.
61 Letter from the Tvl Ch. of Mines to the SAIF, 23 December 1921, 'ARTCM 1921', p.154.
62 Letter from the Tvl Ch. of Mines to the SAIF, 28 December 1921, ibid., p.154.
63 Minutes of meetings of the SAIF, 30 December and 31 December 1921; TUCSA Archs.
64 Letter from the SAIF to the Tvl Ch. of Mines, 9 January 1922; ibid. The vote was 13,500 for, 1,336 against.
65 Minutes of a conference between the Tvl Ch. of Mines and the Augmented Executive of the SAIF in regard to the Chamber's proposals for alterations in working conditions, 9 January 1922; SAEDFA Archs.
66 Minutes of meetings of the SAIF, 30 December and 31 December 1921; TUCSA Archs.
67 Minutes of the conference between the Augmented Executive of the SAIF and representatives of the employers (Curlewis conference), 14-27 January 1922; SAEDFA Archs.
68 Minutes of the Curlewis conference, 12th day's proceedings, 26 January 1922, p.1154 (Mr J. George, of the Reduction Workers' Association); ibid.
69 Press statement of the Tvl Ch. of Mines on the basis upon which the gold mines can restart operations, 29 January 1922, 'ARTCM 1921', pp.157-8.
70 Statement by the Prime Minister on conferences concerning the strike, 6 February 1922, ibid., pp. 159-60.
71 Statement by the Prime Minister, 11 February 1922, ibid., pp.160-1.
72 'Cape Times', 21 February 1922.
73 Ibid., 1 March 1922.
74 'ARTCM 1921', p.161.
75 Letter from the SAIF to the Tvl Ch. of Mines, 4 March 1921, ibid., p.162.
76 Letter from the Tvl Ch. of Mines to the SAIF, 4 March 1922, ibid., pp.162-3.
77 Draft appeal of the Strike Victims Dependants Relief Fund, p.6; SAEDFA Archs.
78 Press statement of the Tvl Ch. of Mines, 11 March 1922, 'ARTCM 1921', p.164.
79 Cope, op. cit., p.263.
80 H.J. and R.E. Simons, 'Class and Colour in South Africa, 1850-1950' (Harmondsworth: 1969), p.294.
81 The official Commission of Inquiry estimated 153

killed (72 government, 39 'revolutionaries or suspected revolutionaries', 42 civilians) and 534 wounded ('Report of the Martial Law Inquiry Judicial Commission' (1922), para.71). The strikers' defence committee estimated the minimum number of killed as 216 (76 government, 78 strikers, 62 civilians), but considered the actual number to be higher (Transvaal Strike Legal Defence Committee, 'The Story of a Crime' (Johannesburg: 1924), p.1).

82 Report of the Executive Committee of the Chamber for 1922, 'ARTCM 1922', pp.43-4.

83 There is, unfortunately and surprisingly, no satisfactory, readily available, study of the events of 1922 to which the reader could be referred. The following works, among others, taken together provide a fairly comprehensive account, though taken singly no one amounts to an adequate study: 'Report of the Martial Law Inquiry Judicial Commission' (1922); Tvl Strike Legal Defence Committee, op. cit.; 'Report of the Mining Industry Board' (1922); B. Hessian, An investigation into the causes of the labour agitation on the Witwatersrand, January to March 1922 (M.A. thesis, Univ. of the Witwatersrand: 1957); S.P. Bunting, 'Red Revolt' (Johannesburg: 1922); Cope, op. cit.; Simons, op. cit.; C.R. Ould, General Smuts' attitude to white labour disputes between 1907 and 1922 (M.A. thesis, Univ. of the Witwatersrand: 1964). Certain works, designed for a popular readership, such as I.L. Walker and B. Weinbren, '2000 Casualties: A History of the Trade Unions and the Labour Movement in the Union of South Africa' (Johannesburg: 1961), and N. Herd, '1922: The Revolt of the Rand' (Johannesburg: 1966), are very superficial accounts, to say the least.

84 In the same period, the numbers of such skilled white workers as winding engine drivers, miners in machine stoping, electricians, fitters, turners and masons showed little change (Tvl Ch. of Mines, Statement showing numbers of workers employed in connection with certain occupations in the mines, 1921 and 1924 (Annexure A of Statement of the Tvl Ch. of Mines to the Mining Regulations Commission); SAEDFA Archs).

85 Statement of the SAEDFA to the Mining Regulations Commission, p.4; ibid.

86 Evidence of the South African Reduction Workers' Association (SARWA) (Mr A.A. Moore, General Secretary) to the Mining Regulations Commission, Evid. of the Min. Regs Comm. (1924-5), p.785; Nat. Archs.

87 Evidence of the Boilermakers' Society (Mr. J.R.

Notes to chapter 3

Oelofse, Organising Secretary) to the Mining Regulations Commission, ibid., pp.494-6.
88 Evidence of the Amalgamated Society of Woodworkers (Mr T. Stark, Organiser) to the Mining Regulations Commission, ibid., p.1863.
89 'Report of the Mining Regulations Commission' (Cape Town: 1925, UG 36/25), p.20.
90 Evidence of Mr A.P. Mellett, miner, to the Mining Regulations Commission, Evid. of the Min. Regs Comm. (1924-5), pp.44, 41; Nat. Archs.
91 Evidence of Mr E. McCormack, ex-miner, to the Mining Regulations Commission, ibid., p.83.
92 Evidence of Mr G.S. Ackerman, miner, to the Mining Regulations Commission, ibid., pp.35-6. E.g. evidence of miners H.R.W. Brown, H.G. Kruger, and P.L. Uys, ibid., p.26.
93 Tvl Ch. of Mines, Statement showing numbers of workers ..., p.2; SAEDFA Archs.
94 Evidence of the SAMWU (Mr H. Day) to the Mining Regulations Commission, Evid. of the Min. Regs Comm. (1924-5), p.530; Nat. Archs.
95 Evidence of Mr. H.W. Hayne, miner, to the Mining Regulations Commission, ibid., pp.258-9.
96 Ibid.
97 Evidence of the SAMWU (Mr D.D. Reich) to the Mining Regulations Commission, ibid., p.532.
98 Evidence of the SARWA (Mr A.A. Moore) to the Mining Regulations Commission, ibid., p.796.
99 Ibid. The Reduction Workers' Association saw it as symptomatic of this extension of the responsibility of white reduction workers (one of whose duties was to guard against theft of gold by African workers during the reduction process) that between 1922 and 1924 the number of prosecutions under the Gold Law for illegal possession of gold rose by 262 per cent (ibid., pp.797-8).
100 White and coloured ratio on the mines, 'South African Mining and Engineering Journal', 10 January 1925, p.492.
101 'Report of the Mining Regulations Commission' (1925), p.8, para.24.
102 Ibid., p.8, para.26.
103 Ibid., p.9, para.27.
104 Sir T. Gregory, 'Sir Ernest Oppenheimer and the Economic Development of Southern Africa' (Cape Town: 1962), p.33.
105 Evidence of the SAMWU (Mr D.D. Reich) to the Mining Regulations Commission, Evid. of the Min. Regs Comm. (1924-5), p.609; Nat. Archs.

Notes to chapter 3

106 Statement by the Tvl Ch. of Mines on the development of the use of the jack-hammer drill, 'South African Mining and Engineering Journal', 17 January 1925, p. 514.
107 Speech of the President, annual general meeting of the Chamber, March 1924, 'ARTCM 1923', pp.59-61.
108 Ibid., March 1926, 'ARTCM 1925', pp.57-8. The increased mechanisation of drilling during the 1920s is evident in a decline between 1920 and 1930 in the numbers of workers per 1,000 tons hoisted per day - 228 whites to 158, and 1,905 Africans to 1,559 (L. Katzen, 'Gold and the South African Economy' (Cape Town: 1964), p.26, Table 4).
109 Tvl Ch. of Mines, Statement showing numbers of workers . . ., p.2; SAEDFA Archs.
110 Evidence of the Superintendent of drill-sharpening on the Crown Mines (Mr W. Hawke) to the Mining Regulations Commission, Evid. of the Min. Regs Comm. (1924-5), pp.1756-62; Nat. Archs. The displacement of the white drill-sharpener was accelerated by the fact that the hollow steel of the new jack-hammer drill was far more difficult to sharpen by hand than the solid steel of the old drills (ibid., p.1775).
111 Table 8.
112 Statement of the SARWA to the Economic and Wage Commission, p.3, Archs of the Eco. and Wage Comm. (1925-6); Nat. Archs.
113 Evidence of the SARWA (Mr A.A. Moore) to the Mining Regulations Commission, Evid. of the Min. Regs Comm. (1924-5), pp.786, 788, 790; Nat. Archs.
114 'Report of the Mining Industry Board' (1922), p.11.
115 Tvl Ch. of Mines, Statement showing numbers of workers . . ., pp.1-4; SAEDFA Archs. This is in itself, of course, not a sufficient measure of the total displacement.
116 Letter from the Under-Secretary of Mines and Industries to the Secretary of Mines and Industries, 13 August 1924; Archs of the Dept of Mines and Inds, File MM 1699/24; Nat. Archs.
117 'Report of the Mining Industry Board' (1922), p.11; 'Report of the Mining Regulations Commission' (1925), p.16.
118 The reorganisation of the mining industry since the strike (Statement of the Tvl Ch. of Mines to the Mining Regulations Commission), 'South African Mining and Engineering Journal', 13 December 1924, p.368.
119 Speech of the President, annual general meeting of the Chamber, March 1923, 'ARTCM 1922', p.62.
120 Transcripts of cases in the Appelate Division of the

Notes to chapter 3

      Supreme Court of South Africa, Transcript of Rex v. G. Hildick-Smith, Magistrate's Court, Johannesburg, 10 August 1923, p.95; Nat. Archs.
121 Ibid., pp.97-123.
122 Ibid., p.96.
123 'Judgements of the Transvaal Provincial Division of the Supreme Court, 1923', Case of Rex v. Hildick-Smith, supporting opinion of P.U. Rissik, p.70.
124 Ibid., judgment of Judge Krause, p.90.
125 Ibid., p.83.
126 Ibid., p.84.
127 Ibid., judgment of Judge Tindall, pp.76-7.
128 Evidence of the Government Mining Engineer (Sir Robert Kotze) to the Mining Regulations Commission, Evid. of the Min. Regs Comm. (1924-5), p.444; Nat. Archs.
129 Evidence of the Inspector of Mines, Germiston (Mr C.F. Hutton) to the Mining Regulations Commission, ibid., p.268.
130 Ibid., p.266.
131 Evidence of the Inspector of Mines, Johannesburg District (Mr C.J. Gray) to the Mining Regulations Commission, ibid., p.56.
132 Evidence of the Inspector of Mines, Brakpan District (Col. H. Bottomley) to the Mining Regulations Commission, ibid., p.367.
133 Evidence of the Inspector of Mines, Johannesburg District (Mr C.J. Gray) to the Mining Regulations Commission, ibid., p.58.
134 Ibid., p.57.
135 Ibid., p.58.
136 Evidence of Mr H.W. Hayne, miner, to the Mining Regulations Commission, ibid., p.260.
137 Evidence of the SAEDFA (Mr R. Tennant) to the Mining Regulations Commission, ibid., p.432.
138 Ibid. (Mr W. Butler), p.327.
139 Ibid. (Mr R. Tennant), pp.379, 430-1.

3. The counter-attack of the white workers

1 Statement of the SAIF, 12 February 1922; TUCSA Archs.
2 Minute Book of the SAEDFA for 1923, 9 September 1923; SAEDFA Archs.
3 Statement relative to the present depression and the trend of South Africa towards a black industrial basis, from the trade unions' point of view, September 1923; ibid.

247 Notes to chapter 3

4   Ibid.
5   Circular letter from the trade unions, 8 September 1923; ibid.
6   The white mine workers also sought action from the government, complaining about the displacement of white workers and stating that 'those who remain are ever haunted by the fear that, as a result of the Court's decision that colour bar Regulations are illegal, many more will be eliminated'. This also met with no success (Letter from the SAEDFA to the Prime Minister, 20 February 1924, and ensuing correspondence; Archs of the Dept of Mines and Inds, File MM 899/24; Nat. Archs).
7   Letter from Creswell to Hertzog, 14 October 1921; Creswell-Hertzog Correspondence, Creswell Papers; Nat. Archs.
8   Letter from Hertzog to Creswell, 26 October 1921; ibid.
9   Creswell, Memorandum of conversation with General Hertzog, 15 July 1922; ibid.
10 Ibid.
11 Letter from Creswell to Hertzog, 12 April 1923; ibid. Hertzog confirmed that Creswell's summary 'truly sums up the substance of our conversation' (Letter from Hertzog to Creswell, 19 April 1923; ibid.).
12 Letter from Creswell to Hertzog, 12 April 1923; ibid.
13 The new government, 'Round Table', September 1924, p.835.
14 Notes of an agreement between the Labour Party and the Nationalist Party; Creswell-Hertzog Correspondence, Creswell Papers; Nat. Archs.
15 Report on the conference of trade union delegates, Cape Town, 1924, Resolution No. 1; Archs of the Dept of Mines and Inds, File MM 2382/24; Nat. Archs.
16 Ibid., Resolutions Nos 2, 6, 8, 9, 10, 12, 16, 18, 20, 24; ibid.
17 This policy was defined and promulgated in a circular from the Prime Minister to all government departments in October 1924: 'The Prime Minister desires it to be understood by all Departments of State that it has been decided as a matter of definite policy that, wherever practicable, civilised labour shall be substituted in all employment by the government for that which may be classified as uncivilised. Civilised labour is to be considered as the labour rendered by persons whose standard of living conforms to the standard generally recognised as tolerable from the

Notes to chapter 3

usual European standpoint. Uncivilised labour is to be regarded as the labour rendered by persons whose aim is restricted to the bare requirements of the necessities of life as understood among barbarians and undeveloped peoples' (P.M. Circular No. 5, 31 October 1924: 'Official Yearbook of the Union of South Africa, 1926-27', p.203).
18 The Customs Tariff and Excise Duties Amendment Act, Act No. 36, 1925.
19 The Wage Act, Act No. 27, 1925.
20 Minutes of a conference between the Minister of Mines and Industries, the Minister of Labour and Dept Secretaries, 28 July 1924; and Circular from the Minister of Labour to other Ministers, 30 July 1924; Archs of the Dept of Mines and Inds, File MM 2157/24; Nat. Archs.
21 Minutes of a conference between a deputation of white mine workers and the Ministers of Labour and of Mines and Industries, 28 August 1924; ibid., File MM 2146/24.
22 'Report of the Mining Regulations Commission' (1925), p.1.
23 Evidence of the SAMWU (Mr D. Reich) to the Mining Regulations Commission, Evid. of the Min. Regs Comm. (1924-5), p.622; Nat. Archs.
24 Ibid., p.161.
25 Ibid., p.166.
26 'Report of the Mining Regulations Commission' (1925), pp.2-14.
27 Ibid., p.14, para.68.
28 Ibid., para.69.
29 Ibid., p.20, para.112.
30 Ibid., para.113.
31 Ibid., pp.20-1, para.115.
32 Ibid., p.20, para.114; p.21, para.116.
33 Ibid., p.17, para.96.
34 Ibid., para.97.
35 Ibid.
36 Ibid., p.18, para.98.
37 Ibid., p.21, para.119.
38 Ibid., pp.21-2, para.122.
39 Ibid., p.22, para.123.
40 Ibid., para.125.
41 Ibid., pp.21-2.
42 Ibid., p.22, para.129. As a long-term solution to the undercutting problem, the Commission favoured a minimum wage per job system (ibid.).
43 Editorial, 'South African Mining and Engineering Journal', 1 November 1924, p.205.

249 Notes to chapter 3

44 The mining industry and its investigators, ibid., 6 December 1924, p.333.
45 Speech of the President, ordinary general meeting of the Chamber, June 1925, 'ARTCM 1925', p.150.
46 Editorial, 'South African Mining and Engineering Journal', 27 June 1925, p.497.
47 Minutes of a conference between a deputation of white mine workers and the Ministers of Labour and of Mines and Industries, 28 August 1924 (Mr R. Butler, of the SAEDFA), p.2; Archs of the Dept of Mines and Inds, File MM 2146/24; Nat. Archs.
48 'Senate Debates 1925', 2 July 1925, cols 562-3.
49 Ibid., 7 July 1925, cols 757-8.
50 'House of Assembly Debates 1925', 25 February 1925, col.273.
51 Ibid., col.275.
52 Ibid. (Minister of Mines and Industries), col.268.
53 'Senate Debates 1925', 2 July 1925, col.568.
54 'House of Assembly Debates 1925', 6 April 1925 (Mr G.A. Hay), col.1941.
55 Ibid. (Mr W.B. Madeley), col.1930.
56 Ibid. (Mr M. Kentridge), col.1902.
57 Ibid., 25 February 1925 (Mr H.W. Sampson), col.286.
58 'Senate Debates 1925', 6 July 1925 (Senator P. Whiteside), cols 670, 672-3.
59 Ibid. (Senator Fraser), col.680.
60 Ibid. (Senator Tucker), col.694.
61 Ibid., 7 July 1925 (Senator Munnik), col.723.
62 'House of Assembly Debates 1925', 6 April 1925, col. 1885.
63 Ibid., 25 February 1925, col.282.
64 Ibid.
65 Ibid., col.285.
66 Ibid. (Sir Drummond Chaplin), col.289.
67 Ibid., 6 April 1925 (Sir Thomas Smartt), col.1890.
68 Ibid. (Mr J.W. Jagger), col.1901.
69 Ibid. (Sir Ernest Oppenheimer), col.1922.
70 'House of Assembly Debates 1926', 27 January-4 February 1926; 'Senate Debates 1926', 16-17 March 1926.
71 'Debate of the Joint Sitting of both Houses of Parliament', 10 May 1926, col.18.
72 Ibid., col.23.
73 Ibid., col.24.
74 Ibid., col.28.
75 Ibid., 11 May 1926 (Sir Thomas Watt), cols 86-7.
76 Ibid. (Senator J.P. Malan), col.58.
77 Ibid., 10 May 1926, col.31.
78 Ibid., col.32.
79 Ibid., col.34.

80 Ibid., 11 May 1926, col.39.
81 Ibid., col.40.
82 Ibid., col.50.
83 Ibid.
84 Ibid., col.51.
85 Ibid., cols 50, 54.
86 Ibid., 12 May 1926, col.130.
87 The Mines and Works Act Amendment Act, Act No. 25, 1926.
88 Correspondence and negotiations, 1926-9; Archs of the Dept of Mines and Inds, File MM 608/26; Nat. Archs.

CHAPTER 4

1. Unrest, conflict and repression

1 Chronological notes on the attitude of natives in the two recent strikes (Memorandum from the Director of Native Labour to the Secretary of Native Affairs), 7 February 1914, pp.1-2; Archs of the Dept of Native Affairs, File NA 98/14/F473; Nat. Archs.
2 Evidence of the General Superintendent of the Native Recruiting Corporation to the Witwatersrand Disturbances Commission, 'Evidence of the Witwatersrand Disturbances Commission' (1913), paras 6837, 6841.
3 Chronological notes on the attitude of natives . . ., p.2.
4 Ibid., pp.2-3.
5 Ibid., p.3.
6 Ibid., p.4.
7 Evidence of the General Superintendent of the Native Recruiting Corporation to the Witwatersrand Disturbances Commission, 'Evidence of the Witwatersrand Disturbances Commission' (1913), para.6853.
8 Chronological notes on the attitude of natives . . ., p.4.
9 Strictly confidential memorandum from General J.C. Smuts to magistrates, 22 July 1913; and Outline of organisation to meet a general industrial crisis; Archs of the Dept of Native Affairs, File NA 98/14/F473; Nat. Archs.
10 Letter from the Chairman of the Native Recruiting Corporation to General J.C. Smuts, 16 July 1913; ibid.
11 Message of General L. Botha to native labourers in mines and works; ibid.
12 Telegram from the Director of Native Labour to the

251 Notes to chapter 4

Secretary of Native Affairs, 4 April 1914; ibid.
13 Ibid.
14 Statement of the Director of Native Labour to the Low Grade Mines Commission, p.11, Evid. of the Low Grade Mines Comm. (1919-20); Nat. Archs.
15 Ibid.
16 'Report of the Native Grievances Inquiry' (Cape Town: 1914, UG 37/14).
17 Among those which the Chamber rejected were those recommending the provision of education for Africans in the compounds, and that an African should only be refused a shift ticket if actually convicted of 'loafing'. However certain others, which it expressed agreement with, such as changes in the wage payment system, it never implemented (Minutes of the Native Grievances Commission Sub-Committee of the Tvl Ch. of Mines, 31 July 1914; Archs of the Nat. Grievs Inq. (1913-14), Archs of the Dept of Native Affairs, File NA 2782/13/F473; Nat. Archs; and Evidence of the Tvl Ch. of Mines (Mr A. French) to the Low Grade Mines Commission, Evid. of the Low Grade Mines Comm. (1919-20), pp.1098-2000; Nat. Archs).
18 E.g. Van Ryn Deep, 20 December 1915; Government Gold Mining Areas, 23 January 1916; New Modderfontein, February 1916.
19 Report by Sub-Inspector, SAP, Benoni to the District Commandant, SAP, Boksburg, 4 February 1916; Archs of the Dept of Native Affairs, File NA 277/16/F473; Nat. Archs.
20 Letter from the Director of Native Labour to the Commissioner, SAP, 11 February 1916; ibid.
21 'Report of the Special Commissioner appointed to Inquire into the Boycotting of Rand Store-keepers by Natives in 1918' (Stanford Report) (Cape Town: 1919, UG 4/19), p.1.
22 Ibid.
23 Ibid., p.3.
24 'Report of the Cost of Living Commission on the Investigation of Accounts of Mine Store-keepers on the Witwatersrand' (Cape Town: 1919, UG 4/19), pp.5-6.
25 'Report of the Special Commissioner . . .', p.3.
26 Report of the Commission of Inquiry into African Unrest on the Witwatersrand in 1918 (Moffat Report), 'Government Gazette', no.1184, 4 September 1918, p.3.
27 Reports of Native Constable Arthur, Sergeant A.N. Turner and Sergeant J. Bland, to the Commissioner, SAP, on the meeting of 19 June 1918; Archs of the Dept of Justice, File 3/527/17; Nat. Archs.
28 Ibid.

252   Notes to chapter 4

29 Circular of the Tvl Nat. Cong. to employers, 20 June 1918; Archs of the Dept of Native Affairs, File NA 737/18/F473; Nat. Archs.
30 Report of Native Constable R. Moorosi on the meeting of 29 June 1918; Archs of the Dept of Justice, File 3/527/17; Nat. Archs.
31 Report of Sub-Inspector F.V. Lloyd to the Deputy Commissioner, SAP, on the meeting of 30 June 1918; ibid.
32 Letter from the Secretary of Native Affairs to the Chief Magistrate of the Transkei, 8 July 1918; Archs of the Dept of Native Affairs, File NA 737/18/F473; Nat. Archs.
33 Letter from the Secretary of Native Affairs to the Tvl Nat. Cong., 2 July 1918; ibid.
34 Report of an Inspector of the Dept of Native Affairs to the Director of Native Labour, 23 July 1918; Archs of the Dept of Justice, File 3/527/17; Nat. Archs.
35 'Rand Daily Mail', 23 July 1918, p.3.
36 Report of the Commission of Inquiry into African Unrest on the Witwatersrand in 1918 (Moffat Report), 'Government Gazette', no.1184, 4 September 1918, pp. 3-4.
37 Report of Native Detective M. Ngwenya to the Commissioner, SAP, on the meeting of 12 January 1919, quoting Mr Ntintili; Archs of the Dept of Justice, File 3/527/17; Nat. Archs.
38 Report of Native Detective M. Ngwenya to the Commissioner, SAP, on the meeting of 26 January 1919, quoting Mr Mvabaza; ibid.
39 Report of Native Detective M. Ngwenya to the Commissioner, SAP, on the meeting of 23 February 1919, quoting Mr C.S. Mabaso; ibid.
40 Telegram from the Director of Native Labour to the Minister of Native Affairs, 31 March 1919; Archs of the Dept of Mines and Inds, File MM 1633/20; Nat. Archs.
41 Report of Sub-Inspector C. Loftus to the District Commandant, SAP, Boksburg, 4 April 1919; Archs of the Dept of Justice, File 3/527/17; Nat. Archs.
42 Report of Native Detective N. Sibisi to the Commissioner, SAP, on the meeting of 3 April 1919; ibid.
43 Ibid.
44 Report of Native Constables W. Jali and N. Sibisi to the Commissioner, SAP, on the meeting of 11 April 1919; ibid.
45 Circular of the Tvl Nat. Cong., April 1919; ibid.
46 Minutes of a conference between the Minister of

253 Notes to chapter 4

Justice and a deputation from the Tvl Nat. Cong., Pretoria, 7 April 1919, p.4; Archs of the Dept of Native Affairs, File NA 389/19/F473; Nat. Archs.

47 Report of the Commission of Inquiry regarding alleged illtreatment of natives by members of the police force during the recent native unrest in Johannesburg (Boyes Report), 7 May 1919, p.6; ibid., File NA 153/20/F473.

48 Letter from Mr G.J. Boyes to the Secretary of Justice, 7 May 1919; Archs of the Dept of Justice, File 3/527/17; Nat. Archs.

49 Various police reports on the meeting at Boksburg, 27 April 1919; ibid.

50 Report of Native Constable W. Jali to the Commissioner, SAP, on the meeting of 20 April 1919, quoting a Miss Kekana; ibid.

51 Report of Native Constable N. Sibisi to the Commissioner, SAP, on the meeting of 18 April 1919, quoting a speaker from Roodepoort; ibid.

52 Report of Native Constable N. Sibisi to the Commissioner, SAP, on the meeting of 1 May 1919, quoting Mr Motsoakae; ibid.

53 Report of the Deputy Commissioner, CID (Tvl Div.), to the Secretary, SAP, on the meeting of 26 November 1919, quoting Mr C.S. Mabaso; ibid.

54 Ibid.

55 Report of the Deputy Commissioner, CID (Tvl Div.), to the Secretary, SAP, on the meeting of 2 January 1920; ibid.

56 Minutes of a conference between various employers of labour and a deputation of Africans at Johannesburg, 9 January 1920, Mr C.S. Mabaso, p.3; Archs of the Dept of Native Affairs, File NA 768/18/F473; Nat. Archs.

57 Ibid., Mr K.K. Pilane, p.9.

58 Ibid., Mr K.K. Pilane, p.10.

59 Report of the Johannesburg Chamber of Commerce to the Director of Native Labour on the results of a conference on 23 January 1920; ibid. (the increases were to be not less than 25 per cent over the pre-war money rates).

60 Report of the Deputy Commissioner, CID (Tvl Div.), to the Secretary, SAP, on the meeting of 1 February 1920; Archs of the Dept of Justice, File 3/527/17; Nat. Archs.

61 Reports of Native Constables W. Jali and N. Sibisi to the Commissioner, SAP, 7 April 1919; ibid.

62 Report of the District Commandant, SAP, East Rand-Boksburg, to the Commissioner, SAP, 10 February 1920; ibid.

63 Speech of the President, annual general meeting of the Chamber, March 1921, 'ARTCM 1920', p.67.
64 Speech of the President, annual general meeting of the Chamber, March 1920, 'ARTCM 1919', p.69.
65 'Report of the Economic and Wage Commission' (1926), Table VIII, p.21; Table H, p.271.
66 Press statement of the Tvl Ch. of Mines on the African strike, 21 February 1920, 'ARTCM 1920', p.88.
67 Report of the Acting Inspector of Labour to the Director of Native Labour, 10 February 1920; Archs of the Dept of Native Affairs, File NA 206/18/F164; Nat. Archs.
68 Press statement of the Tvl Ch. of Mines . . ., 'ARTCM 1920', p.89.
69 Ibid.
70 Ibid.
71 Speech of the President, annual general meeting of the Chamber, March 1921, ibid., p.67.
72 Various reports, Archs of the Dept of Native Affairs, File NA 768/18/F473; Nat. Archs. For brief accounts, see R.K. Cope, 'Comrade Bill: The Life and Times of W.H. Andrews, Workers' Leader' (Cape Town: 1943), p.215; H.J. and R.E. Simons, 'Class and Colour in South Africa, 1850-1950' (Harmondsworth: 1969), pp.231-2.
73 Speech of the President, annual general meeting of the Chamber, March 1921, 'ARTCM 1920', p.68; and correspondence between the Tvl Ch. of Mines and the Johannesburg Chamber of Commerce, ibid., pp.155-7.
74 Press statement of the Tvl Ch. of Mines . . ., ibid., p.89.
75 Letter from the President of the Tvl Ch. of Mines to the Minister of Justice, 25 March 1920, ibid., p.90.

2. The African workers and the class colour bars: structural grievances

1 Statement of the Director of Native Labour to the Low Grade Mines Commission, p.8; Evid. of the Low Grade Mines Comm. (1919-20); Nat. Archs.
2 Evidence of African mine workers and their representatives to the Native Grievances Inquiry (1913-14), the Low Grade Mines Commission (1919-20), the Mining Industry Board (1922), the Mining Regulations Commission (1924-5), and the Economic and Wage Commission (1925-6); Nat. Archs.
3 Evidence of the Chief Induna on the Crown Mines (Mr E.W. Nogaga) to the Mining Industry Board, Evid. of

Notes to chapter 4

   the Min. Ind. Board (1922), p.2750; Nat. Archs.
4 Statement of the Tvl Nat. Cong. to the Low Grade
   Mines Commission, p.16; Archs of the Low Grade Mines
   Comm. (1919-20), Misc. Files; Nat. Archs.
5 Ibid.
6 Ibid., p.17.
7 Evidence of African mine worker Tom to the Native
   Grievances Inquiry, Evid. of the Nat. Grievs Inq.
   (1913-14), 28 October 1913, p.5; Archs of the Dept
   of Native Affairs, File 2782/13/F473; Nat. Archs.
8 Evidence of African mine worker Jaas to the Native
   Grievances Inquiry, ibid., p.25.
9 Evidence of African mine worker Jacob to the Native
   Grievances Inquiry, ibid., p.23.
10 Evidence of African mine worker Jim to the Native
   Grievances Inquiry, ibid., p.3.
11 Evidence of African mine worker Kalaway to the Native
   Grievances Inquiry, ibid., p.19.
12 Evidence of African mine worker Kleinbooi to the
   Native Grievances Inquiry, ibid., p.11.
13 Evidence of African mine worker Mosane to the Native
   Grievances Inquiry, ibid., p.17.
14 Evidence of African mine worker Ngquando to the
   Native Grievances Inquiry, ibid., p.27.
15 Evidence of African mine worker Enoch to the Native
   Grievances Inquiry, ibid., p.4.
16 Report of the Committee of Inquiry into alleged grievances of native labourers in the Crown Mines, July
   1913, p.11; F.S. Malan Papers, Cape Prov. Archs.
17 Ibid., p.16.
18 Evidence of the Chairman of the Native Recruiting
   Corporation (Mr C.W. Villiers) to the Native Grievances Inquiry, Evid. of the Nat. Grievs Inq. (1913-
   14), 3 March 1914, p.12; Archs of the Dept of Native
   Affairs, File NA 2782/13/F473; Nat. Archs.
19 'Report of the Economic Commission' (1914), p.37.
20 Evidence of the Chief Induna of the Crown Mines (Mr
   E.W. Nogaga) to the Mining Industry Board, Evid. of
   the Min. Ind. Board (1922), pp.2754-6; Nat. Archs.
21 Tvl Ch. of Mines, Statement of evidence to the Commissioner appointed to inquire into the recent native
   unrest, 'ARTCM 1918', p.90.
22 Ibid.
23 Ibid., p.91.
24 Report of the Commission of Inquiry into African
   Unrest on the Witwatersrand in 1918, 'Government
   Gazette', no.1184, 4 September 1918, p.4.
25 Ibid.
26 Tvl Ch. of Mines, Statement of evidence to the

Notes to chapter 4

Commissioner . . ., 'ARTCM 1918', p.89.
27 Evidence of Mr D.D.T. Jabavu to the Mining Industry Board, Evid. of the Min. Ind. Board (1922), p.4779; Nat. Archs.
28 Statement of the Tvl Nat. Cong. to the Low Grade Mines Commission, p.16; Archs of the Low Grade Mines Comm. (1919-20), Misc. Files; Nat. Archs.
29 Ibid.
30 Evidence of the Native Mine Clerks' Association (NMCA) to the Mining Industry Board, Evid. of the Min. Ind. Board (1922), p.3027; Nat. Archs.
31 'Report of the Cost of Living Commission on the Investigation of Accounts of Mine Store-keepers on the Witwatersrand' (1919), p.6.
32 Evidence of Mr P.A. Gajana (Chief Compound Clerk, and Secretary of the NMCA) to the Mining Industry Board, Evid. of the Min. Ind. Board (1922), p.2704; Nat. Archs.
33 Ibid.
34 The Pass Laws (a study made by government officials), p.57; Archs of the Dept of Native Affairs, File NA 658/18/F473; Nat. Archs.
35 Evidence of the Native National Congress to the Low Grade Mines Commission (Mr S. Msane), Summary, p.3, Evid. of the Low Grade Mines Comm. (1919-20); Nat. Archs.
36 Minutes of a conference between the Minister of Justice and a deputation of the Tvl Nat. Cong., Pretoria, 7 April 1919, p.16 (Mr J.G. Matshige); Archs of the Dept of Native Affairs, File NA 389/19/F473; Nat. Archs.
37 Statement of the Tvl Nat. Cong. to the Low Grade Mines Commission, p.8; Archs of the Low Grade Mines Comm. (1919-20), Misc. Files; Nat. Archs.
38 Ibid., p.9.
39 E.g. the meeting of 17 December 1918 (Report of Native Constable Philemon to the Commissioner, SAP, on the meeting of 17 December 1918; Archs of the Dept of Justice, File 3/527/17; Nat. Archs).
40 Minutes of a conference between the Minister of Justice and a deputation of the Tvl Nat. Cong., Pretoria, 7 April 1919, p.10 (Mr D.S. Letanka, Vice-Pres. of the Tvl Nat. Cong.); Archs of the Dept of Native Affairs, File NA 389/19/F473; Nat. Archs.
41 Ibid.
42 Ibid., pp.7, 9 (Mr S.M. Makgatho, Pres. of the Tvl Nat. Cong.).
43 E.g. Evidence of African mine worker Frank Page to the Native Grievances Inquiry, Evid. of the Nat.

Notes to chapter 4

Grievs Inq. (1913-14), 28 October 1913, p.9; Archs of the Dept of Native Affairs, File NA 2782/13/F473; Nat. Archs.
44 Statement of the Tvl Nat. Cong. to the Low Grade Mines Commission, p.12; Archs of the Low Grade Mines Comm. (1919-20), Misc. Files; Nat. Archs.
45 Ibid.; and, e.g., Evidence of Mr M. Pelem (labour recruiting agent) to the Mining Industry Board, Evid. of the Min. Ind. Board (1922), pp.4789-90; Nat. Archs.
46 Evidence of the Technical Adviser of the Native Recruiting Corporation (Mr A.W. Stockett) to the Native Grievances Inquiry, Evid. of the Nat. Grievs Inq. (1913-14), 6 March 1914, p.13; Archs of the Dept of Native Affairs, File NA 2782/13/F473; Nat. Archs.
47 Statement of the Tvl Nat. Cong. . . ., p.17.
48 Ibid., p.11.
49 Ibid., p.12.
50 Ibid., p.29.
51 Ibid., pp.8-9.
52 Ibid.
53 Minutes of a conference between the Minister of Justice and a deputation of the Tvl Nat. Cong., Pretoria, 7 April 1919, p.13 (Mr H.N.V. Msane); Archs of the Dept of Native Affairs, File NA 389/19/F473; Nat. Archs.
54 Ibid., pp.12-13.
55 Statement of the Tvl Nat. Cong. to the Low Grade Mines Commission, p.2; Archs of the Low Grade Mines Comm. (1919-20), Misc. Files; Nat. Archs.
56 Ibid.
57 Evidence of the Native Mine Clerks' Association (Mr A.W.G. Champion, Chairman of the NMCA) to the Economic and Wage Commission, Evid. of the Eco. and Wage Comm. (1925-6), pp.2138-40; Nat. Archs.
58 Evidence of the Chief Induna of the Crown Mines (Mr E.W. Nogaga) to the Mining Industry Board, Evid. of the Min. Ind. Board (1922), p.2760; Nat. Archs.
59 Evidence of the NMCA to the Economic and Wage Commission (Mr A.W.G. Champion), Evid. of the Eco. and Wage Comm. (1925-6), pp.2152-3; Nat. Archs.
60 Evidence of Mr P.A. Gajana (Chief Compound Clerk, and Secretary of the NMCA) to the Mining Industry Board, Evid. of the Min. Ind. Board (1922), p.2723; Nat. Archs.
61 Statement of the Tvl Nat. Cong. to the Low Grade Mines Commission, p.4; Archs of the Low Grade Mines Comm. (1919-20), Misc. Files; Nat. Archs.
62 Ibid., p.5.

258 Notes to chapter 4

63 Ibid., pp.6-7.
64 Ibid., p.6.
65 Ibid., p.7.
66 Evidence of the Chief Induna of the Crown Mines (Mr E.W. Nogaga) to the Mining Industry Board, Evid. of the Min. Ind. Board (1922), pp.2750-1; Nat. Archs.
67 Evidence of the Home Native Co-operative Society (Mr M.M. Langa and Mr P.H. Muyayiss) to the Mining Industry Board, ibid., p.5060.
68 Evidence of the Native Mine Clerks' Association (Mr D.F. Mankozana) to the Mining Industry Board, ibid., p.3036.
69 Statement of the Tvl Nat. Cong. to the Low Grade Mines Commission, p.18; Archs of the Low Grade Mines Comm. (1919-20), Misc. Files; Nat. Archs.
70 Evidence of African mine workers and their representatives to the various Commissions of Inquiry during this period; Nat. Archs; Report of the Committee of Inquiry into alleged grievances of native labourers in the Crown Mines, July 1913, pp.5-6; F.S. Malan Papers, Cape Prov. Archs.
71 An investigation by the Chamber of Mines in 1909 found that there was an average of about 300 reported cases of assaults by whites on Africans in the mines per year. This only affected about half of 1 per cent of the African labour force, but these were only reported cases, and the actual number was thought to be considerably larger (letter from the Tvl Ch. of Mines to the Secretary of Native Affairs, 23 December 1909, 'ARTCM 1909', pp.28-9).
72 Report of the Committee of Inquiry into alleged grievances of native labourers in the Crown Mines, July 1913, p.11; F.S. Malan Papers, Cape Prov. Archs.
73 Statement of the Tvl Nat. Cong. to the Low Grade Mines Commission, p.27; Archs of the Low Grade Mines Comm. (1919-20), Misc. Files; Nat. Archs.
74 Evidence of the Native Mine Clerks' Association (Mr A.W.G. Champion) to the Economic and Wage Commission, Evid. of the Eco. and Wage Comm. (1925-6), p.2144; Nat. Archs.
75 Ibid., p.2162.
76 Ibid. (Mr S. Matanga), p.2163.
77 Statement of the Tvl Nat. Cong. to the Low Grade Mines Commission, p.20; Archs of the Low Grade Mines Comm. (1919-20), Misc. Files; Nat. Archs.

CONCLUSIONS

1 This work is to be found in various books and articles, reference to which will be found in the bibliography. See, e.g., R. Horwitz, 'The Political Economy of South Africa' (London: 1967), W.H. Hutt, 'The Economics of the Colour Bar' (London: 1964), and G.V. Doxey, 'The Industrial Colour Bar in South Africa' (Cape Town: 1961). For this stage in the work of non-economists, see, e.g., P.L. van den Berghe, 'South Africa: A Study in Conflict' (Berkeley: 1967), especially chapter 8 (The economic system and its dysfunctions).
2 Hutt, op. cit., pp.99, 135, 174, 180.
3 E.g. Van den Berghe, op. cit., pp.271-4.
4 L. Kuper and M.G. Smith (eds), 'Pluralism in Africa' (Berkeley: 1969), p.3.
5 E.g., Van den Berghe, op. cit., p.270; and J. Rex, 'Race Relations in Sociological Theory' (London: 1970), pp.19-24.
6 Van den Berghe, op. cit., p.267.
7 Ibid., pp.97-9, 266-7, 278.
8 M.G. Smith, Some developments in the analytic framework of pluralism, in Kuper and Smith (eds), op. cit., p.434.
9 Van den Berghe, op. cit., chapter 8, esp. pp.212-13.
10 Horwitz, op. cit., esp. the introductory section.
11 S.T. van der Horst, The effects of industrialisation on race relations in South Africa, in G. Hunter (ed.), 'Industrialisation and Race Relations' (London: 1965), pp.110, 123.
12 Ibid., p.100.
13 Horwitz, op. cit., p.170.
14 D.H. Houghton, Economic development, 1865-1965, in M. Wilson and L. Thompson (eds), 'The Oxford History of South Africa', vol.II: 'South Africa, 1870-1966' (Oxford: 1971), p.31.
15 E.g., Doxey, op. cit., and Doxey, Enforced racial stratification in the South African labour market, in H. Adam (ed.), 'South Africa: Sociological Perspectives' (London: 1971); Hutt, op. cit.; Horwitz, op. cit., and 'The South African Economy' (Cape Town: 1967); Van der Horst, op. cit., and 'Native Labour in South Africa' (London: 1942); F. Wilson, An analysis of the forces operating in the labour market of the South African gold mines, 1936-65 (Ph.D. thesis, Cambridge University, 1967).
16 E.g. in the way in which the above cited works refer to this situation. E.g. Horwitz, on the 1926 'Colour

Bar Act': 'The retrenchment of the colour bar in mining employment by the Mines and Works Amendment Act of 1926 established beyond challenge that the South African ethos and not economic rationality would dictate the ultimate determinants of gold mining costs' (op. cit., p.8).
17 Van der Horst, 'Native Labour in South Africa', p.324.
18 Wilson, op. cit., p.278.
19 Van den Berghe, op. cit., pp.213-15.

Bibliography

OUTLINE

I UNPUBLISHED PRIMARY SOURCES
  1 South African State Archives
  2 Other Archival Sources

II PUBLISHED PRIMARY SOURCES
  1 Reports of Official Commissions of Inquiry
  2 Parliamentary Debates
  3 Census and Statistical Reports
  4 Annual Government Reports
  5 Publications of the Transvaal Chamber of Mines
  6 Newspapers and Periodicals

III SELECT BIBLIOGRAPHY OF SECONDARY SOURCES ON SOUTH AFRICA

IV SELECT BIBLIOGRAPHY OF OTHER SECONDARY SOURCES

I UNPUBLISHED PRIMARY SOURCES

Since most of the archival material that was of use to this study was drawn from the South African State Archives (in the National Archives, Pretoria), and since this material will be referred to here under very general headings, rather than item by item (which would take up an enormous amount of space), a brief note on this source might perhaps be useful.
    The author made extensive research in the State Archives, including research on sources in the officially closed period (after 1920), which he received permission to study. This research yielded a great deal of valuable material. The most useful and important general sources

of information on, and insight into, the groups and situations with which this study is concerned were found to be the archives of certain government Departments and of certain Commissions of Inquiry - the archives of the Department of Mines and Industries, the Department of Native Affairs and the Department of Justice, and the archives of Commissions of Inquiry into socio-economic affairs.

The files of these Departments were found to contain a mass of important material of various kinds. And the Commission archives were also a particularly fruitful source. For there were several important Commissions of Inquiry into the gold mining industry, and into socio-economic affairs generally, during this period, and these Commissions gathered together an enormous amount of data and evidence. The archives of these Commissions contain the verbatim evidence, together with various sorts of useful additional material. All of the groups with which this study is concerned, including the African workers, together with many other people, gave statements and evidence to these Commissions, and were systematically questioned by them.

The State Archives, notably the archives of these Departments and Commissions, constituted the most important source of material for this study. This was the first time that these Department and Commission archives which cover the post-1910 period were systematically researched and studied. The explanation for this is to be found in such factors as the fifty-year rule, the extensive preoccupation of the historiography of South Africa with earlier periods and with politico-constitutional affairs, and the fact that, because of the specific regime prevailing in South Africa, opportunities for higher education and advanced research have been very largely confined to members of the ruling white minority, and consequently the number of inhabitants of South Africa researching into its history has been and remains disproportionately small in relation to its overall size and wealth.

South African State Archives

(1) Archives of government departments

Archives of the Department of Mines and Industries.
Archives of the Department of Native Affairs.
Archives of the Department of Justice.
Archives of the Prime Minister's Department.

Bibliography

(2) Archives of official commissions of inquiry

Archives and evidence of the Transvaal Mining Regulations Commission, 1907-10.
Archives and evidence of the Native Grievances Inquiry, 1913-14.
Archives and evidence of the Low Grade Mines Commission, 1919-20.
Archives and evidence of the Mining Industry Board, 1922.
Archives and evidence of the Mining Regulations Commission, 1924-5.
Archives and evidence of the Economic and Wage Commission, 1925-6.

Other archival sources

Of the various other archival sources consulted, the following were found to be useful:

(1) Trade union and labour movement archives

Archives of the Trade Union Council of South Africa (Head Office, Johannesburg).
Archives of the South African Engine Drivers' and Firemen's Association (Head Office, Johannesburg).
Archives of the South African Boilermakers', Iron and Steel Workers', Shipbuilders' and Welders' Society (Head Office, Johannesburg).
Archives of the South African Reduction Workers' Association (Head Office, Johannesburg).
Archives of the Amalgamated Engineering Union (Head Office, Johannesburg).
Archives of the Amalgamated Society of Woodworkers (Head Office, Johannesburg).
Archives of the South African Labour Party (Johannesburg Public Library).
(The archives of the Trade Union Council, of the Engine Drivers' Association and of the Boilermakers' Society were found to be particularly valuable. The archives of the South African Mine Workers' Union were recently destroyed.)

(2) Private papers

Of the collections of private papers consulted, the following were found to be useful:
F.H.P. Creswell (Nat. Archs, Pretoria).
J.X. Merriman (South African Public Library, Cape Town).

264 Bibliography

J.C. Smuts (Nat. Archs, Pretoria).
F.S. Malan (Cape Provincial Archives, Cape Town).
P. Duncan (University of Cape Town).
M. Alexander (University of Cape Town).
J.F. Herbst (University of Cape Town).

II PUBLISHED PRIMARY SOURCES

1. Reports of official commissions of inquiry

'Report of the Transvaal Indigency Commission' (Pretoria: Government Printing and Stationary Office (GPSO), 1908, TG 13/08).
'Report of the Transvaal Mining Industry Commission' (Pretoria: GPSO, 1908, TG 2/08).
'Interim Report of the Transvaal Mining Regulations Commission' (Pretoria: GPSO, 1909, TG 32/09).
'Final Report of the Transvaal Mining Regulations Commission' (Pretoria: GPSO, 1910).
'Report of the Select Committee of the House of Assembly on the Native Labour Regulation Bill' (Cape Town: Government Printer (GP), 1911, SC 3/11).
'Report of the Commission on the Conditions of Trade and Industry' (Pretoria: GPSO, 1912, UG 10/12).
'Report of the Commission on the Black Peril - The Rape of White Women' (Pretoria: GPSO, 1913, UG 39/13).
'Report of the Witwatersrand Disturbances Commission' (Pretoria: GPSO, 1913, UG 56/13).
'Reports and Minutes of Evidence of the Select Committee of the House of Assembly on European Employment and Labour Conditions' (Cape Town: GP, 1913, SC 9/13).
'Report of the Economic Commission' (Cape Town: GP, 1914, UG 12/14).
'Report of the Native Grievances Inquiry' (Cape Town: GP, 1914, UG 37/14).
'Report of the Commission on Industrial Education' (Pretoria: GPSO, 1917, UG 9/17).
'Report and Minutes of Evidence of the State Mining Commission' (Cape Town: GP, 1917, UG 19/17).
'Report of the Departmental Committee on Underground Mining Contracts (Witwatersrand Mines)' (Pretoria: GPSO, 1917, UG 38/17).
'Final Report of the State Mining Commission' (Pretoria: GPSO, 1918, UG 1/18).
'Report and Proceedings of the Select Committee of the House of Assembly on the Gold Mining Industry' (Cape Town: GP, 1918, SC 3/18).
Report of the Commissioner appointed to inquire into and

report upon the causes which led up to the partial cessation of the municipal sanitary services at Johannesburg . . . and the threatened strike . . ., 'Government Gazette', no.1184, 4 September 1918.
'General Report, and Report on Rents and Housing, of the Cost of Living Commission' (Cape Town: GP, 1919, UG 55/18).
'Profits Report of the Cost of Living Commission' (Cape Town: GP, 1919, UG 1/19).
'Report of the Special Commissioner appointed to Inquire into the Boycotting of Rand Store-keepers by Natives in 1918' (Cape Town: GP, 1919, UG 4/19).
'Report of the Cost of Living Commission on the Investigation of Accounts of Mine Store-keepers on the Witwatersrand and as to the Fixing of Prices of the Chief Articles of Native Trade in the Witwatersrand Area, 1918' (Cape Town: GP, 1919, UG 4/19).
'Report and Minutes of Proceedings of the Select Committee of the House of Assembly on the Cost of Living Commission's Reports' (Cape Town: GP, 1919, SC 13/19).
'Interim Report of the Low Grade Mines Commission' (Cape Town: GP, 1919, UG 45/19).
'Final Report of the Low Grade Mines Commission' (Cape Town: GP, 1920, UG 34/20).
'Interim Report of the Cost of Living Commission' (Pretoria: GPSO, 1920, UG 26/20).
'Report of the Committee of Inquiry into the Closing Down of the Princess Estate Mine' (Pretoria: GPSO, 1920, UG 39/20).
'Report of the Committee of Inquiry into the Simmer Deep and Jupiter Gold Mines' (Pretoria: GPSO, 1920, UG 44/20).
'Report of the Committee of Inquiry into the Probable Closing Down of the Roodepoort United Main Reef Gold Mine' (Pretoria: GPSO, 1920, UG 51/20).
'Report of the Committee of Inquiry into the Closing Down of the Knights Deep Mine' (Pretoria: GPSO, 1920, UG 63/20).
'First Interim Report of the Unemployment Commission' (Cape Town: GP, 1921, UG 16/21).
'Second Interim Report of the Unemployment Commission' (Cape Town: GP, 1921, UG 34/21).
'Final Report of the Unemployment Commission' (Cape Town: GP, 1922, UG 17/22).
'Report of the Martial Law Inquiry Judicial Commission' (Pretoria: GPSO, 1922, UG 34/22).
'Report of the Mining Industry Board' (Cape Town: GP, 1922, UG 39/22).
'Report of the Inter-Departmental Committee on Native Pass

Laws' (Pretoria: GPSO, 1922, UG 41/22).
'Report of the Mining Regulations Commission' (Cape Town: GP, 1925, UG 36/25).
'Report and Minutes of Evidence of the Select Committee of the House of Assembly on the Mines and Works Act 1911 Amendment Bill' (Cape Town: GP, 1925, SC 15/25).
'Report of the Cost of Living Commission' (Cape Town: GP, 1925, UG 47/25).
'Report of the Resumption of Gold Payments by the Union of South Africa' (Pretoria: GPSO, 1925, UG 12/25).
'Report of the Economic and Wage Commission' (Cape Town: GP 1926, UG 14/26).
'Report of the Mining Industry Arbitration Board' (Pretoria: GPSO, 1927).
'Report on the Far East Rand and Features likely to affect the Future of the Witwatersrand Gold Mining Industry' (Cape Town: GP, 1927).
'Report of the Inter-Departmental Committee on the Labour Resources of the Union' (Pretoria: GPSO, 1930, UG 26/30).
'Report of the Carnegie Commission on the Poor White Problem in South Africa' (Stellenbosch: Pro Ecclesia Drukkery, 1932).
'Report of the Low Grade Ore Commission' (Pretoria: GPSO, 1932, UG 16/32).
'Report of the Native Economic Commission' (Pretoria: GPSO, 1932, UG 22/32).
'Report of the Unemployment Investigation Committee' (Pretoria: GPSO, 1932, UG 30/32).
'Report of the Industrial Legislation Commission' (Pretoria: GPSO, 1935, UG 37/35).
'Report of the Witwatersrand Mine Natives' Wages Commission' (Pretoria: GPSO, 1944, UG 21/44).
'Report No. 9 of the Social and Economic Planning Council: The Native Reserves and their Place in the Economy of the Union of South Africa' (Pretoria: GPSO, 1946, UG 32/46).
'Report of the Native Laws Commission' (Pretoria: GPSO, 1948, UG 28/48).
'Report No. 11 of the Social and Economic Planning Council: Economic Aspects of the Gold Mining Industry' (Pretoria: GPSO, 1948, UG 32/48).

2. Parliamentary debates

'Debates of the South African House of Assembly' (Cape Town: GP).
'Debates of the South African Senate' (Cape Town: GP).

Bibliography

(Between 19 November 1915 and 25 June 1923, Parliamentary debates were published in the 'Cape Times'.)
'Printed Annexures, Votes and Proceedings of the House of Assembly' (Cape Town: GP).

3. Census and statistical reports

'Report of the 1904 Census of the Transvaal Colony and Swaziland' (Pretoria: GPSO, 1906).
'Report of the 1911 Census of the Population of the Union of South Africa' (Pretoria: GPSO, 1912, UG 32/12).
'Report of the 1918 Census of the European or White Races of the Union of South Africa' (Cape Town: GP, 1919-21, UG 50/19, UG 56/20, UG 1/21).
'Report of the 1921 Census of the Population of the Union of South Africa' (Pretoria: GPSO, 1923-5, UG 15/23, UG 33/23, UG 35/23, UG 37/24, UG 4/24, UG 37/25).
'Report of the 1926 Census of the European Population of the Union of South Africa' (Pretoria: GPSO, 1927-31, UG 32/27, UG 27/30, UG 4/31). 'Final Report of the 1926 Census' (Pretoria: 1931, UG 4/31).
'Report of the Industrial Census of the Union of South Africa: Statistics of Production - Statistics of Factories and Productive Industries (excluding Mining and Quarrying)' (Pretoria: GPSO, annual, from 1918 onwards, covering the period from 1916-17 onwards; UG 14/18, UG 51/18, UG 17/20, UG 28/21, UG 48/21, UG 40/22, UG 14/24, UG 41/24, UG 35/26).
'Social Statistics: Statistics of Wages and Industrial Matters and of Retail and Wholesale Prices, Rents and Cost of Living' (Pretoria: GPSO, annual).
'Employment in Secondary Industry, Mining and Transportation, 1925-45: Special Report of the Board of Trade and Industries, No. 158' (Pretoria: GPSO, 1946).
'Union Statistics for Fifty Years, 1910-60' (Pretoria: GPSO, 1960).
'Urban and Rural Population of South Africa, 1904-60' (Pretoria: GPSO, 1968; Report No. 02.02.01 of the South African Bureau of Statistics).

4. Other government reports

'Annual Reports of the Department of Mines and Industries' (Pretoria: GPSO).
'Annual Reports of the Department of Native Affairs' (Pretoria: GPSO).
'Official Year Books of the Union of South Africa' (Pretoria: GPSO).

5. Publications of the Transvaal Chamber of Mines

'Annual Reports of the Transvaal Chamber of Mines' (Johannesburg: Tvl Ch. of Mines).
'Statements of Evidence of the Transvaal Chamber of Mines to the Economic Commission' (Johannesburg: Tvl Ch. of Mines, 1913).
'Statements of Evidence of the Transvaal Chamber of Mines to the Economic and Wage Commission' (Johannesburg: Tvl Ch. of Mines, 1925).
'Statements of Evidence of the Transvaal Chamber of Mines to the Mining Industry Arbitration Board' (Johannesburg: Tvl Ch. of Mines, 1927).
'The Mines: What they mean to the Farmer' (Johannesburg: Tvl Ch. of Mines, 1923).
'Party Programmes and the Mines: A Business Statement' (Johannesburg: Tvl Ch. of Mines, 1924).
'The Gold of the Rand, 1887-1927' (Johannesburg: Tvl Ch. of Mines, 1927).
'The Transvaal Chamber of Mines and its Subsidiary Organisations' (Johannesburg: Tvl Ch. of Mines, 1936).

6. Newspapers and periodicals

Various newspapers and periodicals were consulted, the most useful of which were: 'South African Mining Journal' (later 'South African Mining and Engineering Journal'), 'Star', 'Rand Daily Mail', 'Cape Times, 'Cape Argus', 'Round Table', and 'International'.

III SELECT BIBLIOGRAPHY OF SECONDARY SOURCES ON SOUTH AFRICA

ADAM, H., 'Modernizing Racial Domination: South Africa's Political Dynamics' (Berkeley: University of California Press, 1971).
ADAM, H. (ed.), 'South Africa: Sociological Perspectives' (London: Oxford University Press, 1971).
AGAR-HAMILTON, J.A., 'The Native Policy of the Voortrekkers' (Cape Town: Miller, 1928).
ALEXANDER, R. and SIMONS, H.J., 'Job Reservation in the Trade Unions' (Woodstock, Cape: Enterprise, 1959).
ANDREWS, W.H., 'Class Struggles in South Africa' (Cape Town: Stewart, 1941).
ARKIN, M., Strikes, boycotts and the history of their impact on South Africa, 'South African Journal of Economics', 28, 1960.

BALLINGER, M., 'From Union to Apartheid' (Cape Town: Juta, 1969).
BALLINGER, W.G., 'Race and Economics in South Africa' (London: Hogarth Press, 1934).
BARBER, S.H., 'Laws, Volksraad Resolutions, Proclamations and Government Notices relating to Natives and Coolies in the Transvaal' (Pretoria: 1901).
BELL, F.W., 'The South African Native Problem: A Suggested Solution' (Johannesburg: Central News Agency, 1909).
BENSON, M., 'South Africa: The Struggle for a Birthright' (Harmondsworth: Penguin, 1966).
BOSMAN, V. (ed.), 'Industrial Development in South Africa and Facilities for the Establishment of Factories' (Pretoria: GPSO, 1936).
BOYDELL, T., 'My Luck Was In' (Cape Town: Stewart, 1947).
BROOKES, E.H., 'The History of Native Policy in South Africa from 1830 to the Present Day' (Pretoria: Van Schaik, 1927).
BROOKES, E.H., Economic aspects of the native problem, 'Journal of the Economic Society of South Africa', 1, 1927.
BRUTUS (pseud.), 'Never Again! Psychology and the Lessons of the Rand Revolt, 1922' (Johannesburg: Central News Agency, n.d.).
BUELL, R.L., 'The Native Problem in Africa', vol.1 (New York: Macmillan, 1928).
BUELL, R.L., The race problem in South Africa, 'Foreign Affairs', 4, 1928.
BUNTING, B., 'The Rise of the South African Reich' (Harmondsworth: Penguin, 1969).
BUNTING, S.P., 'Imperialism in South Africa' (Johannesburg: Communist Party of South Africa, 1928).
BUNTING, S.P., 'Red Revolt and the Rand Strike' (Johannesburg: Communist Party of South Africa, 1922).
BURGER, J., 'The Black Man's Burden' (London: Gollancz, 1943).
BUSSCHAU, W.J., 'The Theory of Gold Supply, with Special Reference to the Problems of the Witwatersrand' (London: Cassell, 1936).
CAMPBELL, J. and MUNRO, J.R., 'The Great Rand Strike' (Johannesburg: Aldington, 1913).
CARTWRIGHT, A.P., 'Valley of Gold' (London: Methuen, 1961).
CHILVERS, H., 'The Story of De Beers' (London: Cassell, 1939).
CHILVERS, H., 'Out of the Crucible: The Story of the Witwatersrand Goldfields' (London: Cassell, 1929).
CLACK, G., The changing structure of industrial relations in South Africa (Ph.D. thesis, University of London, 1962).

CLAY, H., Competition between European and non-European labour, 'Journal of the Economic Society of South Africa', 3, 1930.
COPE, R.K., 'Comrade Bill: The Life and Times of W.H. Andrews, Workers' Leader' (Cape Town: Stewart, 1943).
COTTON, W.A., 'Racial Segregation in South Africa' (London: Sheldon, 1931).
CRESWELL, F.H.P., 'The Chinese Question from Within' (London: P.S. King, 1905).
CRESWELL, M., 'An Epoch of the Political History of South Africa, in the Life of F.H.P. Creswell' (Cape Town: Balkema, 1956).
DAVIS, A., 'The Native Problem in South Africa' (London: Chapman & Hall, 1903).
DAVIS, J.M. (ed.), 'Modern Industry and the African' (London: Macmillan, 1933).
DE KIEWIET, C.W., 'A History of South Africa: Social and Economic' (London: Oxford University Press, 1966).
DE KIEWIET, C.W., 'The Imperial Factor in South Africa' (Cambridge University Press, 1937).
DE KIEWIET, C.W., Social and economic developments in native tribal life, in 'Cambridge History of the British Empire', vol.VIII (Cambridge University Press, 1936).
DE KOCK, M.H., 'The Economic Development of South Africa' (London: P.S. King, 1936).
DE KOCK, M.H., 'Selected Subjects in the Economic History of South Africa' (Cape Town: Juta, 1924).
DENOON, D.J.N., 'Capitalist influence' and the Transvaal government during the Crown Colony period, 1900-06, 'Historical Journal', 11, 1968.
DENOON, D.J.N., The Transvaal labour crisis, 1901-06, 'Journal of African History', 7, 1967.
DE VYVER, F.T., Labour relations in South African industry, 'Journal of Industrial Relations', 11, 1960.
DIAMOND, C., The Native Grievances Inquiry, 1913-14, 'South African Journal of Economics', 36, 1968.
DOWNES, A.J., 'Printer's Saga' (Johannesburg: South African Typographical Workers' Union, 1952).
DOXEY, G.V., Enforced racial stratification in the South African labour market, in Adam, H. (ed.), 'South Africa: Sociological Perspectives' (London: Oxford University Press, 1971).
DOXEY, G.V., The South African problem: a conflict of nationalism, 'International Journal' (Toronto), 18, 1963.
DOXEY, G.V., 'The Industrial Colour Bar in South Africa' (Cape Town: Oxford University Press, 1961).
DU TOIT, B.M., Color, class and caste in South Africa, 'Journal of Asian and African Studies', 1, 1966.
EMDEN, P.H., 'The Randlords: A Chapter in Empire

Development' (London: English Review, 1935).
ENGLISH EYE WITNESS, 'John Chinaman on the Rand' (London: Everett, 1905).
EVANS, I.L., 'A History of Native Policy in Southern Africa' (Cambridge University Press, 1934).
EVERARD, C.C., 'Botha and Labour: The Iron Heel at Work' (London: Daily Herald, 1914).
FAIR, T.J.D., The core-periphery concept of population growth in South Africa, 1911-60, 'South African Geographical Journal', 47, 1965.
FEIT, E., 'South Africa: The Dynamics of the African National Congress' (London: Oxford University Press, 1962).
FORMAN, L., 'Chapters in the History of the March to Freedom' (Cape Town: New Age, 1959).
FRANKEL, S.H., 'The Tyranny of Economic Paternalism in Africa: A Study of Frontier Mentality, 1860-1960' (Johannesburg: Anglo-American Corporation, 1960).
FRANKEL, S.H., 'Capital Investment in Africa, Its Course and Effects' (London: Oxford University Press, 1938).
FRANKEL, S.H., The position of the native as a factor in the economic welfare of the European population in South Africa, 'Journal of the Economic Society of South Africa', 2, 1928.
FRANKLIN, N., 'Economics in South Africa' (London: Oxford University Press, 1954).
GANDHI, M.K., 'Satyagraha in South Africa' (Madras: Ganeson, 1928).
GANN, L.H., Liberal interpretations of South African history, 'Rhodes Livingstone Journal', 25, 1959.
GEEN, M.S., 'The Making of South Africa' (Cape Town: Miller, 1958).
GIBSON, J.Y., 'The Evolution of South African Native Policy' (Pietermaritzburg: Davis, 1919).
GILBERT, D.W., The economic effects of gold discoveries upon South Africa, 'Quarterly Journal of Economics', August 1933.
GITSHAM, E. and TREMBATH, J.F., 'A First Account of Labour Organisation in South Africa' (Durban: Commercial Printing Co, 1926).
GLANVILLE, E., 'Through the Red Revolt on the Rand: A Pictorial Review' (Johannesburg: Star, 1922).
GLASS, D.V., European population movements in the Union of South Africa, 'South African Journal of Economics', 7, 1939.
GLASS, Y., Industrialisation and urbanisation in South Africa, in Holleman, J.F.K., Mann, J.W. and Heard, K.A. (eds), 'Problems of Transition' (Pietermaritzburg: University of Natal Press, 1962).

GOLDMANN, C.S., 'The Financial, Statistical and General History of the Gold and Other Companies of the Witwatersrand, South Africa' (London: Cassell, 1892).
GOODFELLOW, D.M., 'A Modern Economic History of South Africa' (London: Routledge, 1931).
GRAHAM, M.R., The gold mining finance system in South Africa, with special reference to the financing and development of the Orange Free State goldfield up to 1960 (Ph.D. thesis, University of London, 1964).
GRAY, J.L., The comparative sociology of South Africa, 'South African Journal of Economics', 5, 1937.
GRAY, J., 'Payable Gold' (Johannesburg: Central News Agency, 1937).
GRAY, J. and MCLACHLAN, J., A history of the introduction of the MacArthur-Forrest cyanide process to the Witwatersrand gold fields, 'Journal of the Chemical, Metallurgical and Mining Society of South Africa', 33, 1933.
GREGORY, SIR T., 'Ernest Oppenheimer and the Economic Development of Southern Africa' (Cape Town: Oxford University Press, 1962).
HAHLO, H.R. and KAHN, E. (eds), 'The Union of South Africa: The Development of its Laws and Constitution' (London: Stevens, 1960).
HANCOCK, W.H., 'Smuts', vols I and II (Cambridge University Press, 1962, 1968).
HANCOCK, W.H., 'A Survey of British Commonwealth Affairs', vols I and II (London: Oxford University Press, 1937, 1942).
HARRISON, W.H., 'Memoirs of a Socialist in South Africa, 1903-47' (Cape Town: Author, 1947).
HARTMANN, H., 'Politics and Economics in South Africa' (Princeton University Press, 1962).
HATCH, F.M. and CHALMERS, J.A., 'The Gold Mines of the Rand' (London: Cassell, 1895).
HATTERSLEY, A.F., 'An Illustrated Social History of South Africa' (Cape Town: Balkema, 1969).
HATTERSLEY, A.F., 'South Africa, 1652-1933' (London: Butterworth, 1933).
HEATON-NICHOLLS, G.M., 'The Problem of the Native in South Africa' (Pretoria: GPSO, 1937).
HELLMAN, E., 'Racial Laws versus Social and Economic Forces' (Johannesburg: South African Institute of Race Relations, 1955).
HELLMAN, E. (ed.), 'A Handbook on Race Relations in South Africa' (Cape Town: Oxford University Press, 1949).
HENDERSON, J., The economic conditions of the native people, 'South African Outlook', 57, 1927, and 58, 1928.
HEPPLE, A., 'South Africa: A Political and Economic History' (London: Pall Mall, 1966).

Bibliography

HEPPLE, A., 'The African Worker in South Africa: A Study of Trade Unionism' (London: Africa Bureau, 1956).
HEPPLE, A., 'Trade Unions in Travail' (Johannesburg: Unity, 1954).
HERD, N., '1922: The Revolt of the Rand' (Johannesburg: Blue Crane Books, 1966).
HERTSLET, L.E., 'The Native Problem: Some of its Points and Phases' (Durban: Davis, 1912).
HESSIAN, B., An investigation into the causes of the labour agitation on the Witwatersrand, January to March 1922 (M.A. thesis, University of the Witwatersrand, 1957).
HOERNLE, R.F.A., 'South African Native Policy and the Liberal Spirit' (Johannesburg: University of the Witwatersrand Press, 1945).
HOERNLE, R.F.A., Anatomy of segregation, 'Race Relations Journal', 3, 1936.
HOFMEYR, J.H., 'South Africa' (London: Benn, 1932).
HOLLEMAN, J.F.K., MANN, J.W. and HEARD, K.A., 'Problems of Transition' (Pietermaritzburg: University of Natal Press, 1962).
HORRELL, M., 'South Africa's Workers: Their Organisations and the Pattern of Employment' (Johannesburg: SAIRR, 1969).
HORRELL, M., 'Introduction to South Africa: Basic Facts and Figures' (Johannesburg: SAIRR, 1968).
HORRELL, M., 'South African Trade Unionism' (Johannesburg: SAIRR, 1961).
HORRELL, M., 'Racialism and the Trade Unions' (Johannesburg: SAIRR, 1959).
HORRELL, M., 'South Africa's Non-White Workers' (Johannesburg: SAIRR, 1956).
HORRELL, M., 'Non-European Policies in the Union and the Measure of their Success' (Johannesburg: SAIRR, 1954).
HORWITZ, R., 'The Political Economy of South Africa' (London: Weidenfeld & Nicolson, 1967).
HOUGHTON, D.H., Economic development, 1865-1965, in Wilson, M. and Thompson, L. (eds), 'The Oxford History of South Africa', vol.II (Oxford: Clarendon Press, 1971).
HOUGHTON, D.H., White prosperity and white supremacy in South Africa today: a comment, 'African Affairs', 69, 1970.
HOUGHTON, D.H., 'The South African Economy' (Cape Town: Oxford University Press, 1967).
HOUGHTON, D.H., 'Economic Development in a Plural Society' (Cape Town: Oxford University Press, 1960).
HOUGHTON, D.H., 'Some Economic Problems of the Bantu in South Africa' (Johannesburg: SAIRR, 1938).
HUTT, W.H., 'The Economics of the Colour Bar: A Study of the Economic Origins and Consequences of Racial

Segregation in South Africa' (London: Deutsch, 1964).
HUTT, W.H., Logical issues in the study of industrial legislation in the Union, 'South African Journal of Economics', 3, 1935.
JABAVU, D.D.T., 'Native Disabilities in South Africa' (Lovedale: Lovedale Press, 1932).
JABAVU, D.D.T., 'The Segregation Fallacy' (Lovedale: Lovedale Press, 1928).
JABAVU, D.D.T., 'The Black Problem: Papers and Addresses on Various Native Problems' (Lovedale: Lovedale Press, 1920).
JENSEN, E., 'Poor Relief in Johannesburg' (Cape Town: Stewart, 1928).
JEPPE, C.W.B., 'Gold Mining in South Africa' (London: Todd, 1948).
JOHNS, S., Marxism-Leninism in a multi-racial environment: the origins and early history of the Communist Party of South Africa, 1914-32 (Ph.D. thesis, Harvard University, 1965).
JOHNSTONE, F.A., White prosperity and white supremacy in South Africa today, 'African Affairs', 69, 1970.
JOHNSTONE, F.A., Class conflict and colour bars in the South African gold mining industry, in 'The Societies of Southern Africa in the 19th and 20th Centuries', vol.I (London: University of London, Institute of Commonwealth Studies, Collected Seminar Papers Series, 1971).
JOHNSTONE, F.A., Economic growth, apartheid and social injustice in South Africa, mimeo.
JONES, D.I., 'Communism in South Africa' (Johannesburg: International Socialist League, 1921).
JONES, E.B., South African native land policy, 'Bantu Studies', 14, 1940.
JONES, J.D. RHEINALLT, Industrial relations in South Africa, 'International Affairs', 30, 1953.
JONES, J.D. RHEINALLT, The effects of urbanisation in South and Central Africa, 'African Affairs', 52, 1953.
JONES, J.D. RHEINALLT, The native's role in the economic development of Africa, 'Optima', September 1952.
JONES, J.D. RHEINALLT, The position of the worker under the labour laws of the Union, 'Race Relations', 4, 1939.
JONES, J.D. RHEINALLT, Economic maladjustment and the Civilised Labour Policy, 'Race Relations', 2, 1935.
JONES, J.D. RHEINALLT and HOERNLE, R.F.A., 'The Union's Burden of Poverty' (Johannesburg: SAIRR, 1942).
JOOS, L., 'Histoire de L'Afrique du Sud' (Paris: Le Centurion, 1966).
JOSHI, P.S., 'The Tyranny of Colour' (Durban: E.P. & Commercial Printing Co, 1942).
KADALIE, C., 'My Life and the I.C.U.: The Autobiography

of a Black Trade Unionist in South Africa' (New York: Humanities Press, 1970).
KAHN, E., The right to strike in South Africa, 'South African Journal of Economics', 11, 1943.
KARIS, T.G., South Africa, in Carter, G.M. (ed.), 'Five African States: Responses to Diversity' (Ithaca: Cornell University Press, 1963).
KATZEN, L., 'Gold and the South African Economy: The Influence of the Gold Mining Industry on Business Cycles and Economic Growth in South Africa, 1886-1961' (Cape Town: Balkema, 1964).
KENTRIDGE, M., 'I Recall: The Memoirs of Morris Kentridge' (Johannesburg: Free Press, 1959).
KEPPEL-JONES, A., 'South Africa: A Short History' (London: Hutchinson, 1966).
KEPPEL-JONES, A., South Africa: racialism and republicanism, in Millar, MacLure et al. (eds), 'Africa: The Political Pattern' (University of Toronto Press, 1961).
KEPPEL-JONES, A., 'When Smuts Goes: A History of South Africa from 1952 to 2010' (Pietermaritzburg: Shuter & Shooter, 1947).
KIRK, J., 'Economic Aspects of Native Segregation in South Africa' (London: P.S. King, 1929).
KOOY, M. and ROBERTSON, H.M., The South African Board of Trade and Industries, the South African customs tariff and the development of South African industries, 'South African Journal of Economics', 34, 1966.
KRUGER, D.W., 'The Making of a Nation: A History of the Union of South Africa, 1910-61' (New York: Humanities Press, 1970).
KRUGER, D.W., 'The Age of the Generals' (Johannesburg: Dagbreek Book Store, 1961).
KRUGER, D.W., 'South African Parties and Policies, 1910-60' (Cape Town: Human & Rousseau, 1960).
KUPER, L., 'An African Bourgeoisie: Race, Class and Politics in Southern Africa' (New Haven: Yale University Books, 1965).
KUPER, L., Racialism and integration in South African society, 'Race', 4, 1963.
KUPER, L. and SMITH, M.G. (eds), 'Pluralism in Africa' (Berkeley: University of California Press, 1969).
KUSHKE, G.S.T., 'Industrial Development in South Africa' (Johannesburg: Industrial Development Corporation, 1962).
LEGASSICK, M., Development and under-development in South Africa, Chatham House Seminar Paper, 11 March 1971.
LEGASSICK, M., The frontier tradition in South African historiography, Institute of Commonwealth Studies (London) Seminar Paper, May 1971.
LEHFELDT, R.A., 'Gold, Prices and the Witwatersrand' (London: P.S. King, 1919).

LE MAY, G.H.L., 'British Supremacy in South Africa, 1899-1907' (Oxford: Clarendon Press, 1965).
LESLIE, P., Economics in South Africa, 'South African Journal of Economics', 4, 1936.
LEWIN, J., 'Politics and Law in South Africa: Essays on Race Relations' (London: Merlin Press, 1963).
LIMEBEER, A.J., The group system of administration in the gold mining industry, 'Optima', June 1951.
LOVELL, R.I., 'The Struggle for South Africa: A Study in Economic Imperialism' (New York: Macmillan, 1934).
LUCAS, F.A.W., The determination of wages in South Africa, 'South African Journal of Economics', 1, 1933.
MACCRONE, I.D., 'Race Attitudes in South Africa: Historical, Experimental and Psychological Studies' (Johannesburg: University of Witwatersrand Press, 1957).
MACMILLAN, W.M., 'Bantu, Boer and Briton; The Making of the South African Native Problem' (Oxford: Clarendon Press, 1963).
MACMILLAN, W.M., 'Complex South Africa: Economic Footnote to History' (London: Faber, 1930).
MACMILLAN, W.M., 'The Land, the Native and Unemployment' (Johannesburg: Council of Education, 1924).
MACMILLAN, W.M., 'The South African Agrarian Problem and its Historical Development' (Johannesburg: Central News Agency, 1919).
MALHERBE, E.G., 'Bantu Manpower and Education' (Johannesburg: SAIRR, 1969).
MANSERGH, N., 'Survey of British Commonwealth Affairs', vols I and II (London: Oxford University Press, 1952, 1958).
MANSERGH, N., 'South Africa, 1906-61' (London: Oxford University Press, 1952).
MARAIS, J.S., 'The Fall of Kruger's Republic' (Oxford: Clarendon Press, 1961).
MARKS, S., 'Reluctant Rebellion' (London: Oxford University Press, 1970).
MARQUARD, L., 'The Peoples and Policies of South Africa' (London: Oxford University Press, 1960).
MARQUARD, L., 'The Story of South Africa' (London: Faber, 1955).
MARQUARD, L. and LEWIN, J., 'The Native in South Africa' (Johannesburg: University of Witwatersrand Press, 1944).
MULLER, J.V., 'The History and Growth of the Witwatersrand Gold Mining Industry' (Johannesburg: Central News Agency, 1942).
NIELSEN, P., 'The Colour Bar' (Cape Town: Juta, 1937).
NIELSEN, P., 'The Black Man's Place in South Africa' (Cape Town: Juta, 1922).
OLIVIER, LORD, 'White Capital and Coloured Labour' (London: Hogarth Press, 1929).

OLIVIER, LORD, 'The Anatomy of South African Misery' (London: Hogarth Press, 1927).
OULD, C.R., General Smuts' attitude to white labour disputes between 1907 and 1922 (M.A. thesis, University of the Witwatersrand, 1964).
OULD, C.R., The 'Boksburg Incident' during the strike of 1922, 'Historia' (Pretoria), 5, 1960.
PEARSALL, C.W., Some aspects of the development of secondary industry in the Union of South Africa, 'South African Journal of Economics', 5, 1937.
PEREGRINO, F.Z.S., 'Life among the Native and Coloured Miners in the Transvaal' (Cape Town: Hodgson & Denne, 1910).
PHILLIPS, L., 'Some Reminiscences' (London: P.S. King, 1924).
PHILLIPS, R.E., 'The Bantu in the City: A Study of Cultural Adjustment on the Witwatersrand' (Lovedale: Lovedale Press, 1938).
PIM, H., 'A Transkei Inquiry' (Lovedale: Lovedale Press, 1933).
PIROW, O., 'J.B.M. Hertzog' (London: Allen & Unwin, 1958).
PLAATJE, S.T., 'Native Life in South Africa before and since the European War and the Boer Rebellion' (London: P.S. King, 1916).
PLANT, A., Economic development, 1795-1921, in 'Cambridge History of the British Empire', vol.VIII (Cambridge University Press, 1936).
POLLAK, H., 'Social Development since Union' (Johannesburg: SAIRR, 1959).
PRANCE, C.R., 'Under the Blue Roof: Sketches of a Settler's Life in the Transvaal Backveld, 1908-21' (Bloemfontein: 1944).
PRATT, A., 'The Real South Africa' (London: Holden & Hardington, 1913).
PYRAH, G.B., 'Imperial Policy and South Africa, 1902-10' (Oxford: Clarendon Press, 1955).
RANSOME, S., 'The Engineer in South Africa: A Review of the Industrial Situation in South Africa after the War and a Forecast of the Possibilities of the Century' (New York: Dutton, 1903).
REEVES, J.A., Chinese labour policy in South Africa, 1901-10 (M.A. thesis, University of the Witwatersrand, 1955).
ROBERTS, A.W., 'A Statistical Inquiry into the Population Problem in South Africa' (Cape Town: Royal Society of South Africa, 1926).
ROBERTSON, H.M., 'South Africa: Economic and Political Aspects' (Cambridge University Press, 1957).
ROBERTSON, H.M., The historical evolution of South African wage levels, 'Race Relations', 6, 1939.

ROBERTSON, H.M., 150 years of economic contact between black and white, 'South African Journal of Economics', 2, 1934, and 3, 1935.
ROUTH, G., 'Industrial Relations and Race Relations' (Johannesburg: SAIRR, n.d.).
ROUTH, G., State intervention in the regulation of wages and working conditions in Great Britain and South Africa, 'South African Journal of Economics', 17, 1949.
ROUX, E., 'Time Longer than Rope: A History of the Black Man's Struggle for Freedom in South Africa' (London: Gollancz, 1943).
ROUX, E., 'S.P. Bunting: A Political Biography' (Cape Town: African Bookman, 1944).
SACHS, E.S., 'Rebel Daughters' (London: MacGibbon & Kee, 1957).
SACHS, E.S., 'The Choice before South Africa' (London: Turnstile Press, 1952).
SAMUELS, L.H., HOUGHTON, D.H. and FOURIE, F.C., 'South Africa's Changing Economy' (Johannesburg: SAIRR, 1955).
SCHAPERA, I.S. (ed.), 'Western Civilisation and the Natives of South Africa: Studies in Culture Contact' (London: Routledge & Kegan Paul, 1967).
SCHAPERA, I.S., 'Select Bibliography of South African Native Life and Problems' (London: Oxford University Press, 1941).
SCHREINER, O.D., 'The Nettle: Political Power and Race Relations in South Africa' (Johannesburg: SAIRR, 1964).
SCHUMANN, C.G.N., 'Structural Changes and Business Cycles in South Africa, 1806-1936' (London: King & Staples, 1938).
SHANNON, H.A., Urbanisation, 1904-36, 'South African Journal of Economics', 5, 1937.
SHEPHERD, W.C., 'Recruiting in Portuguese East Africa of Natives for the Mines' (London: P.S. King, 1934).
SILBURN, P.A., 'South Africa, White or Black - or Brown?' (London: Allen & Unwin, 1927).
SIMONS, H.J. and R.E., 'Class and Colour in South Africa, 1850-1950' (Harmondsworth: Penguin, 1969).
SOUTH AFRICAN INSTITUTE OF RACE RELATIONS, The Labour Policy of the Rand Mines, 'Race Relations', 10, 1943.
SOUTH AFRICAN INSTITUTE OF RACE RELATIONS, The civilised Labour Policy and the displacement of non-European labour, 'Race Relations', 11, 1935.
SOUTH AFRICAN TRADES AND LABOUR COUNCIL, 'The Trade Union Movement in South Africa during the Years following Inception' (Johannesburg: National Joint Council, 1939).
STADLER, A., Race and industrialisation in South Africa: a critique of the Blumer thesis, Chatham House Seminar Paper, 28 January 1971.

STEVENS, E.J.C., 'White and Black: An Inquiry into South Africa's Greatest Problem' (Cape Town: Darter, 1914).
TATZ, C.M., 'Shadow and Substance in South Africa: A Study in Land and Franchise Policies affecting Africans, 1910-60' (Pietermaritzburg: University of Natal Press, 1962).
THEAL, G.M., 'South Africa' (London: Fischer Unwin, 1917).
THION, S., 'Le Pouvoir pâle, ou le racisme sud-africain' (Paris: Seuil, 1969).
THOMAS, D.G., A history of the Labour Party in South Africa up to 1924 (B.A. thesis, University of the Witwatersrand, 1963).
THOMPSON, L.M., 'Politics in the Republic of South Africa' (Boston: Little Brown, 1966).
THOMPSON, L.M., 'The Unification of South Africa, 1902-10' (Oxford: Clarendon Press, 1960).
THOMPSON, L.M., The non-European franchise in the Union of South Africa, in Bailey, S.D. (ed.), 'Parliamentary Government in the Commonwealth' (London: Hansard Society, 1951).
TINLEY, J.M., 'The Native Labour Problem of South Africa' (Chapel Hill: University of North Carolina Press, 1942).
TINLEY, J.M., Control of agriculture in South Africa, 'South African Journal of Economics', 8, 1940.
TRANSVAAL LEGAL DEFENCE COMMITTEE, 'The Story of a Crime' (Johannesburg: Transvaal Legal Defence Committee, 1924).
TRAPIDO, S., South Africa in the comparative study of industrialisation, 'Journal of Development Studies', 7, 1971.
TRAPIDO, S., Labour movements and power in South Africa, in 'Collected Seminar Papers on Labour Unions and Political Organisations' (University of London, Institute of Commonwealth Studies, 1967).
TUBERCULOSIS RESEARCH COMMITTEE, 'Tuberculosis in South African Natives, with Special Reference to the Disease amongst the Mine Labourers of the Witwatersrand' (Johannesburg: Institute of Medical Research, 1932).
URQUHART, W., 'The Outbreak on the Rand, March 1922' (Johannesburg: Hortors, 1922).
VAN DEN BERGHE, P.L., Race and racism in South Africa, in Beteille, A. (ed.), 'Social Inequality' (Harmondsworth: Penguin, 1969).
VAN DEN BERGHE, P.L., 'South Africa: A Study in Conflict' (Berkeley: University of California Press, 1967).
VAN DEN HEEVER, C.M., 'General J.B.M. Hertzog' (Johannesburg: APB Bookstore, 1946).
VAN DER HORST, S.T., 'Poverty in Perspective' (Johannesburg: SAIRR, 1967).
VAN DER HORST, S.T., The effects of industrialisation on

race relations in South Africa, in Hunter, G. (ed.), 'Industrialisation and Race Relations' (London: Oxford University Press, 1965).
VAN DER HORST, S.T., The economic implications of political democracy, 'Optima', June 1960.
VAN DER HORST, S.T., The Union of South Africa: economic problems in a multi-racial situation, 'Annals of the American Academy of Political and Social Science', 298, 1955.
VAN DER HORST, S.T., The native in South Africa's industrial revolution, 'Optima', June 1953.
VAN DER HORST, S.T., 'Native Labour in South Africa' (London: Oxford University Press, 1942).
VAN DER HORST, S.T., Some effects of industrial legislation on the market for native labour in South Africa, 'South African Journal of Economics', 3, 1935.
VAN ECK, H.J., 'Some Aspects of the South African Industrial Revolution' (Johannesburg: SAIRR, 1951).
VAN JAARSFELD, F.A., 'The Afrikaner's Interpretation of South African History' (Cape Town: Simondium, 1964).
VAN RHJIN, A.J.R., The importance of the South African mining industry, 'African Affairs', 58, 1959.
WALKER, E., 'A History of Southern Africa' (London: Longmans, 1964).
WALKER, I.L. and WEINBREN, B., '2000 Casualties: A History of the Trade Unions and the Labour Movement in the Union of South Africa' (Johannesburg: South African Trade Union Council, 1961).
WILLIAMS, R. TALBOT, 'White Trade Unionism, Or a Call to the Non-European Workers of South Africa' (Johannesburg: African Political Organisation, 1918).
WILSON, F., An analysis of the forces operating in the labour market of the South African gold mines, 1936-65 (Ph.D. thesis, Cambridge University, 1967).
WILSON, M. and THOMPSON, L. (eds), 'The Oxford History of South Africa', vols I and II (Oxford: Clarendon Press, 1969, 1971).
WOLPE, H., Class, race and the occupational structure, Institute of Commonwealth Studies (London) Seminar Paper, January 1971.
WOLPE, H., Industrialism and race in South Africa, in Zubaida, S. (ed.), 'Race and Racialism' (London: Tavistock, 1970).

IV SELECT BIBLIOGRAPHY OF OTHER SECONDARY SOURCES

ALTHUSSER, L., et al., 'Lire le Capital' (Paris: Maspero, 1965).

Bibliography

ALTHUSSER, L. and BALIBAR, E., 'Reading Capital' (London: New Left Books, 1970).
ARON, R., 'Main Currents in Sociological Thought' (Harmondsworth: Penguin, 1968, 1970).
ARRIGHI, G., Labour supplies in historical perspective, 'Journal of Development Studies', 6, 1970.
ARRIGHI, G., 'The Political Economy of Rhodesia' (The Hague: Mouton, 1967).
BACON, E.F., Race relations in an industrial society, 'Race', 4, 1963.
BANTON, M., 'Race Relations' (London: Tavistock, 1967).
BANTON, M., Race as a social category, 'Race', 8, 1966.
BARAN, P.A. and SWEEZY, P.M., 'Monopoly Capital' (Harmondsworth: Penguin, 1968).
BARZUN, J., 'Race: A Study in Superstition' (New York: Harper, 1965).
BASTIDE, R., Race relations in Brazil, 'International Social Science Bulletin', 9, 1957.
BENDIX, R., 'Work and Authority in Industry: Ideologies of Management in the Course of Industrialisation' (New York: Wiley, 1956).
BENDIX, R. and LIPSET, S.M., 'Class, Status and Power: Social Stratification in Comparative Perspective' (London: Routledge & Kegan Paul, 1966).
BENEDICT, R., Stratification in plural societies, 'American Anthropologist', 64, 1962.
BENEDICT, R., 'Race: Science and Politics' (New York: Modern Age Books, 1940).
BERG, E.J., Backward sloping labour supply functions in dual economies: the Africa case, 'Quarterly Journal of Economics', August 1961.
BETEILLE, A. (ed.), 'Social Inequality' (Harmondsworth: Penguin, 1969).
BETTELHEIM, B. and JANOWITZ, M., 'Social Change and Prejudice' (New York: Free Press, 1966).
BLALOCK, H.M., 'Towards a Theory of Minority Group Relations' (New York: Wiley, 1967).
BLUMER, H., Industrialisation and race relations, in Hunter, G. (ed.), 'Industrialisation and Race Relations' (London: Oxford University Press, 1965).
BOTTOMORE, T.B., 'Classes in Modern Society' (London: Allen & Unwin, 1965).
BRAITHWAITE, L., Social stratification and cultural pluralism, 'Annals of the New York Academy of Sciences', 83, 1960.
BREWTON, B., 'Race and Ethnic Relations' (Boston: Houghton Mifflin, 1965).
BURNS, T. (ed.), 'Industrial Man' (Harmondsworth: Penguin, 1969).

CAMPBELL, E.Q., Moral discomfort and racial segregation - an examination of the Myrdal hypothesis, 'Social Forces', 39, 1961.
CHATER, A., 'Race Relations in Britain' (London: Lawrence & Wishart, 1966).
COLE, G.D.H., 'Studies in Class Structure' (London: Routledge & Kegan Paul, 1955).
COLE, G.D.H., 'A Short History of the British Working Class' (London: Allen & Unwin, 1952).
COLLINGWOOD, R.G., 'The Idea of History' (Oxford: Clarendon Press, 1946).
CORVEZ, M., 'Les Structuralistes' (Paris: Aubier-Montaigne, 1969).
COSER, L., 'The Functions of Social Conflict' (London: Routledge & Kegan Paul, 1968).
COX, O.C., 'Caste, Class and Race: A Study in Social Dynamics' (New York: Monthly Review Press, 1970).
DAHRENDORF, R., 'Class and Class Conflict in an Industrial Society' (London: Routledge & Kegan Paul, 1967).
DANIEL, W.W., 'Racial Discrimination in England' (Harmondsworth: Penguin, 1968).
DANIELS, R. and KITANO, H.H.L., 'American Racism: Exploration of the Nature of Prejudice' (Englewood Cliffs: Prentice-Hall, 1970).
DAVIS, A., GARDNER, B.B. and GARDNER, M.R., 'Deep South: A Social Anthropological Study of Caste and Class' (University of Chicago Press, 1941).
DAVIS, K., 'Human Society' (New York: Macmillan, 1966).
DAVIS, K. and MOORE, W.E., Some principles of stratification, 'American Sociological Review', 10, 1945.
DEIGHTON, H.S., History and the study of race relations, 'Race', 1, 1959.
DE REUCK, A. and KNIGHT, J., 'Caste and Race: Comparative Approaches' (London: J.A. Churchill, 1968).
DOBB, M., 'Studies in the Development of Capitalism' (London: Routledge & Kegan Paul, 1946).
DOLLARD, J., 'Caste and Class in a Southern Town' (Garden City, New York: Doubleday, 1957).
DUCHET, C. and DE COMARMOND, D.P. (eds), 'Racisme et société' (Paris: Maspero, 1969).
DUMONT, L., Caste racism and 'stratification': reflections of a social anthropologist, 'Contributions to Indian Sociology', 5, 1961.
DURKHEIM, E., 'The Division of Labour in Society' (New York: Free Press, 1969).
DURKHEIM, E., 'The Rules of Sociological Method' (Toronto: Free Press, 1968).
EBBELS, R.N., 'The Australian Labour Movement' (Sydney: Australian Book Society, 1960).

EDWARDS, G.F. (ed.), 'Franklin Frazier on Race Relations' (University of Chicago Press, 1968).
ELKINS, S.M., 'Slavery: A Problem in American Institutional and Intellectual Life' (University of Chicago Press, 1959).
EMMET, D. and MACINTYRE, A. (eds), 'Sociological Theory and Philosophical Analysis' (London: Macmillan, 1970).
FONER, L. and GENOVESE, E. (eds), 'Slavery in the New World' (Englewood Cliffs: Prentice-Hall, 1969).
FRANK, A.G., 'Capitalism and Under-Development in Latin America: Historical Studies of Chile and Brazil' (New York: Monthly Review Press, 1969).
FRAZIER, E.F., 'Race and Culture Contacts in the Modern World' (New York: Knopf, 1957).
FRAZIER, E.F., Sociological theory and race relations, 'American Sociological Review', 12, 1947.
FREYRE, G., 'The Mansions and the Shanties: The Making of Modern Brazil' (New York: Knopf, 1963).
FREYRE, G., 'The Masters and the Slaves: A Study in the Development of Brazilian Civilisation' (New York: Knopf, 1946).
FURNIVALL, J.S., 'Colonial Policy and Practice: A Comparative Study of Burma and Netherlands India' (Cambridge University Press, 1948).
FURNIVALL, J.S., 'Netherlands India: A Study of a Plural Economy' (Cambridge University Press, 1939).
GARDINER, P.L., 'The Nature of Historical Explanation' (London: Oxford University Press, 1952).
GENOVESE, E., 'The World the Slaveholders Made: Two Essays in Interpretation' (London: Allen Lane, 1970).
GENOVESE, E., 'The Political Economy of Slavery: Studies in the Economy and Society of the Slave South' (New York: Vintage, 1961).
GERTH, H.H. and MILLS, C.W. (eds), 'From Max Weber: Essays in Sociology' (New York: Oxford University Press, 1946).
GLAZER, N. and MOYNIHAN, D., 'Beyond the Melting Pot: The Negroes, Puerto Ricans, Jews, Italians, and Irish of New York City' (Cambridge: MIT and Harvard University Press, 1963).
GLENN, N.D., Occupational benefits to whites from the subordination of Negroes, 'American Sociological Review', 28, 1963.
GODELIER, M., System, structure and contradiction in 'Capital', in 'Socialist Register, 1967' (London: Merlin Press, 1967).
GUTMAN, H.G., The Negro and the united mine workers of America, in Jacobson, J. (ed.), 'The Negro and the American Labour Movement' (New York: Doubleday, 1968).
HARRIS, M., Caste, class and minority, 'Social Forces', 38, 1959.

HAUG, M.R., Social and cultural pluralism as a concept in social system analysis, 'American Journal of Sociology', 73, 1967.
HEARD, K.A., 'Political Systems in Multi-Racial Societies' (Johannesburg: South African Institute of Race Relations, 1961).
HEPPLE, R., 'Race, Jobs and the Law in Britain' (Harmondsworth: Penguin, 1970).
HOBSBAWN, E., 'Labouring Men: Studies in the History of Labour' (London: Weidenfeld & Nicolson, 1964).
HOBSON, J.A., 'The Evolution of Modern Capitalism: A Study of Machine Production' (London: Allen & Unwin, 1949).
HOBSON, J.A., 'Imperialism' (London: Allen & Unwin, 1902).
HOETINK, H., 'The Two Variants in Caribbean Race Relations: A Contribution to the Sociology of Segmented Societies' (London: Oxford University Press, 1967).
HOETINK, H., The concept of pluralism as envisaged by M.G. Smith, 'Caribbean Studies', 7, 1967.
HOMANS, G.C., 'The Human Group' (New York: Harcourt, 1950).
HOROWITZ, I.L., 'The New Sociology' (New York: Oxford University Press, 1964).
HOSELITZ, B., Interaction between industrial and pre-industrial stratification systems, in Smelser, N.J. and Lipset, S.M. (eds), 'Social Structure, Social Mobility and Economic Development' (Chicago: Aldine, 1966).
HUNTER, G. (ed.), 'Industrialisation and Race Relations: A Symposium' (London: Oxford University Press, 1965).
JACOBSON, J. (ed.), 'The Negro and the American Labour Movement' (New York: Doubleday, 1968).
JOHNSON, C.S., 'Patterns of Negro Segregation' (New York: Harper, 1943).
JORDAN, W.D., 'White over Black: American Attitudes towards the Negro, 1550-1812' (Baltimore: Penguin, 1969).
KERR, C., 'Industrialism and Industrial Man' (Cambridge: Harvard University Press, 1960).
KLINEBERG, O., 'Race Differences' (New York: Harper, 1935).
KLOOSTERBOER, W., 'Involuntary Labour since the Abolition of Slavery: A Survey of Compulsory Labour throughout the World' (Leiden: E.J. Brill, 1960).
LACLAU, E., Feudalism and capitalism in Latin America, 'New Left Review', 67, 1971.
LEGGETT, J.C., 'Class, Race and Labour: Working Class Consciousness in Detroit' (New York: Oxford University Press, 1968).
LEGGETT, J.C., Economic insecurity and working class consciousness, 'American Sociological Review', 29, 1964.

LENIN, V.I., 'Collected Works' (Moscow: Foreign Languages Publishing House, 1963-8).
LEWIN, J., 'The Colour Bar in the Copper Belt' (Johannesburg: South African Institute of Race Relations, 1941).
LEWIS, W.A., Economic development with unlimited supplies of labour, and Unlimited labour: further notes, 'Manchester School of Economic and Statistical Studies', 22, 1954, and 26, 1958.
LIEBERSON, S., A societal theory of race and ethnic relations, 'American Sociological Review', 26, 1961.
LIND, A. (ed.), 'Race Relations in World Perspective' (Honolulu: University of Hawaii Press, 1955).
LIPSET, S.M. and BENDIX, R. (eds), 'Social Mobility in Industrial Society' (Berkeley: University of California Press, 1959).
LOCKWOOD, D., Race, conflict and plural society, in Zubaida, S. (ed.), 'Race and Racialism' (London: Tavistock, 1970).
LOHMAN, J.D. and REITZES, D.C., Deliberately organised groups and racial behavior, 'American Sociological Review', 19, 1954.
LUKÁCS, G., 'History and Class Consciousness: Studies in Marxist Dialectics' (London: Merlin Press, 1971).
LUXEMBURG, R., 'The Accumulation of Capital' (London: Routledge & Kegan Paul, 1951).
MACIVER, R.M. (ed.), 'Group Relationships and Group Antagonisms' (New York: Harper & Row, 1944).
MACIVER, R.M. and PAGE, C.H., 'Society: An Introductory Account' (London: Macmillan, 1965).
MCLELLAN, D. (ed.), 'Marx's Grundrisse' (London: Macmillan, 1971).
MALINOWSKI, B., 'The Dynamics of Culture Change: An Inquiry into Race Relations in Africa' (New Haven: Yale University Press, 1946).
MALINOWSKI, B., 'A Scientific Theory of Culture' (Chapel Hill: University of North Carolina Press, 1944).
MAO TSE-TUNG, 'Selected Readings from the Works of Mao Tse-tung' (Peking: Foreign Languages Press, 1967).
MARSHALL, R., 'The Negro and Organised Labour' (New York: Wiley, 1965).
MARX, K., 'Capital: A Critique of Political Economy' (London: Lawrence & Wishart, 1965).
MARX, K. and ENGELS, F., 'Selected Works' (Moscow: Foreign Languages Publishing House, 1962).
MASON, P., 'Race Relations' (London: Oxford University Press, 1970).
MASON, P., 'Patterns of Dominance' (London: Oxford University Press, 1970).
MASON, P., 'Prospero's Magic: Some Thoughts on Class and

Race' (London: Oxford University Press, 1962).
MASON, P., 'Common Sense about Race' (London: Gollancz, 1961).
MAYER, K.B. and BUCKLEY, W., 'Class and Society' (New York: Random House, 1970).
MEDALIA, N.Z., Myrdal's assumptions on race relations: a conceptual commentary, 'Social Forces', 40, 1962.
MERTON, R., 'On Theoretical Sociology: Five Essays' (Toronto: Collier Macmillan, 1967).
MERTON, R., 'Social Theory and Social Structure' (Chicago: Free Press, 1957).
MERTON, R. and NISBET, R., 'Contemporary Social Problems' (New York: Harcourt & Brace, 1966).
MILLER, D.C. and FORM, W.H., 'Industrial Sociology' (New York: Harper & Row, 1964).
MILLS, C.W., 'The Sociological Imagination' (Harmondsworth: Penguin, 1970).
MONTAGU, M.F.A., 'Man's Most Dangerous Myth: The Fallacy of Race' (New York: Harper & Row, 1952).
MOORE, B., 'Social Origins of Dictatorship and Democracy: Lord and Peasant in the Making of the Modern World' (Harmondsworth: Penguin, 1969).
MOORE, W.E., Slave law and the social structure, 'Journal of Negro History', 26, 1941.
MOORE, W.E. and WILLIAMS, R.M., Stratification in the ante-bellum South, 'American Sociological Review', 7, 1942.
MYRDAL, G., 'An American Dilemma: The Negro Problem and Modern Democracy' (New York: McGraw-Hill, 1964).
MYRDAL, G., 'Value in Social Theory: A Selection of Essays on Methodology' (London: Routledge & Kegan Paul, 1968).
NICOLAUS, M., The unknown Marx, 'New Left Review', 48, 1968.
NORTHRUP, H.R., 'Organised Labour and the Negro' (New York: Harper & Row, 1944).
OLMSTED, F.L., 'The Slave States before the Civil War' (New York: Capricorn, 1959).
OPPENHEIMER, F., 'The State: Its History and Development viewed Sociologically' (New York: Huebsch, 1922).
OSSOWSKI, S., 'Class Structure in the Social Consciousness' (London: Routledge & Kegan Paul, 1963).
PARK, R.E., 'Race and Culture' (Chicago: Free Press, 1950).
PARSONS, T., 'The Social System' (London: Tavistock, 1952).
PARSONS, T., 'Essays in Sociological Theory' (Chicago: Free Press, 1954).
PARSONS, T., SHILS, E., NAEGELE, K. and PITTS, J.,

Bibliography

'Theories of Society' (New York: Free Press, 1965).
PIAGET, J., 'Le Structuralisme' (Paris: Presses Universitaires de France, 1968).
PHILLIPS, U.B., 'Life and Labour in the Old South' (Boston: Little Brown, 1963).
PRICE, A.G., 'White Settler and Native People: An Historical Study of Racial Contacts between Whites and Aboriginal Peoples in the United States, Australia and New Zealand' (Melbourne: Georgian House, 1950).
REUTER, E.B. (ed.), 'Race and Culture Contacts' (New York: McGraw Hill, 1934).
REX, J., 'Race Relations in Sociological Theory' (London: Weidenfeld & Nicolson, 1970).
REX, J., 'Key Problems of Sociological Theory' (London: Routledge & Kegan Paul, 1970).
REX, J., The plural society in sociological theory, 'British Journal of Sociology', 10, 1959.
REX, J., South African society from the standpoint of the comparative study of race relations, Institute of Commonwealth Studies (London) Seminar Paper, October 1969.
REX, J. and MOORE, R., 'Race, Community and Conflict: A Study of Sparkbrook' (London: Oxford University Press, 1967).
ROSE, E.J., 'Colour and Citizenship' (London: Oxford University Press, 1969).
ROSE, P.I., 'They and We: Racial and Ethnic Relations in the United States' (New York: Random House, 1964).
ROSE, P.I., 'The Subject is Race' (New York: Oxford University Press, 1968).
ROSTOW, W.W., 'The Stages of Economic Growth' (Cambridge University Press, 1969).
ROTTENBERG, S., Income and leisure in an under-developed country, 'Journal of Political Economy', 60, 1952.
SCHUMPETER, J.A., 'Social Class and Imperialism: Two Essays' (New York: Meridian, 1955).
SEGAL, R., 'The Race War' (Harmondsworth: Penguin, 1967).
SHIBUTANI, T. and KWAN, K.M., 'Ethnic Stratification: A Comparative Approach' (New York: Macmillan, 1968).
SHUGG, R.W., 'Origins of Class Struggle in Louisiana' (Baton Rouge: Louisiana State University Press, 1939).
SILBERMAN, C.E., 'Crisis in Black and White' (New York: Vintage, 1964).
SIMPSON, G.E. and YINGER, J.M., 'Racial and Cultural Minorities: An Analysis of Prejudice and Discrimination' (New York: Harper & Row, 1965).
SMELSER, N.J., 'Essays in Sociological Explanation' (Englewood Cliffs: Prentice-Hall, 1968).
SMELSER, N.J., 'The Sociology of Economic Life' (Englewood Cliffs: Prentice-Hall, 1963).

SMEISER, N.J. and LIPSET, S.M. (eds), 'Social Structure, Social Mobility and Economic Development' (Chicago: Aldine, 1966).
SMITH, M.G., 'The Plural Society in the British West Indies' (Berkeley: University of California Press, 1965).
SMITH, M.G., Social and cultural pluralism, 'Annals of the New York Academy of Sciences', 83, 1960.
STAMPP, K.M., 'The Peculiar Institution: Slavery in the Ante-Bellum South' (New York: Vintage, 1964).
STAROBIN, R.S., 'Industrial Slavery in the Old South' (New York: Oxford University Press, 1970).
SWEEZY, P., 'The Theory of Capitalist Development: Principles of Marxian Political Economy' (New York: Monthly Review Press, 1968).
TANNENBAUM, F., 'Slave and Citizen: The Negro in the Americas' (New York: Knopf, 1946).
THOMPSON, E.P., 'The Making of the English Working Class' (Harmondsworth: Penguin, 1963).
THOMPSON, E.T., The plantation as a social system, in 'Plantation Systems of the New World' (Washington, DC: Pan American Union, 1959).
THOMPSON, E.T. (ed.), 'Race Relations and the Race Problem' (Durham: Duke University Press, 1939).
THOMPSON, E.T. and HUGHES, E.C. (eds), 'Race: Individual and Collective Behaviour' (New York: Collier Macmillan, 1958).
TIMASHEFF, N., 'Sociological Theory: Its Nature and Growth' (New York: Random House, 1967).
TOBIAS, P.V., 'The Meaning of Race' (Johannesburg: South African Institute of Race Relations, 1961).
TOYNBEE, A., 'A Study of History' (London: Oxford University Press, 1934-54).
TUMIN, M.M., 'Social Stratification: The Forms and Functions of Inequality' (Englewood Cliffs: Prentice-Hall, 1967).
UNITED NATIONS, SUB-COMMISSION ON THE PREVENTION OF DISCRIMINATION AND PROTECTION OF MINORITIES, 'The Main Types and Causes of Discrimination' (New York: United Nations, 1949).
UNITED NATIONS EDUCATIONAL, SCIENTIFIC AND CULTURAL ORGANISATION (UNESCO), 'Race and Science: The Race Question in Modern Science' (New York: Columbia University Press, 1969).
VAN DEN BERGHE, P.L., 'Race and Ethnicity: Essays in Comparative Sociology' (New York: Basic Books, 1970).
VAN DEN BERGHE, P.L., 'Race and Racism: A Comparative Perspective' (New York: Wiley, 1967).
VAN DEN BERGHE, P.L., Dialectics and functionalism: toward a theoretical synthesis, 'American Sociological Review', 28, 1963.

VATTER, H.G., On the folklore of the backward sloping supply curve, 'Industrial and Labour Relations Review', 14, 1961.
WADE, R.C., 'Slavery in the Cities: The South, 1820-60' (New York: Oxford University Press, 1964).
WAGLEY, C. and HARRIS, M., 'Minorities in the New World' (New York: Columbia University Press, 1964).
WALTER, P.A.F., 'Race and Culture Relations' (New York: McGraw-Hill, 1952).
WARNER, W.L., American class and caste, 'American Journal of Sociology', 42, 1936.
WEBER, M., 'The Theory of Social and Economic Organisation' (Toronto: Collier Macmillan, 1969).
WEBER, M., 'The Protestant Ethic and the Spirit of Capitalism' (New York: Scribner's, 1958).
WEINSTEIN, A. and GATELL, F.O. (eds), 'The Segregation Era, 1863-1954' (New York: Oxford University Press, 1970).
WILLIAMS, E., 'Capitalism and Slavery' (London: Deutsch, 1964).
WIRTH, L. and LINTON, R. (eds), 'The Science of Man in the World Crisis' (New York: Columbia University Press, 1945).
WOODWARD, C.V., 'The Strange Career of Jim Crow' (New York: Oxford University Press, 1957).
ZUBAIDA, S. (ed.), 'Race and Racialism' (London: Tavistock, 1970).

Index

Accident compensation, 56
Africans, 21, 168f
African workers, 20-5, 168f, 184f
  amenability of, 60
  and exploitation colour bars, 168f, 185f
  grievances of, 184f
  importation of, 32f, 97, 120
  and job colour bar, 196f
  as labour machines, 85
  mobilisation of, 26f
  in semi-skilled work, 104f, 138f, 157-9
  strikes, 168f
  supply of, 26f, 32f, 38
  ultra-exploitability of, 20f, 34f, 45f, 176f
  ultra-exploitation of, 34f, 45f, 180f
  unrest, 168f
  and white workers, 58f, 104f, 168f, 196f
Afrikaner workers, 62f, 104f, 132
Agents provocateurs, 135
Agriculture, 52-3
Amalgamated Engineering Union, 55
Amalgamated Society of Carpenters and Joiners, 55
Amalgamated Society of Woodworkers, 56

Amalgamations, 16
Amalgamators, 55
Amputations, 172
Ardrey, R., 7
Aristocracy, racial, 62
Armoured cars, 135
Armoured trains, 135
Arms and ammunition, 39
Artillery, 135
Artisans, 55
Assaults, 198-9
Augmented Executive, 131-5

Bakeries, 156
Banksmen, 55
Bank to bank, 100-1
Barbed wire, 39
Basutoland, 32
Bechuanaland, 32
Beds, 189
Bench clearing, 122
Blowing over, 122
Boiler makers, 55
Boilers and Machinery Law, 66
Bolshevik plot, rumours of, 135
Bolsheviks, 127, 155
Bomber planes, 135
Boots, 189
Botha, General L., 170, 175
Boycott of stores, 173
Breach of contract, penal

Index

sanctions for, 24, 35f, 174, 176-7, 191-2
Breweries, 156
Brick layers, 55
Building workers, 55
Business-like methods, 30
Bywoners, 52-4, 107

Candles, 96
Capital:
  concentration, 14-17
  investment, 15, 18-19, 45, 128
  ownership, 13-14
Capitalism, see System of production
Capitalist class, 17
Capitalists, mining:
  and African workers, 20-5, 26f, 168f, 184f
  and exploitation colour bars, 22-5, 26f, 45f, 185f
  interests of, 17-20, 77f, 111f, 119f
  involvement in racial discrimination, 26f, 45f
  and job colour bar, 77f, 104f, 119f, 136f
  and labour costs, see Labour
  and labour supply, see Labour
  organisation of, 13-17
  problems of, 17-20, 93f, 119f
  and white workers, 25, 54-7, 77f, 98f, 104f, 119f, 136f
Capitation fee, 28, 193
Carpenters, 55
Cash nexus, 54
Cattle, 27, 105
Cattle annexation, 28
Cattle trucks, 194
Centralisation, 16
Chamber of Mines, 16; see also Capitalists, mining

Chinese labour, 30, 32-3, 67, 82
Christian spirit, 163
Civilisation, 63, 200
Civilised Labour Policy, 71, 156; see also White Labour Policy
Class, 2-3, 20-5
  analysis, 9-10
  colour bars, 4, 46-7, 215; see also specific class colour bars
  consciousness, 195
  contradictions, 76-7
  formation, 49-54
  interest, 17-20, 26f, 45-9, 71-5, 119f
  structure, 2, 20-5, 46, 49f, 152, 215-16
Clothing, 189
Coal, 96
Coal mining, 29, 97, 131
Cocoa planters, 29
Coffee, 189
Colour bar, usage of term, 46-7, 213-14
Colour Bar Act, 157f
Commandos, 131-2
Competency, certificates of, 66f, 124
Competition, suppression of, 26, 29f, 39f, 193
Competition for labour, see Labour
Complements, labour, see Labour
Complements Committee, 31
Compounds, 38-9
Compound system, 35f, 171-2, 193
Compulsion:
  economic, 20f, 29, 51-4
  extreme extra-economic, 22f, 34f, 45f, 176f, 190f
Concentration camps, 53
Contracts, see Labour
Contract shift, 43-4, 186-7
Cooling off periods, 112, 115

Corduroy extraction process, 142-4
Cost(s):
 development, 18-19
 inflation, 19, 94f, 130
 labour, see Labour
 of living, 96, 98, 172f, 179f, 188f
 materials, 19-20, 96
 minimisation, 19-20, 136f
 overhead, 18-19, 101
 structure, 17f, 29, 32, 93, 180-4
Craft unions, 55-6
Credit, see Debt inducement
Creswell, F.H.P., 84, 97, 153-7, 166
Crop failure, 27, 53
Curlewis conference, 132
Cyanide, 96
Cyanide process, 94

Debt, 28
Debt inducement, 27-9, 193
Deferred pay, 172
De-nationalisation, of working class, 34
Department of Native Affairs, 194-5
Dependants, 190
Dependence, economic, 20-4, 27-9, 51-3, 57-8
Desertion, 36-7
Diamond mining, 13-14, 29, 38
Differential exploitability of labour, 58f
Dingaan's Day, 32, 138
Director of Native Labour, 39, 169f, 185
Discrimination, racial, 3-4, 8, 22-4, 26f, 45-9, 64f, 76f, 89, 104f, 119f, 136f, 168f, 201-2, 203f, 215-16
Displacement from jobs, see Labour
Dolly hammer machine, 143
Domination, system of, 1, 20-4
 legitimisation of, 23-4
 mystification of, 6-7, 23-4
Doxey, G.V., 204
Dressing down, 122
Drilling, 43-4, 186-7, 193
Drill sharpening, 55, 121, 143
Drought, 54
Dying workers, screening-off of beds of, 172

Eating cats, 179
Economics, 1, 203f
Efficiency of labour, capitalist penalisation of, 42-5
Electricians, 55
Empiricism, 8
Employment colour bars, 64f
Environmentalism, 7-10
Evening-up, see Labour rationing
Eviction, 52
Exploitability, ultra-, see Compulsion, extreme extra-economic
Exploitation, 21-4, 34f, 180f
 colour bars, 23-4, 26f, 45f, 86-8, 176f, 185f
 legitimisation of, 24
 mystification of, 24
 ultra-, see Labour costs, ultra-minimisation of
Eysenck, H.J., 7

Face to face, 100-1
Far East Rand, 97
Farmers, 29, 97
Fitters, 55
Forced labour, see Compulsion, extreme extra-economic
Fragmentation of working

class, 34, 38-9
Franchise, discriminatory, 24
Free labour, see Labour, politically free

Gangs, combination of, 123, 159
Gelatine, 96
Gelignite, 96
Genetic determinism, 7
Geology of gold fields, 13-14, 17-18, 31, 51, 102-4
Gold fields, 13
Gold Law of the Transvaal, discrimination in, 23
Go slows, 114
Government, discrimination in, 24
Grade of ore, 17-18, 95, 102-4, 131
Groups, 14-16
Guns, 27

Hanging of workers, 136
Harbours, 29, 70
Heaven, place in, 175
Hertzog, General J.B., 165-6
Hildick-Smith case, 145f, 162
Hole marking, 122
Hole plugging, 122
Holidays, paid, 56
Home-brewed drink, 27
Horwitz, R., 204, 210
Hose fixing, 122
Hospital services, 156
Houghton, D.H., 204
Human chattel, 194
Hunger, 179
Hutt, W.H., 204
Hut tax, 27

Idealism, 8, 206
Ideology, racist, 22-4

Import substitution, 97
Independence, economic, 26, 28-9, 57-8
Industrialisation, 2, 97
Industrial relations, 111f
Industrial union, 56
Investment, see Capital
Iron Moulders' Society, 56
Isolation of workers, 38-9

Jack-hammer drill, 142-3
Jensen, A., 7
Job colour bar:
    extension of, 104f, 157f
    grievances of African workers, 196-8
    historical development of, 66f
    and mining capitalists, 77f, 101, 104f, 119f, 138f
    reduction of, 119f, 138f
    secondary importance of, 183, 184f, 213
    structural genesis of, 57f
Johannesburg, 53-4, 177
Johannesburg Soviet, 126
Juvenile employment underground, 82

Keeping the King, dying in the sea while, 178
Kidnapping, 171

Labour:
    aristocracy, 55
    competition, 26f, 40-1, 97
    complements, see Labour rationing
    contracts, 33-4, 35f, 191-2
    control, see Compulsion, extreme extra-economic
    costs, 19, 29, 93f, 100,

136-8
costs, ultra-minimisation of, 19-20, 25, 32, 34f, 45f, 180-3, 184f
costs, white labour, 25, 33, 56, 83-4, 98-100, 136-8
displacement, 59, 107f, 144-5, 157-8
distribution, 24, 31, 34
emigration, 104-5
force, of gold mines, 25 55, 104f
forced, see Compulsion, extreme extra-economic
importation, 26, 29f, 97
mobilisation, 26f
non-white, ultra-exploitability of, see Compulsion, extreme extra-economic
non-white, ultra-exploitation of, see Labour costs, ultra-minimisation of
politically free, 25, 36, 50
power, 2, 17
productivity, 19, 42-4, 100, 145, 186-8, 193
rationing, 31, 34
recruiting, 27f, 189, 193
recruiting agencies, 16, 29f
recruiting monopsony, 29f, 193
semi-skilled, 70, 105f, 142-3
shifts, 43-4, 186-7, 193
shortage, 26, 32, 51, 97, 104-5
skilled, 25, 51, 54-6, 58-9
substitution, 20, 58-9, 123f, 138f, 157f
supply, 20, 26f, 38, 55
unpaid, 43-4, 186-7, 193
unskilled, white, 59-64, 70-1

Land:
access to, 21-2, 51-4, 57-8, 179
ownership of, 20-4, 51-4, 105-6, 179
splitting of tribal holdings, 27
subdivision, 51-2
Language, 199
Languishing of mines, 44
Lashing, 43-4, 186-7, 193
Latitude 22, 32, 97, 120
License rights, discrimination in, 23
Loafer ticket system, 43-4, 186-7, 193
Loan advancement, see Debt inducement
Locusts, 54
Low grade mines, 17-18, 95, 102-4, 131

Machine guns, 135
Machinists, 55
Manufacturing, 97
Masons, 55
Master and Servant Laws, 24, 35-6, 174, 176-7, 190-2
Materialism, dialectical and historical, 9, 217
Maximum average system, 42-5, 186-8, 193
May Day, 132, 138
Mealie meal, 96
Means of production, 2, 9, 17, 20-5, 27-9, 51-4, 57f
Mechanics, 55
Merchants, 29
Migrant workers, 57-8; see also Labour importation
Millwrights, 55
Miner, general, 141
Mineral trading rights, discrimination in, 23
Miner's phthisis, 56
Miner's Phthisis Act, 99
Mines and minerals, discrimination in access to, 23

Mines and Works Act, 68, 146, 157f
Mining, deep level, 18-19, 25, 122
Mining Industry Commission, 84
Mining Regulations, 66-70
 contravention of, 147-50, 157-61
Mining Regulations Commission, 66, 157-61
Mining rights, discrimination in, 23
Mining work, unpopularity of, 32
Mobilisation:
 of army, 169, 194
 of labour, see Labour
 of police, 116-17, 169-70, 194
Moffat Commission, 175-6, 188
Money, 185f
Monopsony, see Labour
Moulders, 55
Movement control, see Regimentation of non-whites, and Pass system
Mystification, 6, 24

Nationalist Party, 152-6
Native Affairs Department, 194-5
Native Grievances Inquiry, 171-2, 186-8
Native Labour Regulation Act, 35
Native Land Act, 23
Native Recruiting Corporation, 16, 30-2, 39-40
Native wars, see Wars, South African
Nyasaland, 32

Oligopoly, 14, 45
Output, 18-19
 falling, 19, 94-5, 100-4

 maximisation, 19, 26, 138f
Over-production, crises, 18
Overtime, see Wage rates
Ownership, 13-17, 21-2
 non-, 21-2, 27-9, 51-4, 57f
 private, 21-2, 51-4, 57f

Pact:
 electoral, 152-5
 Government, 155-7
Pass:
 Laws, 24, 35-9
 system, 35-9, 171, 176-9, 191-4
Passive resistance, 176-9
Pawn brokers, overseas, 151
Peace Conference, 176
Piecework, 42-5, 186-9, 193
Pigmentation, see Skin pigmentation
Pigsties, 107
Pipefitting, 55, 141
Plate amalgamation, 143
Pluralism, 206-11
Pneumonia, 97
Politically free labour, see Labour
Political rights, discrimination in, 24
Poor whites, 59-64
Population growth, 27, 54
Porridge rations, 171, 186
Portuguese East Africa, 32-4
Postal services, 70
Powerlessness, extreme, see Compulsion, extreme extra-economic
Prejudice, preoccupation with, 1, 8, 166, 206
Premium price, 95, 119
Preparation of jumpers, 122
Preparation of working place, 122
President Wilson, 176
Price of gold, 14, 17-18, 95, 119

Pricing system, 40
Production for use, 57-8, 127
Profit, 17, 145
  mass of, 45
  -output ratio, 18-19, 101
  rate of, 45
Profitability:
  crisis, 59, 93f, 119f, 145
  imperatives, 17-20, 26, 45, 94
Prohibition:
  of labour importation, 97
  of Sunday milling, 82
Proletarianisation, 50-3, 57-8
Property:
  colour bars, 23
  laws, discrimination in, 23
  owners, 20-5
  rights in mining areas, discrimination in, 23
Protectionism, 64f
Pull factors, 193
Pumpmen, 55
Push factors, 27, 193

Race, 5-10
Race relations, field of, 5-10
Racial discrimination, see Discrimination, racial
Racism, see Ideology, racist
Racism, preoccupation with, 1, 8, 166
Railways, 29, 53, 70
Raw chaps, 105
Reclamation, 55
Recovery rate, 94
Redundancy, 123, 159-60
Regimentation of non-whites, 24, 35f
Relations of production, 2, 9, 20-5, 26f, 50-4, 58, 185f, 215-16
Residence rights in mining areas, discrimination in, 23
Rex, J., 206
Rhodesia, 32
Riggers, 55
Rigging up, 122
Rinderpest, 53
Risk, 185
Road construction, 32
Robinson, H.W., 204
Rock breaking, 55
Rock drill steel, 96
Roman-Dutch law, 52

Safety valve, 79
Scab labour, 132
Scramble for labour, 30
Secondary sector, 29, 97
Semi-skilled work, see Labour
Shaft sinking, 55
Shaft stewards, 114-15, 131
Share cropping, 22
Shift ticket, 43-4, 186-7, 193, 199
Shops, rights of establishment, discrimination in, 23
Shop stewards, 114-15, 131
Skilled work, see Labour
Skills, 25, 51, 54-6
Skin pigmentation, 3, 22-4, 50
Skipmen, 55
Small man, disappearance of, 54, 154
Smith, M.G., 207
Smuts, General J.C., 129, 132, 163, 170
Social formation, South African, 11, 21, 49
Social inequality, 1, 5-10
Soil erosion, 27
South African:
  Engine Drivers' and Firemen's Association, 56, 69-70, 138
  Industrial Federation,

56, 131-5, 151
Labour Party, 56, 152-6
Mine Workers' Union, 56
Reduction Workers'
  Association, 56
South West Africa, 32
Squatting, 20-1
  Laws, 24, 28
Standard of living, 189
Status Quo Agreement, 70,
  82, 104f, 129, 133
Stock decimation, 27
Stoning, 175
Stoping, 55
Strikes, 36, 107f, 125f,
  168f, 180-4
  wildcat, 114f
Striking force, 117
Structural insecurity, 57f,
  152
Structuralisation of
  grievances, 195
Subsistence, 20-2, 26-7,
  57-8, 188-9
Sugar, 189
  planters, 29
Surface works, 141
Surplus, 2, 21
Swaziland, 32
System of production, 2,
  20-5, 45, 50, 51-4, 89,
  215-16
  reinforcement of, 22-5
  reproduction of, 22-5

Taboo, labour, 60-1
Tax measures, 24, 27
Technological innovation,
  20, 94, 142-4
Tenancy, terms of, 22
Tertiary sector, 29
Theft, 179
Timbering, 107, 141
Time work, 41-2
Track laying, 107
Traders, 28
Trade unions, 25, 55-6
Trading rights, discrimination in, 23
Traffic in human flesh, 194
Tramming, 43-4, 186-7, 193
Transport riders, 53
Transvaal:
  Chamber of Mines, see
    Federation of Trades, 56
  Labour Importation
    Ordinance, 67, 82
  Miners' Association, 56
  Native Congress, 174f
Tropical Africa, 32, 97, 120

Ultra-exploitability, see
  Compulsion, extreme
  extra-economic
Ultra-exploitation, see
  Labour costs, ultra-
  minimisation of
Ultra vires, 69, 82, 145f
Union Jack, tearing up of,
  175
Unsavoury methods, 193
Unskilled work, see Labour
Urban areas, 53-4
Urbanisation, 51-4

Van den Berghe, P., 206, 214
Van der Horst, S.T., 204,
  210
Van Ryn Deep, 107

Wage fixation, 39f, 185f
Wage rates, 29f, 39f, 56,
  137-8, 180-3, 185f
  inelasticity of, 32, 39f,
    180-3, 185f
  and labour importation,
    33
  overtime, 56, 98
  ultra-minimisation of,
    see Labour costs
  unskilled labour, 60, 83
War, South African, 53, 94
War, world, 2, 43, 59, 94,
  104f, 178

Wars, South African, 21
Waste packing, 107
Watering down, 122
White areas, 23
White Labour Policy, 70-1, 82-6, 97, 156; see also Civilised Labour Policy
White man, superior intelligence of, 85
White workers, 25, 49f, 86-8, 150f
  and African workers, 58f, 71f, 168-70, 196
  displacement of, 20, 58-9, 123f, 138f, 157f
  and employment colour bars, 58f, 64f, 119f, 150f
  and exploitation colour bars, 86f
  in gold mines, 54-7, 66-70, 93f
  involvement in racial discrimination, 58f, 64f, 71f
  proletarianisation, 21-2, 27, 51-4, 57-8
  semi-skilled, 70, 105f, 142-3
  skilled, 25, 51, 54-6, 58-9, 66f, 138f, 157f
  strikes, 125f, 168-71
  structural genesis of, 25, 51-4
  structural insecurity of, 57-8, 71-5
  unskilled, 51-4, 59-64, 70-1, 82-6, 97, 156
  uprising by, 135-6
Wilson, F., 203
Winch drivers, 55
Winding engines, 66
Witwatersrand:
  Mine Employees' and Mechanics' Union, 55
  Native Labour Association, 16
  Trades and Labour Council, 56
Work extension, 20, 121f, 138f
Working hours, 56, 82, 98-9, 101, 121f
Works Committees, 114

Zinc, 96

For Product Safety Concerns and Information please contact our EU
representative GPSR@taylorandfrancis.com
Taylor & Francis Verlag GmbH, Kaufingerstraße 24, 80331 München, Germany

www.ingramcontent.com/pod-product-compliance
Lightning Source LLC
Chambersburg PA
CBHW071803300426
44116CB00009B/1192